HOVELS, HACIENDAS, AND HOUSE CALLS

HOVELS, HACIENDAS, AND HOUSE CALLS:
The Life of Carl H. Gellenthien, M.D.

Dorothy Simpson Beimer

Dorothy Simpson Beimer

Sunstone Press
Santa Fe, New Mexico

To my mother Audrey

First Edition

Printed in the United States of America

Library of Congress Cataloging in Publication Data:

Beimer, Dorothy Simpson, 1944—
    Hovels, haciendas, and house calls.

    Bibliography: p. 295
    Includes index.
    1. Gellenthien, Carl H. 2. Physicians (General
practice)--New Mexico--Biography. 3. Tuberculosis--
Patients--New Mexico--Biography. I. Title.
R154.G342B45   1985   610'.92'4 (B)   85-14881
ISBN: 0-86534-074-9

Published in 1986 by SUNSTONE PRESS
              Post Office Box 2321
              Santa Fe, NM 87504-2321 / USA

TABLE OF CONTENTS

ACKNOWLEDGEMENTS

The author wishes to thank Dr. Carl H. Gellenthien for his cooperation in providing information for this book. Appreciation is also extended to members of his family, including Editha Bartley, for invaluable help. The author is indebted to many friends for their assistance. Grateful appreciation is also extended to the Institute of Research of New Mexico Highlands University for support and encouragement.

AUTHOR'S NOTE

A physician's code of ethics dictates that he must maintain the confidences of his patients, guarding them scrupulously at all times. Accordingly, no patient records or case histories have been disclosed without regard to the privacy of the patient. The patient stories recorded in this book, although based on real experiences of actual persons, have been rendered totally unidentifiable in order to protect the privacy of the persons concerned where any breach of confidence might otherwise be incurred. Names of persons and places, consequently, have been changed although actual case histories remain accurate. Any resemblance to actual persons, living or dead, is purely coincidental, is not intentional, and should not be inferred. Where no breach of confidence is involved, e.g., in non-medical contexts, actual names are used. Names of places or of historical personages where no breach of confidence is involved, have not been changed.

There will be some who may say that this fact or that date is inaccurate. As far as possible, I have verified my information with more than one source. Often I had to rely on the memories of those past their 70th decade, memories which are, as all memories, colored with individual perceptions. Thus, if some versions differ with the details herein, it is probably quite natural in view of the fact that each perspective may be entirely different. The facts are related accurately insofar as they were presented to me. My primary source for most of the information has been Dr. Gellenthien himself. Each fact or incident was verified insofar as possible with at least one other source. However, not all information was verifiable. In such cases, Dr. Gellenthien's memory has been the only source available.

— D.S.B.

INTRODUCTION

This is the story of a man, not a disease, but because the disease affected the man's entire life, a brief background on the nature of tuberculosis was deemed necessary. A review of the terminology connected with the illness provides an interesting insight into the nature of the disease itself.

"Phthoe" was the name given by the Greeks to the individual who was "shriveling up under intense heat."[1] The father of medicine, Hippocrates, (circa 460-370 B.C.) was probably the first to write an elaborate description of the disease which he named Phthisis, meaning "to waste away or lose weight."[2] One of his patients, the daughter of Euryanax, died of the disease, and her case history is still viewed as an accurate description.[3] The word "phthisis" came to designate the wasting and melting away of the body caused by disease of the lungs.[4]

In early Hindu writings the disease is referred to by a word meaning "a consumption."[5]

The Latin word tabes, used in a general sense to denote wasting, was used in the seventeeth century. "Words expressing the emaciation of tuberculosis patients occur in all languages, but probably none has been more widely used than 'consumption'."[6] To describe the process that caused their patients to burn up with fever and lose weight, English physicians of the early seventeenth century adopted the Latin verb consumere, meaning to eat up or devour; later they formed the habit of referring to wasting disease as "a consumption."[7] The word "consumption" was used as early as 1398 when John of Trevisa wrote, "Whan the blode is made thynne, soo folowyth consumpcyon and wastyng."[8]

The word "tuberculosis" comes from the Latin tuberculum, the diminutive of tuber, bump, or swelling.[9] Autopsies done in the seventeenth century revealed small, hard nodules in the diseased lungs about the size of an eye of a potato. Because of this resemblance to the potato tuber, the name "tuberculosis" came into common usage.[10]

When performing an autopsy in 1700 the French physician Jean Jacques Manget saw tubercles so small, they resembled "millet seed" present in all parts of the body. His description led to the naming of this type of disseminated disease as "miliary" tuberculosis. [11]

Involvement of certain lymphatic nodes is one of the constant manifestations of tuberculosis. The expressions "scrofulous" and "strumous glands" were often used to describe those tuberculosis nodes, especially of the neck. The adjective "scrofulous" suggests resemblance to a sow, and "strumous" means "something built up." Although the disease can be limited to a certain part of the body, tubercule bacilli can become widely distributed throughout the body, causing a generalized infection called "miliary tuberculosis" which is characterized by the formation of very small nodules in most organs. [12] Thus, the adjective "scrofulous" referred to the tubercular patient. It has also been used at times as a noun.

The American slang expression "lunger" and the French word *poitrinaire* epitomize a type of patient with a chronic, debilitating disease of the lungs. [13]

"Galloping consumption" was used when the disease ran a fulminating course, bringing about extensive destruction of lung tissue in a few months. It was spoken of with fear as it was rapidly fatal. Usually, however, the disease waxes and wanes with long periods of apparent remission followed by periods of exacerbation. [14]

Physicians described the emaciation of the patient, an exhaustion of the reserves of the body that they traced to the "vehement" or "hectic" fever characteristics of the disease. Such descriptions often used the adjective "hectic."

> Tuberculosis was…unquestionably the greatest single cause of disease and death in the Western world, and one finds it masquerading throughout medical and nonmedical writings under a bewildering variety of names. Besides the words "phthisis," "consumption" and "scrofula," the expressions "asthenia," "tabes," "bronchitis," "inflammation of the lungs," "hectic fever," "gastric fever," "lupus," and many more, referred in most cases to conditions now known to have been caused by tubercle bacilli. [15]

The term most commonly used for the disease in the nineteenth century was probably "consumption." The term "tuberculosis" (or TB) became widely used in the twentieth century. It was said that in TB, the patient was "consumed," or burned up. "TB is a disease of time; it speeds up life, highlights it, spiritualizes it. In both English and French, consumption 'gallops'." [16]

The American expression "lunger" implies that tuberculosis is a disease of the lungs, which is true, but not exclusively so. Severe

9

pulmonary tuberculosis is often accompanied by the production of lesions in the intestines and in the larynx. Laryngeal tuberculosis or aphonia renders swallowing very painful and can bring about an almost complete extinction of the voice, while intestinal tuberculosis causes an exhausting diarrhea.[17] The "chalky" voice quality, characteristic of some TB victims, betrayed the attack of the tubercule bacilli on the vocal chords, even when laryngeal TB was not evident. TB seldom isolates itself, preferring to infest every part of the body.

Tuberculosis can manifest itself in any part of the human body. *Inflammation of the membranes surrounding the brain (meningeal tuberculosis), destruction of kidney tissue (renal tuberculosis), the infirmity of the hunchback known as gibbus or Pott's disease (tuberculosis of the spine), lupus (tuberculosis of the skin), fistula-in-ano and several other pathological conditions illustrate the power of tubercle bacilli to cause destructive lesions in practically all tissues and organs.*[18]

The initial stages of TB cause little discomfort. Thus, the disease usually remained unnoticed by the patient until it had reached its most advanced stages. Hippocrates taught that phthisis began as a respiratory catarrh, with chest pains, increasing malaise, and a cough yielding yellow sputum. These symptoms occurred only after the lesions had become extensive. The Greek and Roman physicians recognized that evening fever and night sweats, blood spitting, a small pulse, clubbed fingers and curved nails, pleurisy followed by empyema, extinction of the voice, and diarrhea were signs of pulmonary phthisis.[19]

Aretaeus, a Greek from Asia Minor, described an advanced case of tuberculosis with such detail that the account is considered unequalled. It follows, in part:

Voice hoarse; neck slightly bent, tender, not flexible, somewhat extended; fingers slender but joints thick...the nails of the fingers crooked, their pulps are shriveled and flat, for, owing to the loss of flesh, they neither retain their tension nor rotundity...the nails are bent, namely, because it is the compact flesh at their points which is intended as a support to them; and the tension thereof is like that of solids. Nose sharp, slender; cheeks prominent and red; eyes hollow, brilliant and glittering; swollen, pale or livid in the countenance; the slender parts of the jaws rest upon the teeth, as if smiling; otherwise of a cadaverous aspect. So in all other respects; slender, without flesh...One may not only count the ribs themselves, but also easily trace them to their terminations; for even the articulations at the vertebrae are quite visible and their connections with the sternum are also manifest; the intercostal spaces are hollow and rhomboidal, agreeably to the configuration of the bone...the spine of the vertebrae, formerly hollow, now protrudes, the muscles on either side being wasted; the whole shoulder blades apparent like wings of birds. [20]

Galen (*circa* 131-20 A.D.) believed phthisis was incurable and that it was contagious. He prescribed the bleeding of patients, an ample diet including milk, and a cool, well-ventilated room. His methods were used with few changes for the next 1500 years. [21]

There was no known cure for the disease in the early 1900s except rest and fresh air, the same treatment recommended 460 to 370 years before Christ by a contemporary of Hippocrates. The Greek physician wrote, "If I had the consuming disease, I would plant my tent on the southern slope of the mountain, would get myself a goat and rest there." [22] The tent signified fresh air and rest. The southern slope meant altitude and sunshine. And the goat represented milk and good nutrition. Until the middle 1900s that is all anyone knew of the treatment of tuberculosis. [23]

Throughout the years rememdies included such items as red roses and honey, tar, myrrh, opium, arsenic, chalk, sulpher, creosote, digitalis, tea, coffee, chocolate, tobacco, and various herbs. [24] Exercise, including horseback riding, was sometimes recommended. During the eighteenth century, physicians began recommending warm, mild climates.

In 1833, George Bodington's revolutionary ideas on pure, fresh air saved his patient's life and influenced doctors of his day to value the fresh air treatment. [25] Dr. Edward Livingston Trudeau made the idea even more popular. In 1875 he went to Saranac Lake expecting to die of his tuberculosis. But he recovered and attributed his good fortune to the pure, cold mountain air. He then founded the sanatorium at Saranac Lake for TB sufferers. It became one of the most renowned sanatoria in the entire country. Saranac Lake was called the "Switzerland of America." Dr. Trudeau's rabbit experiment in 1885 gave credence to the notion that fresh air and sunshine, along with proper diet, brought about "the cure." The rabbits were divided into three groups in lots of five. The first lot was inoculated with pure tuberculosis cultures, supplied with plenty of food, and allowed to live freely in the fresh air and sunshine. The second lot was also inoculated but was put in a dark, damp place, confined in a box with very little food. The third lot shared the second's conditions but was not inoculated. In lot one, all but one rabbit survived. In lot two, four rabbits died within three months with evidence of tuberculosis. The third lot of rabbits emerged emaciated but with no signs of disease.[26] Thus, Saranac Lake's cool, mountain air and altitude were endorsed. The climate of the southwest was believed to be equally salubrious. Great hotels, spas, and sanatoria sprang up all over the west. Tent cities grew up overnight.

The idea of rest was also pioneered by Dr. Trudeau. One of his TB patients, Charles R. Armstrong, went bobsledding in 1892 and broke his leg. He had to spend 20 weeks in bed. To his doctor's surprise, not only did his leg heal, but his lungs healed as well. His case drew important comment on the value of rest. Armstrong recovered and became superintendent at Trudeau.[27]

Nevertheless, statisitics were not encouraging. When Dr. Trudeau arrived at Saranac Lake, TB was the leading cause of death in America. Fifty years later, 80,000 Americans were still dying of it annually.[28] In the 1920s every third person between the ages of 15 and 60 in America — or about one in ten — died of tuberculosis.[29]

The scourge of TB came on the scene long before the nineteenth century. Ancient papyri scripts describe the disease, as do old Chinese writings, indicating that TB stalked the human race from the beginning. The skeleton of a man about 20 years of age at death was found in a grave of Neolithic or Stone Age. The vertebrae were found to be fused, indicating Pott's disease or TB of the spine. Egyptian mummies, including one of a priest of Ammon from about 1,000 B.C., show evidence of TB. When scientists X-rayed the mummy Tutankhamen (King Tut), TB of the spine was evident. The pathology of preserved bones on the plains of the Ganges in India show the presence of the disease there, also.[30]

Throughout the years the disease was attributed to various causes including personality types, humours, blood disorders, excesses, irritants, stress and overwork. Jean Villemin, a French physician, proved TB was infectious, but not until 1882 was it known that a specific organism caused the disease. A German doctor, Robert Koch, discovered and isolated the tubercle bacillus. The most momentous lecture of nineteenth century medicine was delivered before the Berlin Physiological Society when Koch announced his discovery. A colleague who heard the lecture, Dr. Paul Ehrlich, immediately began assisting Koch in his research. But there was no known cure for TB except rest and fresh air. Not until 1944 was streptomycin discovered. In that year Selman Waksman, who was working at the New Jersey State Agricultural Experimental Station in New Brunswick, developed streptomycin through studying the bacteria of highly manured soil. It was the first successful chemotherapy for TB patients, but it was not without harmful side effects. It did, however, destroy the reproductive abilities of the bacilli, giving the patient's natural resistance a chance to overcome the enemy. Later, a drug which actually killed the bacilli, Isoniazid, was developed, followed by numerous such drugs.

TB was feared in the early twentieth century as leprosy was in Biblical times. John Bunyan wrote: "Yet the Captain of all these men of death that came against him to take him away, was the Consumption, for 'twas that that brought him down to the grave."[31] It wiped out entire families including the Emersons and the Brontes. The Reverend Patrick Bronte survived his wife and six children but was probably the source of the infection which destroyed them all.[32]

Paul de Kruif cited many examples of the white death's contagious terror. One story was of how a consumptive father, refusing to be hospitalized, had coughed three of his own children into tuberculous death, had infected two more of them, and had paid for his homicide by his own consumptive dying.[33]

> Detroit's people were told how any citizen with open, active TB, not discovered, not followed by constant x-ray checkup, not isolated, was more dangerous than any machine-gun gangster. Here was the horrid history of a deadly Aunty. In exchange for her keep she'd gone to live with her married sister who had eight children. And so had sprayed her own white death on all of them, infecting every last one of them, killing the youngest — a six-month old baby who had just strangled in TB death.[34]

Although it was known that tuberculosis was infectious, little was done to prevent its spread in the early days. Edgar Allan Poe, John Keats, and E.L. Trudeau himself nursed their dying brothers respectively, each housed in small, closed rooms. Virginia Poe's well-attended parties were interrupted only by her most profuse hemorrhages. School children drank from common cups.

> In 1844, all 78 boys and 91 of the 94 girls in a workhouse in Kent were found to be suffering from it (TB), although only a few of them had shown obvious signs before being admitted to the institution. Similarly, 53 percent of the children in a Berlin orphanage were found to be scrofulous.[35]

It was estimated that approximately half of the English population at one time had tuberculosis.[36]

In 1886, tuberculosis accounted for 12 out of 100 deaths in the United States. In 1907, one person out of every 60 in the U.S. had TB. In the 1920s, one in 10 persons between the ages of 15 and 60 died of tuberculosis.[37] Tuberculosis was the most prominent cause of death between the ages of 20 and 40 years, responsible for one-third of the deaths of young and middle-aged adults, people in their most productive years.[38] In 1934 de Kruif wrote that in Detroit TB was killing three times more young people of 20 and under than all other contagions put together. "It is sending to cadaverous, coughing death more Detroiters in the prime of life — fifteen years old to forty — than any sickness whatsoever."[39] It struck the rich, poor, young, old, brilliant, retarded, educated, ignorant, healthy, and weak. It killed equally well kings and paupers, priests and prostitutes — and it killed children.

The fragile eight-year-old daughter of cartoonist John Gruelle of the *Indianapolis Star* was one of its victims. Just before Christmas of 1914 Marcella Gruelle found an old doll of her grandmother's in an attic and took it to her father who was working to meet a deadline at his newspaper office. She wanted a name for the doll — and a face. Her father drew a simple one-lined smile with his red ink and attached two old buttons to her face for eyes. Inspired by their poet friend James Whitcomb Riley who had written about the raggedy man and about Orphan Annie, they decided on the name "Raggedy Ann." One more addition made the doll complete. With his red pen John painted a heart on the doll's chest and printed, "I love you" right under it.

Marcella loved the doll. When she couldn't sleep because of her persistent cough, her father made up stories about how Raggedy Ann would have adventures of her own after Marcella slept. On March 21, 1916, with Raggedy Ann in her arms, the little girl died of tuberculosis. After that John kept Raggedy Ann perched up on his desk at the office and began writing down the stories he'd told his little daughter.

Just as the literary world might never have received a novel concerning the adventures of a boy who grew up on the Mississippi had Samuel Clemens' son, Tom, not died in infancy, so, too, millions of children throughout the world might never have heard of Raggedy Ann had the daughter of a political cartoonist not died.

Raggedy Ann was begotten with love. She was created between deadlines in a newspaper office by a father who cared more for his little girl than he did for political cartoons.

As a result, Raggedy Ann has returned that love to countless children throughout the years. [40]

Early in this century, one out of every 500 infants born in the United States was destined to die of tuberculosis before living a year.[41] In 1927, there were 600,000 cases of TB annually, 70,000 deaths a year. The TB death rate per 100,000 population declined from 245 in 1890 to 200 in 1904 to 100 in 1921 to 41.3 in 1944 and to 39.7 in 1945 as health care improved.[42] In 1904 there were only six tuberculosis control programs and 100 sanatoria maintaining about

10,000 beds. By 1942 these had multiplied over eleven times to 115,351 beds. Diagnostic methods improved and patients were treated early.[43]

The prevailing attitudes regarding TB during the Victorian era carried over to the twentieth century. Fear was one of those attitudes. Another was the romantic mythology with its accompanying beliefs.

Romantic mythology surrounding tuberculosis was perpetuated by stricken writers who claimed that TB was accompanied by creativity. Percy Bysshe Shelley consoled John Keats, both stricken, saying that "this consumption is a disease particularly fond of people who write such good verses as you have done."[44] Indeed, it had been said that no one weighing more than 99 pounds could be a true poet.[45]

Because so many famous and successful people of the eighteenth and nineteenth centuries had tuberculosis, it was thought that highly creative people were more likely to get the disease. Someone asked Elizabeth Barrett Browning's physician, "Is it possible that genius is only scrofula?" It seemed logical to postulate the existence of a microbial toxin capable of causing, through a cerebral intoxication, the mental alertness exhibited by so many infected individuals. Although it is now realized that the classical *spes phthisica* is not as universal a characteristic of TB as was once thought, many doctors still believe there is something peculiar about the psychology of TB patients, recognizing the flickering intelligence which brightens up suddenly for a while but is then followed by mental depression or fatigue. Such behavior "gives to the consumptive a close resemblance to the person who is under the influence of moderate doses of alcohol or of a narcotic drug."[46]

Tuberculosis was known as a disease of extreme contrasts: white pallor and red flush, hyperactivity alternating with languidness.[47]

Tuberculosis was as double-headed as the jack of spades — on the one hand, it was referred to as the tired disease, and on the other, the fever burning from the lung infection stimulated energy in the frail bodies of the patients which they could ill afford to expend.[48]

Thus, in spite of a doctor's advice to the contrary, a creative person would work intensely in bursts of energy as Keats did.

Apparently the toxin of the disease — tuberculin — like a higher alcohol, causes a kind of euphoria, a blind optimisim, especially evident just before death. It was distressing for a doctor to see his patient *in extremis*, the body approaching death while the mind was blithely engaged in optimistic plans for the future, convinced that recovery was imminent. Often death would overtake the patient even as he babbled happily about the great successes he would achieve tomorrow.[49]

In *The Magic Mountain* by Thomas Mann, written in 1927 about a patient confined to a tuberculosis sanatorium, a description of Joachim, a dying patient, stated that "he was living fast, his life whirred away like the mechanism of a watch; he passed at a gallop through stages not granted him...time to reach."[50] Toward the end he no longer realized his state and spoke of returning soon to his life as a soldier, saying he felt well and happy. "This though he had scarcely any pulse, and at the end could no longer feel the hypodermic needle."[51] This condition, the illusion of well-being, "is as regular as it is pathetic, this forgetful, credulous self-deception, that attacks even masculine spirits as the hour of the lethal process nears its culmination."[52]

Mann describes Joachim's dying moments. The patient sank down in bed and then curtly ordered his family to prop him up, stating hurriedly that he must write out an application for an extension of his leave and hand it in at once. "And even while he said this, the 'short crossing' came to pass."[53]

Joachim's physician, Hofrat Behrens, stated that the patient was lucky to have such an easy death.

> "The heart is giving out rapidly, lucky for him and for us; we can do our duty with camphor injections and the like, without much chance of drawing things out. He will sleep a good deal at the end, and his dreams will be pleasant...even if he shouldn't go off in his sleep, still it will be a short crossing, he'll scarcely notice...It's so in the majority of cases...I know what death is, I am an old retainer of his; and believe me, he's overrated. Almost nothing to him. Of course, all kinds of beastliness can happen beforehand — but it isn't fair to count those in, they are as living as life itself, and can just as well lead up to a cure. But about death...we don't realize it.[54]

Romantic mythology was perpetuated by literary figures such as Lord George Byron, stricken by myth rather than disease, who said to his consumptive friend Tom Moore that he would like to have consumption himself because then all the ladies would notice his condition and remark that poor Byron looked so interesting in dying.[55]

The contemporaries of Byron, Shelley and Keats believed that consumption made a writer more sensitive, more creative; and thus the romantic agony myths of the Romantic Period were kept alive. Edmond and Jules de Goncourt, literary critics, believed that ill health created favorable conditions for finer human attributes. Despite their admiration for Victor Hugo, for instance, the Goncourts believed that Hugo would have been a greater writer had he not been in such robust health.[56]

The profound agony of the sensitive young artist stricken by tuberculosis in Eugene O'Neill's *Long Day's Journey Into Night* was undoubtedly inspired by the playwright's personal acquaintance with the disease. Little Eva in Harriet Beecher Stowe's *Uncle Tom's Cabin* could hardly have elicited so many tears if she had died less romantically.

Similarly, Emily Bronte, ill with consumption, made her character Frances Earnshaw in *Wuthering Heights* die a glorious death in her husband's arms. No less poignant was the death of Mimi in the opera *La Bohème* by Giacomo Puccini. Mimi visited her lover Rodolfo one last time before dying, apparently of tuberculosis. Rodolfo prayed that Mimi would not die, turned away for a moment, and then discovered that she had slipped away. Inconsolable with grief, he held her in his arms, crying out her name.

Although Keats and Shelley have been regarded as symbolic of the romantic and consumptive youths of the nineteenth century, many other writers were also victims of tuberculosis. The long list includes William Cullen Bryant, Washington Irving, Jane Austin, Emily and Charlotte Bronte, Robert Louis Stevenson, Elizabeth Barrett Browning, Ralph Waldo Emerson, Henry David Thoreau, William Sidney Porter, Stephen Crane, D.H. Lawrence, Eugene O'Neill, Katherine Mansfield, and Ernest Christopher Dowson. Though many of them died young, these writers produced works of genius because they labored intensely. Some, like Sidney Lanier, a nineteenth century Southern poet, believed infirmity caused a consuming restlessness that drove one on to artistic creation. Believing he would die soon, Lanier worked feverishly, feeling that his spirit was singing its swansong. He wrote a poem, "Sunrise" when he was on the verge of death. The French playwright Molière, too, died at his work, almost onstage, driven to the last by his consumptive obsession in the face of approaching death.[57]

> The doctors recognized this (restless) characteristic of TB even while they imperfectly understood the disease. Some said it was the outgrowth of increased mental activity stimulated by constant rest and the fear of death. Others said it was due to actual toxic agents manufactured by the TB bacilli and spilled into the nervous system.[58]

Many writers, who claimed that TB enhanced their perceptions and emotions, described the disease with various metaphors. Elizabeth Barrett Browning described the febrile excitement as "a butterfly within fluttering for release." John Addington Symonds said that tuberculosis gave him a wonderful "Indian summer of experience." Ralph Waldo Emerson said, "A mouse is gnawing at my chest."[59]

Falling leaves symbolized the destruction of young lives. Charles Hubert Millevoye in "The Fall of the Leaves" regarded the mournful hue of autumn as a forewarning of his own doom. He died consumptive in 1816 when he was 39 years of age.[60] William Sydney Porter (O. Henry) also had TB and wrote a short story called "The Last Leaf" in which a leaf was painted on the wall outside the bedroom window to "protect" a young woman from dying with the falling of the last leaf when all hope would be gone.[61]

Many writers, acutely aware of the short time left to them, reflected such fears in their poems. Even the title of Ernest Dowson's famous poem is an obsession with time: *"Vitae summa brevis spem nos vetat incohare longam"* — "The brevity of life forbids us to entertain hopes of long duration."[62]

Keats, worried that he would not have time to finish all he wanted to write, penned his well-known words:

> When I have fears that I may cease to be
>   Before my pen has glean'd my teeming brain...[63]

Keats wrote to Fanny Brawne in February of 1820, a year before his death, that in the sleepless hours of the night an anxious thought intruded upon him — that if he should die, he would have left no immortal work behind him, nothing to make his friends proud of his memory. He lamented that if he'd had the time, he would have made himself remembered. Keats was forbidden by his doctors to write poetry, even to read it, but he continued to work intermittently. "If my health would bear it, I could write a Poem which I have in my head, which would be a consolation for people in such a situation as mine."[64] His unwritten poem will never be known to the world. Within the lines of "Endymion" Keats expressed the hope of being able to complete his work before his time ran out.

> Many and many a verse I hope to write...
> O may no wintry season, bare and hoary,
> See it half finish'd: but let Autumn bold,
> With universal tinge of sober gold,
> Be all about me when I make an end.[65]

It was not to be. Keats died in the spring of his life, not in the autumn, at the age of 25. He left behind the sublimity of his thoughts:

> A thing of beauty is a joy for ever:
> Its loveliness increases; it will never
> Pass into nothingness; but still will keep
> A bower quiet for us, and a sleep
> Full of sweet dreams, and health, and quiet breathing.[66]

"The following day autopsy showed the lungs to be almost entirely destroyed, his physician wondering how he had managed to survive during the last few months."[67]

How many unwritten poems, unsung operas, and unpainted portraits were denied the world by the disease which was the most common cause of death in the nineteenth century! Yet the intensity with which the stricken worked may have been the key that unlocked the genius for so many.

Myths surrounding tuberculosis kept pace with increasing numbers of deaths. It became fashionable to wear a consumptive appearance, to be pale and drained. It was glamorous to look sickly and rude to eat heartily. The "tubercular look" was considered attractive, a mark of distinction.[68] In 1852 Thoreau wrote in his *Journal* that decay and disease are often beautiful like the hectic glow of consumption.[69] The Russian artist, Marie Bashkirtsev, wrote in her *Journal* in Paris in 1887, prior to her death at 24, that she coughed constantly, but instead of making her look ugly, it gave her an air of languor that was most becoming. What was the fashion for aristocratic *femme fatales* and young artists became the general custom, the fashion of nineteenth century manners.[70]

Edgar Allan Poe's wife Virginia was the personification of the romantic heroine, the ideal of nineteenth-century feminine beauty. In January of 1842 she gave a party. Dressed in white, she sang and played the harp in the glow of the lamplight. Suddenly Virginia stopped singing and clutched her throat. Crimson blood ran down her neck and chest. Poe thought his wife's illness added to her charm and rendered her more ethereal. Her chalky pallor and her haunted, liquid eyes made her more delicate, more morbidly angelic.[71]

Twentieth-century women's fashions with their standards of thinness originate from the Victorian ideas associated with the romanticizing of tuberculosis. The statement that no woman can ever be too rich or too thin is probably a carry-over from that era. Perhaps, too, the early twentieth-century fashion in make-up was an attempt to capture the "tubercular look" which was big-eyed and hollow-cheeked, lips too full in contrast to the cheeks, and eyes, deep in their bony sockets, large and bright. Thus, women used pale foundation covered with ivory face powder to create the translucent, almost transparent, look of the tubercular. Dark eyebrow pencil heightened the face's pallor. Red rouge spotted high on the cheeks made the "hectic flush" and gave the cheeks the hollow appearance. Mascara, eye liner, and eye shadow enlarged the eyes while making them appear sunken. Lip liner enlarged the lips, and red lipstick accentuated the pale face. Only in recent years have women's fashions attempted to show a healthy look rather than a consumptive appearance.

For those like Carl Gellenthien who suffered the ravaging effects of it, tuberculosis was no romantic drama. The medical student knew he would be just as dead whether taken by the glorified "romantic agony" or not. Knives, spears, ropes, hemlock, and tuberculosis kill equally well; and there is no romance in a cold corpse.

Charles Dickens described tuberculosis accurately when he wrote in *Nicholas Nickleby* that it is a dread disease which prepares its victim for death in a gradual, quiet, solemn struggle between soul and body.

> ...day by day, and grain by grain, the mortal part wastes and withers away, so that the spirit grows light and sanguine with its lightening load, and, feeling immortality at hand, deems it a new term of mortal life; a disease in which death and life are so strangely blended, that death takes the glow and hue of life, and life the gaunt and grisly form of death; a disease which medicine never cured, wealth never warded off, or poverty could boast exemptions from; which sometimes moves in giant strides, and sometimes at a tardy sluggish pace, but, slow or quick, is ever sure and certain. [72]

Dickens described the character Smike with "the sunken eye.... too bright, the hollow cheek too flushed, the breath too thick and heavy in its course, the frame too feeble and exhausted." [73]

Indeed, the disease would often make its insidious attack in such gradual stages that the victim was unaware of his illness until it had reached advanced stages. To the laboring masses, TB was not the aristocratic inspiration of artistic works, leading painlessly to an ethereal release of the soul among the falling autumn leaves. It was the breeder of destitution — a killer. Had writers described the disease with realism, they would have observed the sick and the poor in slums and hospitals, their bodies wasted and ravished, their minds haunted by impending death.

There were three classifications of pulmonary tuberculosis identified by the National Association for the Study and Prevention of Tuberculosis. Lesions were identified and then the patient was assigned a classification.

Minimal meant slight infiltration, limited to the apex of one or both lungs, or a small part of one lobe with no tuberculosis complications.

Moderately Advanced meant marked infiltration, more extensive than minimal, with little or no evidence of cavity formation and no serious tuberculosis complications.

Far Advanced meant extensive localization infiltration or consolidation in one or more lobes or disseminated areas of cavity formation with serious tuberculosis complications. [74] Classifications after treatment, as when the patient was to be discharged, were the following:

(a) Apparently cured. All constitutional symptoms and expectoration with bacilli absent for a period of two years under ordinary conditions of life.

(b) Arrested. All constitutional symptoms and expectoration with bacilli absent for a period of six months; the physical signs to be those of a healed lesion.

(c) Apparently arrested. All constitutional symptoms and expectoration with bacilli absent for a period of three months; the physical signs to be those of a healed lesion.

d) Quiescent. Absence of all constitutional symptoms. Expectoration and bacilli may or may not be present. Physical signs stationary or retrogressive. The foregoing condition to have existed for at least two months.

(e) Improved. Constitutional symptoms lessened or entirely absent; physical signs improved or unchanged; cough and expectoration with bacilli usually present. (Note: Artificial pneumothorax cases are not classified better than improved.)

(f) Unimproved. All essential symptoms and signs unabated or increased.[75]

Advice given to patients leaving the sanatorium included a warning and specific instructions. Patients were told to remember to rest and to eat well.

Most patients break down because they are careless or because others persuade them that they are not sick. The man who gets well is the man who never forgets he has Tuberculosis. Many "Advanced" cases have become well through constant carefulness and persistence. Many "incipient" cases have died on account of carelessness.[76]

Patients were advised to avoid overexertion, lack of rest, and neglected colds and dissipation. "Remember, you are NOT cured. Not matter how well you feel, the longest part of your 'cure' lies ahead of you."[77] Drs. Brown and Gellenthien stressed the importance of a continued awareness of the disease because frequent relapses occured after a patient left the sanatorium and its quiet life style. Patients were urged to keep in touch with the Valmora staff in the future and to ask for help at any time. The fact that they left the sanatorium grounds to return to their homes did not lessen the concern of the doctors and staff.

Before modern drugs there was no "cure" for TB, so when a patient left Valmora, he was "improved," "arrested," or "apparently cured," but never free of the stigma of being a consumptive. And the percentage of "cures" of any kind was not high. Thus, to receive a diagnosis of tuberculosis was not unlike receiving a sentence of death.

The movie "Honky-Tonk Man," starring Clint Eastwood, depicted the last weeks of a consumptive seeking success as a singer in Nashville. He had chosen not to go to a sanatorium, preferring freedom on the road, though it might hasten his death. Whether a victim chose to go to a sanatorium or not, he lived under a death sentence, in bondage to the "Captain of the Men of Death."

It was under this death sentence that Carl Gellenthien was sent to Valmora in 1924 with a diagnosis of "Far Advanced Pulmonary Tuberculosis." The prognosis was "guarded." In other words, he had the worst kind of TB and, in reality, the prognosis was hopeless.

NOTES

1. Rene Dubos and Jean Dubos, *The White Plague: Tuberculosis, Man and Society* (Boston: Little, Brown and Company, 1952), p. 71.
2. Lois Reiser Emerick, "Valmora: The Story of an Institution" (unpuplished M.A. thesis, Department of History and Social Science, New Mexico Highlands University, 1962), p. 2.
3. "Parallel Cases, Tuberculosis: Hippocrates," *MD* (March, 1964), p. 195.
4. Dubos and Dubos, *op. cit.*
5. *Ibid.*, p. 5.
6. *Ibid.*, p. 72.
7. *Ibid.*
8. Susan Sontag, *Illness as Metaphor* (N.Y.: Farrar, Straus and Giroux, 1978), p. 9.
9. *Ibid.*, p. 10.
10. Carl H. Gellenthien, Interview at Valmora Clinic, Valmora, New Mexico, December 29, 1980.
11. Dubos and Dubos, *op. cit.*, p. 73.
12. *Ibid.*, p. 4.
13. *Ibid.*, p. 1.
14. *Ibid.*, p. 4.
15. *Ibid.*, p. 10.
16. Sontag, *op. cit.*, p. 14.
17. Dubos and Dubos, *op. cit.*, p. 1.
18. *Ibid.*, p. 4.
19. *Ibid.*, p. 70.
20. *Ibid.*, p. 71.
21. Emerick, *op. cit.*,
22. "Modern Methods of Tuberculosis Discussed: Valmora Medical Superintendent Tells of Development by Science in Fighting Disease," n.t., n.d., newspaper clipping in Scrapbook 1, Valmora Library, Valmora, New Mexico, p. 57.
23. Carl H. Gellenthien, "Gellenthien Says Climate Is Great Aid," *The Health City Sun* (Albuquerque, New Mexico), November 20, 1931, p. 1.
24. Emerick, *op. cit.*, p. 3.
25. "Parallel Cases, Tuberculosis: George Bodington," *MD* (March, 1964), p. 195.

26. Elizabeth Mooney, *In the Shadow of the White Plague* (N.Y.: Thomas Y. Crowell, Publisher, 1979), p. 36. (Reprinted by permission of Harper & Row, Publishers, Inc.)

27. "Tuberculosis: A Menace and a Mystery and $4,500,000 in Christmas Seals," *Life Magazine* (November 29, 1937), p. 32.

28. Mooney, *op. cit.*, pp. 7-8.

29. *Ibid.*, p. 24.

30. "Modern Methods of Tuberculosis Discussed: Valmora Medical Superintendent Tells of Development by Science in Fighting Disease," *op. cit.*

31. John Bunyan, *Life and Death of Mr. Badman and The Holy War*, ed. John Brown (Cambridge: The University Press, 1905), p. 157.

32. Dubos and Dubos, *op. cit.*, p. 38.

33. Paul de Kruif, *The Fight for Life* (N.Y.: Harcourt, Brace and Co., 1938), pp. 236-237. (From *The Fight for Life* by Paul de Kruif, copyright 1937, 1965 by Harcourt Brace Jovanovich, Inc., Reprinted by permission of the publisher.)

34. *Ibid.*

35. Dubos and Dubos, *op. cit.*, pp. 9-10.

36. *Ibid.*, p. 9.

37. Newspaper clipping from *The Chicago Tribune*, n.t., n.d., in Scrapbook 10, Valmora Library, Valmora, New Mexico, p. 2.

38. *Ibid.*

39. de Kruif, *op. cit.*, p. 224.

40. Evelyn Witter, "The Story of Raggedy Ann," *The Book-Mart* (April, 1983), p. 6.

41. Annual Report of the National Tuberculosis Association for the Year Ending March 31, 1961, "The People Behind the Big Push," New York: National Tuberculosis Association, 1961, p. 2.

42. Carl H. Gellenthien, "New Methods in the Treatment of Tuberculosis," Reprinted from *Industrial Medicine*, 16 (March, 1947), p. 117, in Scrapbook 3, Valmora Library, Valmora, New Mexico, p. 69.

43. *Ibid.*

44. Sontag, *op. cit.*, p. 32.

45. *Ibid.*, p. 29.

46. Dubos and Dubos, *op. cit.*, pp. 59-60.

47. Sontag, *op. cit.*, p. 11.

48. Mooney, *op. cit.*, p. 51.

49. Carl H. Gellenthien, interview at Valmora Clinic, Valmora, New Mexico, July 24, 1983.

50. Thomas Mann, *The Magic Mountain*, trans. H.T. Lowe-Porter (N.Y.: Alfred A. Knopf, 1939), p. 686.

51. *Ibid.*

52. *Ibid.*, p. 674.

53. *Ibid.*, p. 677.

54. *Ibid.*, p. 685.

55. Sontag, *op. cit.*, p. 31.

56. Dubos and Dubos., *op. cit.*, p. 60.
57. Mooney, *op. cit.*, p. 52.
58. Ibid., p. 52.
59. *Ibid.*
60. Dubos and Dubos, *op. cit.*, p. 45.
61. *Ibid.*, p. 51.
62. Ernest Dowson, "Vitae summa brevis spem nos vetat incohare longam," *The Poems of Ernest Dowson* (London: John Land, the Bodley Head, MDCCCV), p. 2.
63. H. Buxton Foreman, ed., *the Poetical Works of John Keats* (N.Y.: Thomas Y. Crowell & Co., 1865), p. 376.
64. Lionel Trilling ed., *The Selected Poems of John Keats* (N.Y.: Farrar, Straus and Young, Inc., 1951), p. 268.
65. Foreman, *op. cit.*, pp. 72-73.
66. *Ibid.*, p. 71.
67. Dubos and Dubos, *op. cit.*, p. 17.
68. Sontag, *op. cit.*, p. 28.
69. *Ibid.*, p. 20.
70. *Ibid.*, p. 29.
71. Dubos and Dubos, *op. cit.*, p. 55.
72. Charles Dickens, *The Life and Adventures of Nicholas Nickleby* (N.Y.: Hurst and Company, Publishers, n.d.), pp. 632-633.
73. *Ibid.*, p. 632.
74. W.T. Brown and C.H. Gellenthien, *Valmora Sanatorium*, Booklet 4, Valmora Sanatorium, Valmora, New Mexico, n.d., in Scrapbook 1, Valmora Library, Valmora, New Mexico, p. 3.
75. *Ibid.*, p. 26.
76. *Ibid.*, p. 26.
77. *Ibid.*, p. 26.

CHAPTER
I
Room #8

The condemned man waited in a 12' by 15' room for the hour of his death.

Room #8 was not a prison cell, for the man had committed no crime. His executioner was not the hangman or the firing squad. His death sentence was not mandated by the laws of men.

Whether languid and feverish or convulsed in paroxysms of coughing, the wasting frame of the man languished day after day in the small room. The exiled man had seen his executioner face to face. The killer wore a pale countenance with scarlet spots burned into the cheeks, a sunken chest, an emaciated, near-transparent body. The man knew well the face of his executioner. He had seen the dilated black pupils staring back at him from the mirror — the face of tuberculosis etched across his own.

The man was Carl Herman Gellenthien. The year was 1924. The small room was one of many sanctuaries of hope at Valmora Industrial Sanatorium nestled in a canyon of mountainous northern New Mexico. In Room #8 Carl Gellenthien stared back at the gaunt figure in the mirror, the pallid image of his enemy, and saw the mask of death across his face.

Yet he did not die. Somehow, one day soon after his confinement, a subtle change began to take place. How or why he did not know, but the young man knew he was to be granted a reprieve. He knew he would have to earn it. But there was no doubt. He would fight the enemy and he would win.

Carl Gellenthien knew the fight he was up against. He understood his enemy. He had been a senior in medical school at the University of Illinois. He and other aspiring young doctors had shuddered at the very sight of the "death house," the tuberculosis wing of Cook County Hospital, a building set apart from the main hospital where the hopeless cases of TB were sent to die. Even the Chicago Municipal Tuberculosis Sanatorium offered more hope than the dismal Cook County Hospital. Yet Carl was not afraid of his own death. Once he hemorrhaged so severely on a Chicago streetcar he was certain death gripped him. Coughing up mouthfuls of blood, he thought that if it was God's will for him to die now, he would accept it. But though death clutched at him, the enemy did not pull him away. His foe waited for him to face it squarely in Room #8. He did.

Gellenthien's arrival at Valmora was an unforgettable experience for the Chicago youth. He had heard of "the wide open spaces" with its cowboy lore and easy lifestyle. But crossing the line into New Mexico was like crossing the borders of a foreign land. The first thing he noticed was the space — wide grasslands without a house in view. Then he noticed the clear, blue sky above the rugged Rocky Mountains. This was all in contrast to Chicago's closely spaced concrete, glass, brick and steel and to its overcast, smoke-tinged skies. He noticed the clean, fresh smell of pine and sage in contrast to the industrial air of stockyards and steel mills. New Mexico air was dry. That, too, was different from the air currents off the lake which bathed Chicago in humidity. There was another difference, too. The change in altitude, from Chicago's 500 feet to Valmora's 6,200 feet was not so obvious, but the Sangre de Cristo mountain range captured Gellentien's attention as he looked out the window.

When the train stopped at Valmora, Gellenthien was greeted by a friendly man named Theodore Hoffman, the Business Manager of Valmora. Later he would be known to Gellenthien as "Hoff." As they approached the hospital nearly half a mile from the train stop, Gellenthien thought, "How soon will I be able to leave this place?" It was not because the place was dismal or that he was met with unfriendly greetings that he had such thoughts; it was because he was compelled to stay there, a prisoner in the bondage of disease. He began to count the days, hoping that each would bring him closer to his departure time. All the patients counted. Unfortunately, some never left; they died. However, between 1904 when Valmora was established and 1924, statistics showed that 85 percent of the patients went home free of tuberculosis. [1]

Gellenthien's first impression of Dr. William T. Brown, Valmora's founder and superintendent, was one of awe at the enormity of the man who stood six foot four in his stocking feet. Adding to his height were the cowboy boots and big "ten gallon" western hat. To Gellenthien, who stood 5'10" and weighed considerably less than his normal 150 pounds due to his illness, Brown's gigantic appearance was awesome but not intimidating. Brown was not only a big man; he was a big source of hope. On him the future hinged, for this man could advise him how best to recover his health and enable him to return to medical school.

Carl Gellenthien was not alone among the members of his profession to develop TB. Gellenthien was the 14th member of his class to drop out of school with TB. Of the 14 students who left the University of Illinois College of Medicine that year, only two went west, Gellenthien to Valmora, his classmate to Colorado Springs. Those two alone recovered. The other 12 succumbed.[2]

At first the twenty-four-year old wondered if he would ever see his Chicago home again, if he would become the medical missionary he hoped to be. Lying in bed reading and thinking, Gellenthien planned specific goals. He mapped out his life in three major parts: he would become an internist, a medical researcher, and a country doctor. He might even marry and have a family. Whatever he did, he would not succumb to America's number one killer. He looked in the mirror and told himself that his doctors were wrong. He would not die. He would fight the enemy.

Complete bed rest was an essential part of the treatment. When Dr. Brown ordered bed rest, he meant absolute bed rest, usually for at least six weeks, but longer if fever persisted. Activity was taboo. Even raising the arms was forbidden. A deep breath was discouraged because the lesion in the lungs might be stretched and ruptured. The idea was to slow the pace to near hibernation so the lungs could heal. Even when patients were allowed to be up, they were cautioned against any strenuous movements. Dr. Brown advised:

> Unless otherwise specified "exercise" means walking. Other forms of exercise such as playing croquet, etc., should not be taken without special permission. One can take considerable exercise by getting in and out of his chair. Violent exertion is injurious. When a patient's temperature reaches 99.5 he should...take no further "exercise."...The "exercise" prescribed for someone else may in no way fit your case, and irregularity in this regard will not only fail to benefit you, but may prove detrimental to your welfare.
> NEVER HURRY.[3]

Dr. Brown did not allow patients to get up to use the bathroom until they were deemed well enough to do so. Later, when Gellenthien became Medical Director at Valmora, he also cautioned against exercise, but he changed that particular rule and gave his patients bathroom privileges as he felt that the emotional benefits of getting up to use the bathroom outweighed the unpleasantness and stress of "having to wrestle with a bedpan."[4]

Consumptives were told to repress coughing as much as possible in order to conserve their energy and place less stress on the lungs. They were cautioned not to laugh too hard or to weep because even that emotional activity consumed energy and placed stress on the respiratory system.

When Bess Comstock, a TB victim, was sent to Saranac Lake in the 1920s, she discovered the standard treatment for TB — absolute bed rest for a minimum of six weeks but longer if fever persisted. A fever of 100 degrees Fahrenheit meant bed rest.

> At first she wept, thinking of the two children at home, the parties going on without her, the maples turning silver and red outside the door of her new home. But they warned her against tears, pointing out that an infant crying doubles his metabolic rate, a bad thing for a consumptive. [5]

A deep breath was not allowed because the lesion in the lungs might be stretched and pour out its poisons. In order to give the body's defenses every chance to work against the invading bacilli, the pace had to be slowed to near hibernation while the battle raged within the patient. At first Bess was not allowed to hold a book and read. She simply had to lie on her back and look out the window at the mountains. Later she was allowed to read and to write one letter a day but it was a long time before she was allowed to take up her sewing because sewing expends nine calories per hour. [6]

Coughing was to be suppressed as much as possible. Bess Comstock's doctor warned that a man who coughs hard all day does as much work as a man who climbs a mountain, and every bit of energy was needed to fight the disease. [7] Patients were sometimes given ice to hold in their mouths to help suppress coughing.

At Valmora, too, patients were advised to suppress coughing.

> The exertion of coughing may raise the temperature and pulse, and hinder the healing process in the lung. Seventy-five percent of all coughing is unnecessary. It can and should be suppressed as much as possible. [8]

Besides the danger to the patient himself, coughing was discouraged because it gave the bacilli a vehicle for travel. Unable to move independently, the bacilli could travel several feet if a cough was not covered. Patients were asked to cover their mouths with a cloth if coughing could not be avoided.

> Everyone, of course, understood that coughing spread the germs, which lingered in the room for three hours and projected three feet from the cougher's mouth. But the germs were also transmitted from spit in the streets, brought indoors on shoes or long skirts, where they set up housekeeping and...were redistributed when the maid swept. As early as 1920 the doctors had figured out if you lay on a couch

*which a tubercular had just vacated, you ran a risk of infection. But no
one really knew why some resisted the obviously frequent exposure
and remained healthy, and others, living under sanitary and affluent
conditions, succumbed.* [9]

Patients were allowed to cough in the morning upon waking to
obtain a sputum sample for the laboratory but were to try to suppress
couging for the rest of the day.

Everything was done to encourage the patients to eat and gain
weight. Most TB patients had poor appetites and even with high
calorie diets gained little. When it came time to weigh in, they would
do everything they could to make the scales show another pound or
two. They would drink several glasses of water before weighing in or
would put silver dollars in their pockets to add to their weight.

The two main objectives in the treatment of tuberculosis were: 1)
to promote physical rest by a prolonged stay in bed and, in selected
cases, to rest the diseased lung by some form of collapse or compres-
sion therapy; and 2) to promote mental and psychological rest and a
positive mental attitude.

Although there were more than forty individual factors involved
in the treatment of TB, the most important individual factor was rest,
the closest thing to a specific therapy available. With the diseased
lung at rest, the lymph flow was impeded and there was tendency to
fibrosis; the disease then became localized. [10]

*The rationale of the rest treatment is best demonstrated by analogy.
Let us suppose that the palm of the hand has been cut to the bone. It
has been sutured. If the fist were opened and closed from twelve to
thirty times a minute it is evident that the cut would have a hard time
healing.*

*And so it is with the lungs. Tuberculosis causes ulcers, and as we
breathe twelve to thirty times a minute, or approximately 30,000
times a day, the scar tissue is constantly torn by this contraction and
expansion of the lung, and the healing process is retarded.*

*Patients should be in bed because less work is required of the lungs
when lying than when sitting or standing.* [11]

Besides the general body rest provided by bed rest, there were four
non-surgical and fifteen surgical methods for promoting local rest.
The non-surgical methods included lying on the affected side, placing a weight on the chest over the affected side, and using appliances
such as casts, adhesive straps and binders to limit chest motion and
control diaphragmatic breathing. [12]

Chest surgery was done to put the lung at rest just as one would
put a broken bone in a cast to promote healing. The various techniques included pneumolysis or separation of an adherent lung from

30

the costal pleura; pneumoperitoneum where gas or air was artificially injected into the peritoneal cavity when pneumothorax was impossible; and phrenectomy, limiting the expansion of the lung by paralyzing the hemi-diaphragm by resecting the phrenic nerve. Sometimes the nerve was just crushed or severed rather than removed. Regardless of what was done, the nerve usually grew back in time. The most common procedure was artificial pneumothorax. Nitrogen was introduced into the chest wall to force the lung to collapse and rest. Later it was discovered that ordinary air would work just as well as nitrogen and without the cost. Elizabeth Mooney gave a vivid description:

> It was an exceedingly traumatic operation, for, like all surgery for consumptives, it had to be done with the patient fully conscious.
>
> In the operation a long needle was inserted between the ribs to pierce the chest wall. The sound was one of the worst things about it — rather like a knitting needle going though heavy cardboard. Patients who had undergone pneumothorax often suffered noisy breathing afterwards. [13]

Another method of resting the lung was to insert foreign bodies. Wax was tried, but it melted and slipped beneath the diaphragm. Other substances such as olive oil were tried. Even ping pong balls were used in the attempt to plug the yawning cavities in the lung. The idea was that the ping pong balls would squeeze the lung into submissive rest. But this procedure also proved unsuccessful because foreign bodies in the chest cavity introduced pressure and caused necrosis or gangrene and fistulae. Dr. Gellenthien once walked down the hall of a hospital where he saw surgeons putting in ping pong balls in one operating room and in the next operating room surgeons were busy taking them out.

Collapsing the chest wall by thoracoplasty, removing ribs, was another method. If the periosteum (the fibrous membrane which forms the investing covering of the ribs) was left intact, the ribs would grow back in time. If not, the condition would be permanent. The procedure often left the patient with a severely crippled hand due to the unavoidable involvement of the brachial plexis. [14]

Mooney described the operation:

> Thoracoplasty was hard even on the doctors — a long, long operation which was a terrible shock to the patient. Of course it had to be done under local anesthetic, so the patient missed nothing of what was going on. It was usually done in three stages because it was so demanding of both patient and doctor.
>
> A long incision was made down the back a few inches from the backbone. The physician then removed nine ribs in order to collapse

the lung permanently. *Often the infection spilled from the bad lung into the good because the patient was forced to lie on his side during the
operation. The sound of rib removal was enormously loud in the
operating room, and the fully conscious patient suffered unbelievable
mental anguish.* [15]

Finally, surgical techniques became sophisticated enough to
allow resecting lobules, lobes, or the entire lung.

A chronological outline of the development and use of various
surgical techniques follows:

1905-1915: Pneumothorax was employed...

*1915-1925: ...chest surgery, especially phrenic exairesis and
thoracoplasty, became more popular. Tuberculin tests were first used
in mass surveys making this period the time when modern control
measures began.*

*1925-1939: The next 10 years...brought great emphasis on the
epidemiological phases of tuberculosis. Contacts were more frequently examined and morbidity and mortality statistics became more accurate...Pneumothorax was being used more intelligently and selectively. Pneumolysis, oleothorax and bronchoscopy became more
frequent.*

*Chest x-rays became more common and were claimed to be the
most accurate diagnostic procedure we possessed.*

*1935-1945: The development of the photo fluorograph and the
automatic phototimer made mass x-ray studies possible. The search
for a "specific" treatment was directed to chemotherapy and the antibiotics...In surgery, thoracoplasty procedures were refined and used
more intelligently and selectively. Pneumonectomy and lobectomy
became more common.* [16]

After the discovery of chemotherapy, surgical procedures were rare-
ly used. The introduction of streptomycin, dihydrostreptomycin,
PAS (para-aminosalicylic acid), INH (isoniazid) and other such drugs
made surgery unnecessary.

Before drugs were discovered, the three essentials of treatment
were rest, food, and fresh air.

*It has been said that the length of stay necessary in a sanatorium or
the length of time required to cure or arrest the disease is in inverse
proportion to the number of hours spent in the open night air at rest.*

*Night air is not harmful and your room should never, even when
you are dressing or disrobing, be entirely closed.*

Drafts and crowded rooms should be avoided.

*Remember that a porch is the most essential feature of the
cottage.* [18]

Gellenthien's credo became, "Fresh air! Internally! Externally!

and Eternally!" Some nights would get as cold as 40 degrees below zero. Patients used newspapers on the mattresses for insulation and piled on blankets and coats. They wore warm clothing from head to toe. But they left the windows open, and not one caught pneumonia. Colds were a rarity. Dr. Lawrason Brown of Trudeau Sanatorium was one of the many specialists of the early days who recommended cold, pure mountain air for consumptives and insisted they sleep out on their porches even in the bitter winter weather. At Valmora patients would get out in the sun and even take nude sunbaths in the winter was well as in the warmer months, enjoying the solarium which was built for that purpose.

Foot warmers were used to help warm the beds. There was a heavy round bed warmer made of stone that could be filled with hot water. It was supposd to warm the bed all night, but often in the morning it would be cold and would make the bed even more uncomfortable. This item was called a "pig."

Climate was a large part of the cure. Climate is made up of temperature, barometric pressure, humidity, precipitation, evaporation, winds, clouds, sunshine, pollutants, pollens and electrical conditions in the air. All of these various meteorological elements affect the health, either adversely or beneficially. Recommended locations for "lungers" included Italy, the Mediterranean, the South Pacific, and the American southwest. "Lungers" began coming in large numbers in the 1800s, "chasing the cure," seeking the high, dry, cool air and the germ-killing sunlight of the Rockies. The argument was that cold, humid winters with little sunshine consumed the patient's energy and depleted his resistance and ability to combat the invading tubercle bacilli. Thus, a warm, dry, mild climate at high altitudes was thought to be beneficial.

New Mexico was especially attractive. The climate in the State ranges from arid to semi-arid and from warm to temperate, depending on the altitude which varies from the lowest elevation of 2,280 to more than 13,000 feet in the northern mountains. The State's average altitude is 5,700 feet. Winters are mild, and summers are marked by warm days and cool nights. Humidity is low and the sun shines nearly every day. The high altitudes cause definite body changes attributable to the lowered pressure of oxygen and lower barometric pressure.[18]

The benefits of high altitude were explained in a booklet prepared for Valmora patients:

> White corpuscles of the blood are the body's defenders against those invading enemy germs, and red corpuscles are the transportation units rushing food and ammunition to the army on the field of battle.

> Red bone marrow is the manufactory of red corpuscles. As the
> pressure of oxygen falls in the surrounding air, compensation is ef-
> fected by increased activity of the red bone marrow, speeding up pro-
> duction of its red corpuscles. With more of these available, there is an
> increased flow of blood through the lungs. The army of white cor-
> puscles then begins to pick up, to fight with renewed vigor and greater
> efficiency; supplies have come in, reinforcements, food,
> ammunition. [19]

Thus, when enemy germs invade the body, a struggle between in-
vader and defender ensues, as powerful and dramatic as any of the
wars of the nations of the world. In order to be victorious, the
defenders must destroy the enemy or, if that is impossible, to im-
prison them to starve and die in an impregnable wall of scar tissue. [20]

The role of high altitude in the healing process was significant.
In high altitudes, a cubic foot of air contains a higher percentage of
oxygen by volume than a cubic foot of air in lower altitudes. This is
largely due to lesser concentrations of smoke and other impurities. [21]
In other words, more oxygen is taken in with no greater effort in
breathing.

> A further advantage of this favorable altitude is the lowered
> barometric pressure. Lungs, naturally, are supposed to fill the thoracic
> cavity in which they are enclosed. They contract or expand in accor-
> dance with outside air pressure. At sea level this pressure is fifteen
> pounds to the square inch, while...at Valmora, for example,
> barometric pressure is eleven pounds to the square inch. It can be
> understood...how this four pounds less pressure would be less in-
> jurious, less apt to tear the delicate tissue struggling to heal itself. [22]

Sunshine was another significant factor for those "chasing the
cure." "At Valmora, the 6,200 foot altitude means one mile less of air
to weaken the bacteria-killing light; thus, the actinic ray is more
powerful than at Chicago's 500 foot altitude." [23]

Patients were urged to go where the air was clean and free from
low altitude congestion of impurities and dampness. Many came
from cities where they had been unaccustomed to seeing the sun,
especially during the winter months. At Valmora it was discovered
in three years of observation that there had been only two sunless
days a year. Thus, patients were able to be out nearly every day, and
the psychological effect was evident. People are happier and more
optimistic when they are able to relax in the warm sunshine and feel
its healing light fall upon overtired, overstrained bodies. [24]

It was found that sunlight treatment was especially helpful in
tuberculosis of the bone, throat and intestines. In 1902 the first experiments were tried in Switzerland by exposing tubercular wounds

to direct sunlight. As a result of the success of this heliotherapy, tubercular arms and legs which ordinarily would have been amputated were cured.

Long light rays and heat rays given out by the sun do their share as well as the ultra-violet. Being out of doors in the sunshine for so much of the time, the patient gradually acquires a tanned, light-absorbing skin, in place of his white, light reflecting one. There is mental stimulation, too; greater cheerfulness is evidenced in keener appetite, more restful sleep, and a marked improvement in general health. [25]

In all types of pulmonary tuberculosis, the use of sunlight had to be restricted. When it was used, in selected cases, the greatest care had to be taken to avoid hemorrhage. For bone, throat and intestinal TB, however, sunlight was almost a specific. Heliotherapy was used in many non-tuberculous conditions also. [26]

It was believed that mountain air generally contains twice the amount of ultra-violet rays as does the atmosphere of low places. The sun was called "nature's great disinfectant and curing assistant." [27] It was known that tubercular germs directly exposed to the sunlight would die. The rays of the sun assisted the vaso-dilation of the tissues, aiding in breaking down blockades and hurrying the blood along in its work of destroying the invading enemy germs. Less congestion in the internal organs, less interference with the blood-cell fights, and certain alterations for the better in the blood chemistry could all be directly attributed to the rays of the sun. [28]

It was also believed that the sun's rays were assisted by air movement and that cool air in motion was beneficial. The overtaxed heat regulating mechanism of the fevered body had a better chance for balancing the inner with the outer temperature when exposed to moving air that is neither too hot nor too cold. It was thought that low humidity, coolness, purity, and motion of the air kept the skin working at its highest efficiency. Fresh air was thought to be essential to recovery: out-of-door air which was cool and dry rather than damp, diverse in temperature rather than uniform and monotonous, moving rather than still. Moderate temperature and low humidity profoundly affect one's physical and mental well-being. [29]

It was believed that TB was primarily an indoor disease where the germs could overcome the body's fighting forces. The dusty, overheated air of crowded places would lessen the defenses of the respiratory tract membranes, and the germs spread more easily in a crowd. Cool air increases the blood flow and encourages the secretion of germ-killing fluids. But in hot, moist climates the mucous membrane lining of air passages is less active. [30]

The results of Valmora's salubrious climate were evident in

statistics. Of 800 patients who entered between the ten year period of September 15, 1927 to September 14, 1937, three-fourths, or 597 patients, were diagnosed as having pulmonary TB. Somewhat over half had reached the far-advanced stage and the rest of the pulmonary cases were equally divided between minimal and moderately advanced. Thirty-eight or 4.8 percent were diagnosed as having some other type of TB. (The other 20.6 percent, or 165 persons, were admitted for other illnesses.) The record of discharge showed that eighty-four percent, or 672 or all the TB cases, were improved or better. Only 46 or 5.8 percent left unimproved, and 60 or 7.5 percent died. (Twenty-two or 2.7 percent were not included as they came for diagnosis only.) Compared with general results of TB hospitalization in the United States, only 57 percent of over 40,000 cases in 278 civilian sanatoria became improved or better. In 29 veterans' sanatoria only 37 percent of the 3,294 cases showed progress. Valmora's 84 percent "cure" rate was far superior. [31]

Thus, when Carl Gellenthien arrived in 1924 he was met with the best treatment available at the time. Valmora had the best in climate for the invalid: sunlight, fresh air, high altitude, cool breezes, dry air and pleasant surroundings. Carl was given bed rest to begin with. He was given the best in nutrition and encouraged to gain weight. He was allowed to read after the first long days of bed rest had passed. While he was taking the cure, he thought and planned, mapping out his life with the hope that only a 24-year-old youth can have. At Valmora, his hopes were fed as he was stimulated and encouraged by the staff as well as his fellow patients, and those hopes flourished.

The psychological benefits of sunshine and fresh air have already been mentioned. Robert Louis Stevenson, who retreated to a Pacific exile, found this psychological element significant.

"By a curious irony," Stevenson wrote, "the places to which we are sent when health deserts us are often singularly beautiful...I daresay the sick man is not very inconsolable when he receives sentence of banishment, and is inclined to regard his ill-health as not the least fortunate accident of his life." [32]

So it was that Carl Gellenthien, though 1,180 miles away from home, found his prison was not without beauty. The door of his room opened onto a well-lighted porch looking out into the lovely green patio where sun and breeze and scent of growing things cheered him. The sounds of birds moving among the flowers and trees beckoned the invalid back to life.

But the charm and beauty of nature are not enough, of themselves, to effect a cure. All of nature's most bountiful attractions may not stay the insidious executioner's hand. Stevenson wrote that in spite of the beauty of his surroundings, tuberculosis wore him down.

> For fourteen years I have not had a day of real health. I have awaken-
> ed sick and gone to bed weary, yet I have done my work unflinchingly.
> I have written in bed and out of bed, written in hemorrhages, written
> in sickness, written torn by coughing, written when my head swam
> from weakness — and I have done it so long that it seems to me I have
> won my wager and recovered my glove. Yet the battle still goes on; ill
> or well is a trifle so long as it goes. I was made for a contest, and the
> Powers-That-Be have willed that my battlefield shall be the inglorious
> one of the bed and the medicine bottle. [33]

Beauty was conducive to recovery but could not itself turn death away. Keats, who worshipped beauty, failed to recover in spite of his beautiful surroundings in Rome. Doomed to death even as his genius came into full power, Keats knew the cup was being taken from him. His mother and brother Tom had preceeded him in death from TB. At the age of 24 his self was nearly maddened by the knowledge of certain extinction.

It must have been so for Carl Gellenthien. At the age of 24 he had great hopes for a full life as a medical missionary. He wanted to finish school, to see the scourge of tuberculosis — his mortal enemy — conquered once and for all. He wanted to repay his parents who had financed his stay at Valmora. But he had to recover first, and his prognosis was not good. His disease was so advanced that his doctors told him not to make any plans. They expected him to be dead within two years.

In Room #8, the first room to the left at the top of the hospital stairs, Gellenthien reflected on how he had discovered his own tuberculosis. He had been attending classes all day at the Univeristy of Illinois, spending his evenings working as Secretary at the YMCA, and his nights working as City Surgeon at the Iroquois Memorial City Hospital taking care of emergency cases from the downtown Chicago loop. As a senior in medical school, his studies were increasingly demanding and he was fatigued from his long hours. The winter of 1923 he had suffered from "wet" pleurisy. His doctor had tapped his chest to drain off the fluid, but he did not recognize the insidious tuberculosis lurking there. The summer of 1924 Carl enjoyed the YMCA summer camp in Wisconsin but noticed his energy waning. In the fall when he returned to his classes, he thought his symptoms meant the return of the pleurisy he had suffered the winter before. But he told no one of his concern.

One day in October, while working in the clinical laboratory along with a classmate, Earl Ewert, Carl coughed into a handkerchief and then excused himself. Earl, who later became Chief of the Urology Department of Boston's Lehey Clinic, worried about Carl. Later he learned what had happened. Carl had gone into the private laboratory and made a slide of his own sputum. Then he showed it to his professor. The slide disclosed multitudes of the acid-fast, rod-shaped bacteria, many more than the average TB patient's specimen would ordinarily show. It was the kind of slide that lab technicians said could "practically walk away by itself." Remarking on the fine quality specimen of tubercle bacilli, the professor inquired where Carl had procured the slide of this advanced case of TB. The young man confessed that the specimen was his own.

Earl didn't see his classmate again for two years. The promising young medical student was examined by the best specialists in Chicago and given a diagnosis of "far advanced submiliary pulmonary tuberculosis" — with a guarded prognosis. He was a "plus four," a person whose body was so overrun with bacilli that he was certain to have a short future. Lab technicians told lurid tales of the short futures of the highly contagious "plus fours," a name "for those whose sputum samples were so jammed with bacilli they could scarcely be counted."[34]

But it was Carl himself, not a lab technician, who first saw that bacilli-jammed slide. He had no idea where or when he had contracted the disease. Perhaps he had picked up the germs in the autopsy room in one of his lab sessions. Perhaps he had caught the disease from a patient. Certainly his fatigued body was susceptible enough to illness under the stress of his heavy schedule. Whatever the cause, the disease changed his life.

On November 1, 1924, Gellenthien arrived at Valmora with the words of his highly renowned professors haunting his memory: "You'd better not make any plans, young man. You probably won't be back." When he pressed them for more answers, they said that with his kind of advanced TB, he could expect less than two years to live.

How then did the young man recover from an illness that should have killed him?

To know why the condemned man did not die, to understand how he lived to become one of the conquerors of his enemy, one must understand something of who he was, how he came to be there, and what influences directed him.

NOTES

1. "Valmora in Chicago," *Las Vegas Daily Optic*, October 10, 1932, p. 4.
2. Carl Gellenthien, interview at Valmora Clinic, Valmora, New Mexico, September 10, 1982.
3. William T. Brown and C.H. Gellenthien, *Valmora Sanatorium*, Booklet 4, *op. cit.*, p. 7.
4. Carl H. Gellenthien, interview at Valmora Clinic, Valmora, New Mexico, September 5, 1981.
5. Mooney, *op. cit.*, p. 32.
6. *Ibid.*, p. 50.
7. *Ibid.*, p. 33.
8. W.T. Brown and C.H. Gellenthien, *Valmora Sanatorium*, Booklet 4, *op. cit.*, p. 9.
9. Mooney, *op. cit.*, p. 81.
10. C.H. Gellenthien, "'Rest,' the Most Important Aid in 'Curing' T.B.," *The Valmora Sun*, January, 1939, p. 6, in Scrapbook 3, Valmora Library, Valmora, New Mexico, p. 23.
11. *Ibid.*
12. *Ibid.*
13. Mooney, *op. cit.*, p. 185.
14. Carl H. Gellenthien, interview at Valmora Clinic, Valmora, New Mexico, August 10, 1983.
15. Mooney, *op. cit.*, pp. 187-188.
16. Carl H. Gellenthien, "New Methods in the Treatment of Tuberculosis," *op. cit.*, pp. 1-2.
17. Carl H. Gellenthien, interview at Valmora Clinic, Valmora, New Mexico, December 29, 1980.
18. Carl H. Gellenthien, interview at Valmora Clinic, Valmora, New Mexico, June 15, 1982.
19. Carl H. Gellenthien, *Valmora Sanatorium*, Booklet 6, Valmora Sanatorium, Valmora, New Mexico, n.d., in Scrapbook 3, Valmora Library, Valmora, New Mexico, p. 47.
20. Carl H. Gellenthien, interview at Valmora, New Mexico, July 29, 1981.
21. Carl H. Gellenthien, *Valmora Sanatorium*, Booklet 6, *op. cit.*
22. *Ibid.*
23. Carl H. Gellenthien, interview at Valmora, October 21, 1981.
24. *Ibid.*

25. Carl H. Gellenthien, *Valmora Sanatorium,* Booklet 6, *op. cit.*
26. *Ibid.*
27. Carl H. Gellenthien, interview at Valmora, October 20, 1981.
28. *Ibid.*
29. *Ibid.*
30. *Ibid.*
31. "Statistical Report Tells Graphic Story," *the Valmora Sun,* February, 1939, p. 8, in Scrapbook 3, Valmora Library, Valmora, New Mexico, p. 25.
32. Sontag, *op. cit.,* p. 33.
33. "The Power of Art Over Disease," *Robins Reader* (Richmond, Virginia: A.H. Robins Company, Spring-Summer, 1982). p. 6.
34. Mooney, *op. cit.,* p. 84.

CHAPTER II

Crossing the Bridge

The trip from Chicago to Valmora was not an easy one. On the train headed west, Carl Gellenthien had time to think about the disease that had caused him to drop out of medical school and to wonder if he would ever return home again. He had time to reflect on the events of the past few years and to think about his family. The hopes and dreams of his boyhood returned to him. The memories of his home and his neighborhood flickered across his mind with each passing mile.

He thought about the fateful day he had discovered his tuberculosis and the diagnosis had been confirmed. That was the day he'd had to tell his father he had TB and would have to drop out of school. It was a dismal moment when he left the University campus to go to the post office where his father worked. All his hopes and dreams seemed extinguished. His house of cards had collapsed around him. His parents' sacrifices were to be futile, he thought.

As Carl crossed the bridge over the Chicago River on the elevated train that day, he looked down at the water and it seemed inviting. It was the only time Carl ever seriously considered suicide. The thought occurred to him that he should jump. But he would not allow the thought to linger. He went on across the bridge and up to his father's office to tell him the news. The bridge he crossed that day was not just the span across the Chicago River. It was the bridge that took him from his life as a Chicago medical student to his destiny as a world-famous doctor.

Charles Gellenthien's love for his son was evident that day in October when the youth came unexpectedly into his father's office. It was a crushing blow but Charles would not allow his son to entertain hopelessness. He told his son that he would recover and return to complete medical school. And he believed it. In fact, Charles staked all his earthly possessions on that belief. He mortaged his home to send Carl to Valmora.

As he reflected on that day and thought of his family, Carl Gellenthien, traveling west for the first time in his life, realized that there was a ray of hope. He was on his way to the best tuberculosis sanatorium in the southwest. He thought of his family and realized that he had strong ancestors. If his genes carried the courage and strength of his grandparents and parents, then heredity factors were in his favor. Both sets of grandparents had come to America from Germany in the middle 1800s with the hope of finding freedom and prosperity. His grandfather, Karl Gellenthien, was a stubborn man who insisted on speaking English, proud that he could speak the language of his new home though he murdered the language unmercifully at times.

Like most immigrants, the Gellenthiens had two goals: to own a home and to educate their children. To them, real estate and education were the most valuable assets a family could have, and they were willing to work hard to attain them. Karl Gellenthien got up early each morning, took his daily "schnapps" or spirits to warm his blood and, to save street car fare, often walked the six miles to the tannery/furriery on Goose Island where he toiled until dark.

The Gellenthien home where Carl was born was located on the corner of Marshfield and Haddon. The home on Chicago's northwest side, 1103 North Marshfield Avenue, was just down the street from the YMCA located where Ashland Avenue, Milwaukee Avenue and Division Street form a triangle. The older Gellenthiens lived on the ground floor of their three-story home and rented the upper stories for extra income.

Karl's son, Charles, who was born March 16, 1873, was a cabinet maker when he met Bertha Beeskow, the daughter of John Beeskow. After Charles and Bertha were married, Charles became a postal clerk. Bertha, born March 29, 1877, was a seamstress with her own successful sewing school before she married. After marriage she concentrated on her tasks as a homemaker. There were two boys and two girls to be fed, clothed and cared for. Charles supported his family on $40.00 a month.

While his parents lived on the first floor of the Gellenthien home, Charles and his wife lived in the basement. It was there that their first child, Carl Herman Gellenthien, was born on November 27, 1900. Two years later Henry was born. Irma, the oldest daughter, was born July 13, 1905, and the youngest, Elvira, was born October 15, 1909.

Like Charles, Bertha valued education and believed in continual learning. She wanted her children to learn to play the piano. Carl thought boys who played the piano were sissies, and he hated going to his teacher's house for music lessons, hated more the recitals. One day on his way to his teacher's house to practice for a recital, Carl saw a terrible accident. A boy had grabbed the back of a truck, slipped under the wheels, and was killed. Carl went home and told his mother he couldn't possibly go to his music lesson after seeing that mishap. In fact, he could not take part in the recital because the song he had to play would remind him of the accident and make him ill. He might never be able to play the piano again, he reasoned, because music lessons would remind him of the accident too. Carl's mother was sympathetic as Carl pleaded piteously to be allowed to skip his lessons. Consequently, he never had to take piano lessons again, something he regretted later in life.

The lofty goals of Carl's family helped him to determine his future. Through his German-Lutheran religion classes at St. John's Elementary School, Carl learned the language of his ancestors. He attended Wells Grade School and was active in the YMCA. It was, in fact, the influence of the YMCA near his home that made Carl decide to become a social worker. He wanted to sleep in the "flop house" on West Madison Street where the homeless milled around during the day looking for work or handouts and slept on cots lined up in the big room at night, separated only by chicken wire. Carl thought he ought to sleep there himself to prepare himself to become a good social worker. But his parents would not allow him to spend even one night in the "flop house." They told him he'd bring home lice. He'd have to get his practical experience elsewhere.

Throughout his life, Carl would fight if it came to defending his rights or someone else's. His instinctive reflex action to defend himself was displayed when he was about 17 years old. As he stood near a corner drug store awaiting a streetcar, two fellows intent on robbing him approached. The front doorway was slanted and the concrete was icy. When Carl saw the robber pull a gun, demanding money, he punched the thug on the jaw, knocking him back. The thief slipped on the icy walk, fell, and blacked out when his head hit the concrete. As the other fellow pulled his gun, Carl began to run. He ran two blocks toward an oncoming streetcar, weaving in and out, while the thief yelled, "Stop or I'll shoot!"

Carl ran past the conductor who began to protest that the youth had not paid his nickel fare. But Carl ran on toward the policeman he'd spotted on the front platform of the car. Advised of the situation, the cop had Carl guard the unconscious thief with the hold-up man's gun. The officer proceeded after the fleeing gunman who took cover in an alley, stuck his gun around the corner, and shouted that he'd shoot if the cop came any closer. The officer kept after him and arrested him in the alley. Later Carl's father accompanied him down to the police station to tell the Captain his story.

"Just how much did you have in your pockets?" the Captain asked.

"A dollar Ingersol watch and 15 cents," Carl answered.

The Captain scolded him, saying it wasn't worth risking his life for that. But he couldn't deny that two robbers were apprehended because of the courage of an officer and a young man.

Like other boys his age, Carl was expected to do his share of work. He made ten cents a day working after school and on Saturdays at his uncle's grocery store and meat market. This was a good addition to the penny-a-week allowance he received from his father. With the prospect of collecting many pennies, Carl tolerated the complaints from customers when he inexpertly cut off 9 cents' worth of cheese instead of the requested 10 cents' worth. He was soon able to weigh out a pound of butter expertly. As a cashier, he learned to add columns. Carl had a little pony and cart, and he delivered groceries all over the neighborhood. He visited the merchants in the area, selling a wax his uncle had developed to keep hot flat-irons from sticking to cloth. He also helped his grandfather herd milk cows. They would take the cows up to Humboldt Park. There was a lake in the Park where the children enjoyed rowboats in the summer and skating in the winter. It was probably there that Carl first experienced the cold Chicago wind which he dubbed "marrow bite."

Carl found other ways to supplement his penny allowance. The Jewish women were not allowed to work on the Sabbath, so Carl would go to their homes Friday evenings to light the gas stoves for cooking kosher meals. He received a penny from each woman for doing such chores.

Sometimes Carl's methods were of the Tom Sawyer tradition. When Haley's Comet appeared, he made a newspaper telescope. He and his companions charged a penny for anyone to look through it to see the comet. The customers would lie down on the sidewalk and look up through the telescope. Then the boys would pour cold water down the telescope into the faces of the unsuspecting customers. Needless to say, there were few repeat customers.

Another boyish prank was to trick the peddlers who came through selling junk. The boys called them "Gypsies." One boy would distract them by throwing snowballs at them while the other boys would steal items from the back of the wagon. Then the boys would bring the items they'd taken and sell the junk back to them. The peddlers had so much junk they never knew the difference and gladly paid the boys — or perhaps they knew and gladly paid the boys to leave them alone!

Carl's teachers at the parochial school were strict. A rap on the knuckles with the ruler was almost a daily ritual. For especially inattentive boys, a favorite punishment was to shut the offender in the closet with his hands tied up to the hangers. He'd have to stay there for hours. After Carl experienced this a time or two, he began to play hooky. For a while his truancy went undiscovered, especially when he forged his report cards. When he was finally caught and given a whipping, he went to bed feeling so miserable he hoped he'd die so that all his relatives would realized how mean his parents were. He wanted to run away but was hurting too much. By the next day he had changed his mind.

One winter day Carl and his friends skipped school, built a fire by the Butler Building Paper Company, and decided to chew tobacco as they sat around the fire. Carl became ill after this first experience with tobacco and went home. His mother put him to bed, greatly worried and wondering what disease had stricken her little boy. When Carl's father got home, the sympathy ended.

"You've been chewing tobacco!" he declared.

Carl never figured out how his father knew what he'd done, but he never forgot the whipping he got for it.

One Sunday evening Carl went to hear Al Jolson sing at a Vaudeville show. It was considered a sin to attend such a show, especially on Sunday. Carl's teacher turned him in and he was punished. Later Carl wondered how the teacher knew he'd been there unless the teacher had been there too!

Carl's school was more than a mile from home and the school bus had not yet been introduced. However, the West Side Brewery was located at Marshfield Avenue and Augusta Boulevard. So Carl would catch a ride on the beer wagon to go to school, standing on a keg and studying his catechism along the way. Pastor Succop saw him and told Carl's parents it was sinful for the boy to ride on a beer wagon, studying his religion, instead of walking to school. Carl was reprimanded.

The youth did manage do a few things his parent's didn't find out about. When they weren't looking he and the other youngsters would gather sticky tar from the street and chew it. They thought it was a good substitute for the penny-stick of gum they couldn't afford.

The boys used to jump from one roof top to another where the buildings were only a few feet apart. One slip would have resulted in a three-story fall but the boys were unmindful of the danger just as they were careless enough to hook on to the cable wire and ride down the street behind the streetcar.

On the Fourth of July one year the boys made their own "fireworks," using carbide powder. The powder was carried in a small barrel on the running boards of cars and was used to light the headlights. The boys collected carbide gas by putting a big tin milk can over the carbide. After putting in a home-made fuse and adding water, the boys lit the fuse and dashed away. The milk can exploded with a huge bang and flew nearly two stories high before crashing to the ground.

When Carl was a teen-ager, the family sold their home on North Marshfield and moved to 4937 West Huron Street about five miles away. His parents could no longer afford to send Carl to the private German-Lutheran school, and they believed the public schools were sinful. Pastor Succop tried to convince Charles that since he couldn't afford to send Carl to the parochial school beyond the eighth grade, there was no need for Carl to coninue his education; he should get a job. But Carl was determined to finish high school. Since he wanted to graduate with his buddies from the old neighborhood, he took the street car every day, from 1914 to 1918, to attend Murray-Tuley High School.

The new home was a two-story, brick "row" house. The buildings were about 10 feet apart, not close enough for young boys to jump from one roof to another. But by that time Carl had outgrown such activities and was busy with his studies and part-time jobs. He was secretary for the Division Street YMCA and had a part-time job at Marshall Field's, the largest department store in Chicago, in the men's clothing department. He made a dollar a day but had to spend 5 cents' fare each way for the streetcar and 25 cents for a meal at a nearby restaurant.

Left with only 65 cents a day, Carl decided to ask for a 25 cent raise. His boss told him he wasn't worth it. Some years later when Carl was nationally recognized for his medical work, the President of Marshall Field, one of Valmora's sponsors, wanted to take Dr. Gellenthien on a tour of the store. Gellenthien replied that he was already familiar with the store as he had worked there as a youth. Then he told the President about his unsuccessful request for a 25-cent raise and they had a good laugh about it.

Carl graduated from high school on a Thursday night and started working at Wahl-Henius Institute of Fermentology the next morning. As assistant chemist at the brewmaster's school, Carl tested beer for turbidity, amount of lactic acid, alcohol, and so on. Carl attended Crane College, a junior college in the Chicago School System, taking chemistry and biology, graduating in 1921. Although his goal had been to become a social worker, he now decided to become a doctor.

Carl realized how much a doctor is able to help people when he was about ten years old. He fell over a curbstone while chasing a ball and broke the femur of his right leg. There were no X-rays then. The family doctor came to the house and did the best he could. Carl had his first experience as a patient on the kitchen table. His father acted as the anesthetist and gave him chloroform while the doctor set the leg. Thus, Carl's experience with the kind old family doctor, along with the high ideals he developed through the YMCA, led to his determination to become a doctor.

It was through the YMCA that Carl became an expert swimmer and a Red Cross Life Guard. He received more than a dozen medals from the Red Cross for life saving. His own life was saved, however, when at the age of 14 he attempted a fancy dive, the half gainer, and hit his face on the diving board. He was unconscious in eight feet of water when his instructor quickly pulled him out.

Once Carl saved a man who was caught in the whirlpool current under one of the locks of the Illinois/Michigan canal southwest of Chicago. He was able to hold the fellow up above the water until someone could throw a rope down to them.

Carl began to sense a divine call to find a special place in the world. He greatly admired Dr. Albert Siegmund Gustave Doederlein. Dr. Doederlein was a medical missionary in India for the Lutheran Church, and Carl wished to be like him. His dream was to take his place as a missionary in India when the older doctor retired.

There was, indeed, a special place for Carl Gellenthien, but it was not to be in India. The place was to be New Mexico. God used circumstances to place Carl there, conditions as adverse as those that placed Joseph in Egypt when he was sold into bondage. Carl, too, was brought under bondage, not unto men but unto "the Captain of the Men of Death." God took a tubercular pariah, a refugee in a strange land, and used him to help conquer the very disease that was supposed to have killed him.

Along the way there were events in Carl's life that reminded him that he was supposed to live and to serve others. On his way to his eight o'clock anatomy class one morning, the elevated train was rammed by another from behind. The young medical student was holding his textbook in one hand and his lunch bag in the other. The apple in his bag was literally squashed to applesauce when the collision sent Carl sprawling under a human landslide. Carl got to his feet and began to assist in lifting passengers out the side windows to the train platform. When the car jumped the track, the power was knocked out, rendering the third rail harmless. There were many injuries:

cuts, bruises, fractures, severed limbs. In their zeal to assist, Carl and another fellow stepped out onto the cat walk where the electric current of the third rail would have killed them instantly if the current had not been severed in the accident. Not until someone shouted for them to get off did they realize their carelessness. Carl continued assisting until help arrived. Tragically, the brakeman died as he was being carried away.

Why hadn't Carl been killed? He was visibly shaken as he arrived at his anatomy class. His professor demanded to know why he was late, why his coat was torn and bloodstained, why he was so pale, and why he had not brought his textbook. After giving his explanation, Carl was sympathetically excused. Fortunately, his textbook was recovered.

Even though he had to work his way through school, Carl had a scholarship of $109.00 a year. He had to buy his books and rent a microscope. He had to work at three different jobs to get through medical school. But his parents encouraged him and helped as much as possible. When the bottom dropped out the day Carl learned he had TB, his parents were there to support him.

Carl was able to repay his parents for their sacrifices by helping them pay off their home a few years later and by financing a vacation for them. Neither had been out of Illinois before. When Carl was well established as Valmora's director, he financed a trip that took them down to New Orleans, west to Valmora, then on to California, up to Astoria, Seattle, and Victoria, over to Vancouver, across Canada and back home. It was a fabulous vacation for them, the last one for Charles who died just six months before he was to retire. He contracted typhoid fever and died at 64.

Charles left his legacy in the form of the wisdom, humor, and sound philosophy he gave his children. When Carl joined "The Dill Pickle Club" in college, his father tolerated his questions about religion for a while. Carl wondered about the theory of evolution and the Bible. His father let him talk on about it until Bertha became disturbed at her son's questions. Then Charles would say quietly, "I think that's enough now, Carl." Yet he never discouraged his son from thinking, learning, and seeking. He was the man who taught Carl to work, to play, to be gentle but strong, to laugh and to care. It was he who spanked his son for chewing tobacco, who served as anesthetist for his son's surgery, who accompanied him to the police station, who met him at the door of his despair on the dark day he had to leave college. It was he who gave his son the courage to go on. It is no wonder when he died his children felt that their world had come to an end.

48

Bertha lived to be 93 but it was only through Carl's medical skill that she did not die years earlier. When she was in her 80s she began to experience stomach pains. Her doctors found nothing amiss. When Carl examined his mother's X-rays, he saw a dim shadow that was too nebulous to define. It could be something or might turn out to be nothing. The physicians told Carl it was up to him to decide if exploratory surgery should be done on a woman of her age. It was one of the most difficult decisions Carl ever had to make. As a doctor himself, he knew how traumatic exploratory surgery would be for an elderly woman. But Carl told the surgeons to go ahead, relying on the instinct that told him there was a problem. He stood at the operating table and watched the procedure. His instinct had been right. There was a malignant growth there, the kind that spreads fast, but they got it out in time to assure no spread of malignancy.

When Bertha was taken to her room following surgery her real problems began. The reputation of the hospital in Chicago was excellent. The personnel were competent and the best doctors practiced there. In fact, they were Carl's friends and colleagues. The patients there could afford the best of care. That was why Carl was utterly shocked when he walked into his mother's room shortly after her surgery to find her shamefully neglected. She lay unconscious with the bandages up around her neck. The incision, which was supposed to be covered with bandages, was exposed. Not only was it exposed but it was covered with feces. The bed was filthy. The room was a mess. The nurses were visiting at their station, oblivious of the unconsicous patient's condition. Carl took one look at his mother and charged to the nurses' station like an angry lion. The head nurse was too busy chatting on the phone to notice him, so Carl slammed his fists down on her desk and shouted, "Get off your fat ass and find my mother's chart!"

She jumped then, and the entire staff soon knew the power of Dr. Gellenthien's wrath. He was livid with anger and demanded an explanation. There was none. When his mother developed complications due to the bacteria that had entered her body under such deplorable conditions, Carl was thrown into one of the most emotionally charged situations he'd ever faced. He was ready to sue the hospital and its staff; he would have if his mother had not recovered.

Bertha was in a coma for three months. She had repeated convulsions. One cold winter night he was feeling discouraged after sitting with his mother for some time in her very warm room. The patient could not be kept covered, so the room had to be kept very warm to prevent pneumonia from setting in. About two a.m. Carl and the nurse were suctioning out the trachea through the tracheostomy, the opening in the throat, to keep Bertha's chest clear of mucus. Seeing his mother in a coma for so long, Carl was depressed. He turned to the nurse.

"Do you think it's right to keep on like this? What would you do if this was your mother lying here?" he asked. "Would you keep on?"

"Yes, Doctor. You see, I have been through this before." Then she told of caring for her husband who had been in a similar coma for months.

"And what happened?" he asked.

"He died," she replied simply.

She had done the right thing and she felt good about it. Knowing that someone else had dealt with the same situation encouraged Carl. He never forgot how that nurse lifted his spirits by sharing her own ordeal with him.

Finally a diagnosis was made. The bacteria was identified as Staphylococcus aureus. Unfortunately, it had invaded Bertha's brain. Proper antibiotics were administered, and Bertha made a complete recovery. She lived at Valmora for the rest of her life, becoming acquainted with her grandchildren and great grandchildren. She enjoyed making braided rugs, painting, and enjoying the beauty of nature in Valmora's lovely valley.

As Carl Gellenthien left Illinois that fateful year, 1924, headed west on a thin hope that he might recover at Valmora, he realized that his family had a great faith in God and in Carl's determination to overcome his illness. To some, it was evident that this young man's dream of becoming a medical missionary would probably end in death. But to Carl and his family, it was a temporary setback, just another obstacle to overcome before reaching his goal.

The boy who grew up on Chicago's northwest side had already come a long way. And after he became a nationally recognized physician, a newspaper cited him as one of the many successful citizens who had grown up in the neighborhood long known among social workers as "the area of greatest juvenile delinquency."[1]

The story stated that when William A. Wiebolt gave $100,000 to the building of the division Street YMCA, he hardly realized how many future citizens would benefit, including Phil Cavarretta, star in the 1935 World Series. The champion baseball player claimed that he owed his success to the YMCA which taught him how to play "fair and square." Johnny Weismuller, the famed Tarzan star, was cited as a man whose big dream came true out of the 'Y' swimming pool.[2]

Likewise, Division Street folks can't quite realize the national reputation and eminence, in anti-tuberculous work, which has come to Dr. Carl Gellenthien, as head of the internationally famous Val-A-

Mora [sic] sanatarium in New Mexico; for Carl himself was just a little "Y" kid, a few years ago, trying hard to get along, studying medicine in spare time and sick with T.B. himself from overwork and lack of means. [3]

The article concluded by stating that the YMCA branches which served "under privileged" neighborhoods had been working on a new plan for the last few years with notable success, "indicating that it is possible to turn out more Cavarrettas and Weismullers...and Gellenthiens, and not so many of the Al Capone and Baby Face Nelson type." [4]

As the train approached Raton pass, taking Carl to Valmora, he thought of the many obstacles he had already overcome. He was not convinced that he would die. He was disappointed, realizing that God could not use him as a medical missionary to India because of his tuberculosis. Later, however, he would see that it was precisely because he had TB that God was able to use him as a medical missionary in a very special place.

Nor did his parents give up hope. Carl remembered his father's voice on that dismal day in the post office where he had broken the news of his illness: "Carl, you always did want the moon with a fence around it. Well, this is only a setback. You're going to make it. And I'm going to help you."

Crossing the bridge over a gorge in one of the deep canyons, Carl remembered the bridge over the Chicago River where he'd thought of ending it all. Now he realized that he'd crossed bridges before and he would cross the one ahead of him. He was to find that he could build on his experiences. His job at the Wahl-Henius Institute, for instance, gave him a background in chemistry and led him to become a member of the American Chemical Society. It helped him later, too, when he achieved a score of 88.6 (general average) on his New Mexico board exams in application for a New Mexico medical license. Carl received his license, No. B-2 100, from the New Mexico Board of Medical Examiners on October 10, 1927.
license, No. B-2 100, from the New Mexico Board of Medical Examiners on October 10, 1927.

Traveling to Valmora for the first time, Carl had no idea what the future held. But he believed he would recover his health and live to achieve his goals. He knew he would conquer his enemy.

NOTES

1. R.M. McFarland, "All's Quiet on Boy Gang Line; 'Y' is Reason," n.t.,n.d., newspaper clipping in Scrapbook 1, Valmora Library, Valmora, New Mexico, p. 83.
2. *Ibid.*
3. Dorothea Nicholas, "Division Street 'Y' Marks First 50 Years of Work," *Chicago Daily Tribune*, September 29, 1960, p. 4., in Scrapbook 1, Valmora Library, Valmora, New Mexico, p. 87.
4. *Ibid.*

CHAPTER III

On Whom the Pale Moon Gleams

Carl was having breakfast in the dining car on the train taking him to Valmora when a companion at the table asked where he was headed.

"Valmora," Carl replied.

"Oh. What do they mine there?" the fellow inquired.

"It's not a mining town," Carl explained. "It's a tuberculosis sanatorium."

The man blanched. "Do you have tuberculosis?"

When Carl affirmed that he did, the fellow made a hasty exit, his half-eaten breakfast forgotten. Carl knew then for the first time what it was like to be a leper.

The incident taught Carl that he must not allow the fears of others to upset him. His own fear and loneliness had to be replaced by faith and a sense of purpose. He knew that thousands of others had fought the same battle. The list of victims is endless, but a few well-known names stuck in his mind:

Frederic F. Chopin, Harold B. Wright, John Wesley, Washington Irving, Johann F. von Schiller, William E. Henley, Honore de Balzac, Baruch Spinoza, Thomas Hood, Benjamin Rush, Andrew Jackson, Lawrason Brown, St. Francis of Assisi, U. S. Grant, Leigh Hunt, Jean Jacques Rousseau, John Locke, Mohandas K. Gandhi, Jay Gould, Edith Rockefeller McCormick, William MacLeod Raine, Queen Victoria of Sweden, Paul Ehrlich, H. G. Wells, Claude Achille Debussy, Joseph Addison, Marie Curie, Alexander Graham Bell, Josiah Gregg, W. C. Fields, and Wolfgang Mozart.[1]

Young Carl probably felt something like Chopin as he traveled so many miles away from home. In his last days Chopin had said, "If only I could leave off spitting blood for awhile, if only I weren't a prey to an idiotic homesickness. I vegetate, simply and patiently await my end."[2] Chopin had become ill when he was 27 years old, his sickness characterized by hemoptysis, fever, weakness, and weight loss. The summer of 1838 he had a serious attack of cough, fever, and bloody sputum. By 1840, at the age of 30, Chopin weighed only about 100 pounds. He gave a final concert in Paris in 1848 and died October 17, 1849 in Paris.[3]

As a victim of the white plague, Carl Gellenthien was in good company.

> We conjure up recollections of John Keats, the Bronte sisters, and any number of bright, sensitive, young writers, painters, and musicians who coughed away their lives in a garret. We think of such literary representations as Violetta in Dumas' *La Dame aux camélias*, who was transformed by Verdi into Violetta in *La Traviata*, and to poor little Mimi, whose hands were cold in *La Bohème*.[4]

But that was little consolation. In the larger sense, Carl was alone, for each individual must fight his personal battle for survival. Carl had learned to be a survivor, but even the strongest individuals had succumbed to the Captain of the Men of Death. Why Carl survived TB while many others failed is a question worth exploring.

Many patients were sent to Valmora to die. They had all left homes and families to live in isolation, surrounded only by those of their own kind like outcasts in a leper colony.

> Like leprosy victims, the tuberculosis patient...was often shunned. (Oddly enough, the bacilli for the two diseases are not unalike.) Many were the patients in Saranac whose families brought them thankfully to Trudeau Sanitarium, departed with relief and were never heard of again.[5]

Carl Gellenthien's experience on the train's dining car that morning on the way to Valmora had an impact on him that was difficult to describe. He wondered if he would be treated this way by everyone for the rest of his life. How could he complete his medical training even if he overcame his illness? Who would want a doctor with TB? Certainly he would not be able to live a normal life. A dozen images crossed his mind. If he applied to get into the military service, he would be turned away. In public restaurants if his condition were known, he would be shunned. Could he ever get a job of any kind, anywhere?

Indeed, after it had been established that TB was an infectious disease, some states blocked entrance to tuberculosis patients in fear of its spread. Bess Comstock suffered the stigma of the curse when she was finally able to leave Saranac Lake's ground. Private clubs posted signs outside their doors to bar her kind. Where she had been welcomed before, she now saw the signs: "No Tuberculars." When her children were allowed to visit her, they stood against the wall as far as possible from her bed. She was not allowed to hug or kiss them. Her daughter wrote:

> She must have been aware that it was possible she would never be able to put her arms around us again lest she jeopardize our future. It was well documented that children were far more susceptible to TB than adults. The best thing she could do for us was to stay safely across the room. [6]

Always, there were the statistics to remind them of how contagious TB was. In 1920 alone, 121,500 died from TB in the United States. [7]

> The nineteenth century saw consumptives as romantic, wan and wasting, marked for an early grave, but interesting as they feverishly burned themselves out writing novels and poetry. But the early part of the twentieth century understood consumption to be dangerously contagious and its cure only a pedestal to a position not unlike that of the leper. Under the circumstances, its victims did what they could with the life their ostracization left them. [8]

Sometimes after a slow climb to apparent health, the patient would slip back down again, for TB was never "cured." Relapse was common and added to the fear surrounding the disease. Lawrason Brown, physician at Saranac Lake, said, "The disease is treacherous. The germ slumbers not nor does it sleep." [9]

Approximately fifty percent of patients discharged from the sanatoria of the United States were dead five years after discharge. However, eleven years after discharge from Valmora, only 12.75 percent had died. Patients were taught that they must be ultra-conservative for several years after discharge from Valmora even though they felt well, looked well, and were assured by their attending physicians that their lesions were under control. [10] Patients were gravely warned before they left Valmora:

> Unfortunately, you are not able to leave with the thought that your physical trouble has been eradicated, and that you can forget, as you can the appendix after an appendectomy. Medical science does not know how to remove all the tubercle bacilli from the human body, nor does it know how to remove the cause of chronic ulcerative colitis, and the other chronic diseases. Your stay at Valmora has brought the invading organisms under control and you have learned how to live in order to keep them under control. Whether you succeed or not depends entirely upon you and your ability to live within your physical means. [11]

On July 30, 1939, approximately two-thirds of the patient body at Valmora was discharged as physically fit to return to their homes. This was a gratifying figure. Of the 130 patients receiving treatment during the 1938-39 fiscal year, only 7 patients or 5.4 percent died. For the rest of the sanatoria in the U.S., the death rate while in the sanatorium was 23 percent. This "cure" rate was accomplished at Valmora despite the fact that 56 percent of the group were in the far advanced stage on admission. [12]

Patients leaving in 1939 were gently admonished by the doctor to continue to protect their health.

> While at Valmora, your breaking of training and of rules was done only by our own deliberate action. Instead, however, of the satisfaction of getting away with something, you found yourself enjoying the disapproval of the staff and the ridicule of your fellow patients.
>
> They were amused at your stupidity in spending your money and time to regain your health and then throwing away your opportunity. You only did that once.
>
> After you leave Valmora, however, well meaning friends and relatives will bring tremendous and insidious pressure to bear on you to break training. Your future well-being depends on your ability to resist these temptations and to swim against the tide, that you may continue the daily regime you learned at the sanatorium. [13]

Leaving Valmora to re-enter the world brought patients the problem, also, of dealing with the fear of TB. The stigma of having spent time in a TB sanatorium would go with them everywhere, and the fear of TB was widespread. Elizabeth Mooney, whose mother Bess Comstock spent years at Saranac Lake, developed phthisiphobia, the dread of tuberculosis. "The whole country in the twenties had phthisiphobia, but it completely possessed me." [14] She described the kind of fear so many people in the twenties had:

> Many a car passed through Saranac in those days exceeding the speed limit as the driver pressed the accelerator to the floor and a clean handkerchief to his nose. The custom so irritated one old-time resident that one day he stood on the curb on Main Street and bawled after a disappearing car, "The tuberculars we got here probably came from your hometown!" [15]

Benny Valdez, who began work at Valmora in 1950, stated that his family constantly worried about the possibility of his catching the disease. [16] One patient's son went to great lengths to avoid his father, who was under the care of Dr. Gellenthien. The patient overcame his TB long before the son overcame his phthisiphobia.

In spite of the fear of TB, consumptives were welcomed in New Mexico because the State was poor and in need of immigrants. They came like refugees from the battlefield, but the battle raged within them and they could not escape it. Many undoubtedly felt the loneliness described in Arthur O'Shaughnessy's poem:

> We are the music-makers,
>> And we are the dreamers of dreams,
> Wandering by lone sea-breakers,
>> And sitting by desolate streams;
> World-losers and world-forsakers,
>> On whom the pale moon gleams:
> Yet we are the movers and shakers
>> Of the world for ever, it seems. [17]

Many of those "world-losers and world-forsakers" became New Mexico's most productive citizens. Many returned to their home states, but of those who chose to remain the list includes successful businessmen, lawmakers, artists, writers, bankers, teachers, and doctors. It was known that they were not "cured." They were "apparently arrested" after two years without symptoms and after another two years were "apparently well." Many remained in New Mexico because they wanted to retain the health they had recovered or to be near the sanatorium in case of a relapse. They felt that remaining in New Mexico's salubrious climate would heighten their chances for remaining well. Among those who remained were Ivan Hilton and Jerry Myers, both bankers; Senator Bronson Cutting; Edward and Frank Byrne, priests; John Ransdell, Baptist minister; Dr. H.M. Mortimer and Dr. Leroy Peters, both physicians; and Paul Frank, a successful businessman. Marjorie "Marge" Shea, Valmora's secretary since 1934, came as a very young girl to seek the "cure." At the present time she has been Valmora's secretary and bookkeeper for over 50 years.

The Valmora sanatorium was designed for a capacity of 75 but had twice that many at its height. When Carl Gellenthien was a patient in 1924, there were about 75 patients. In the ten year period from September 15, 1927 to September 14, 1937, there were 800 patients who came from all walks of life: bankers, engineers, nurses, physicians, merchants, railroad workers, clerks, students, housewives, newspaper correspondents, tennis players, pianists, aviators, nuns, night club entertainers, artists, and so on.

Sixty-two percent of the total 800 patients in that ten year period were of the male sex. The average age of the men was 33 years and of the women was 27 years. For all patients the average age was about 31 years. The span of age ranged from ten months for the youngest patient treated at Valmora to 79 for the oldest. [18]

Over the ten year period, forty-four percent remained from six months to over one year. The average duration for the entire 800 patients was about seven months. The records indicated: [19]

Condition on Admission Valmora Sanatorium, 1927-1937:

Pulmonary TB	597 or 74.6 percent
Other TB	38 or 4.8 percent
All other	165 or 20.6 percent

Condition on Discharge Valmora Sanatorium, 1927-1937:

Improved or better	672 or 84.0 percent
Unimproved	46 or 5.8 percent
Dead	60 or 7.5 percent
Diagnosis Only	22 or 2.7 percent

When Carl Gellenthien arrived at Valmora in 1924, he found the environment conducive to recovery. It was beautiful, peaceful, and self-sufficient. This self-sufficiency meant that there were few disturbances or distractions from the outside world. Eventually Valmora had its own Western Union facilities, its own post office, electricity generating power base, meterological station, general store, and Bell Telephone. The natural spring water supply was abundant, and each room had hot and cold running water, electric lights, steam heat, and bathroom. Each had windows and French doors opening into the sunny sleeping porch. There was an intercom system that was monitored when necessary. The hospital's Spanish Colonial Style was constructed around a large patio. There was a big recreation hall where dances, parties, and theatrical productions were held. A chapel was built and church services were held frequently. There was a separate solarium for sunbathing, and a spacious park with a fountain, swings, and lovely shade trees. A farmer who lived in a house at the far end of Valmora cultivated enough vegetables to feed Valmora's population and more. Milk was supplied by Valmora's dairy cows. Valmora was a State Game Reserve, and patients enjoyed watching protected wildlife and birds.

In addition to the Administration Building, the main dining hall, and the hospital, Valmora consisted of rows of cottages grouped around the park. Each cottage had a screened outdoor sleeping porch where patients could sleep, even in mid-winter. Most of the cottages were constructed for double occupancy, although a few were three and four bed cottages and some patients arranged for single occupancy.

The hubbard tanks used in physiotherapy were built of stainless steel at the sanatorium. Construction work was done on site. As Valmora grew, the range of services increased. The facility was expanded in 1930 to accommodate more non-tuberculosis patients such as those with cancer or gangrene of the lung. The new hospital had a laboratory and X-ray room, surgical and physiotherapy equipment, and facilities for collapse therapy, surgery, and heliotherapy.

Finally, isoniazid was available and reduced TB from the number one cause of death in the 1930s to as low as the 20th cause of death by the 1950s.[20] The sanatorium remained open.

During the 1940s, new and better methods of treating TB were finally developed. Since the need for the treatment facilities at Valmora decreased, Gellenthien had to decide whether to remain at Valmora and keep the sanatorium open, or to move elsewhere. He chose the former. The reasons for his choice were quite clear. First, Gellenthien did a study which included information on all patients treated at Valmora since 1927. The study showed that many patients were not treated for TB, but for other illnesses which required high altitude and dry climate as treatments. Gellenthien felt that this alone justified the continued existence of Valmora. Another reason that he stayed was because he and his wife loved Valmora and had no desire to leave.[21]

Dr. G. was offered many positions elsewhere, some of them highly tempting. He was asked to go to the Mayo Clinic as head of the Internal Medicine Department there. He had worked closely with his friend Charles Mayo, Jr. — "Chuck" and felt at home at the Clinic. Another offer came from Monroe Dunaway Anderson who established the M.D. Anderson Foundation and started the M.D. Anderson Hospital and Tumor Institute in Houston, Texas after his wife died of cancer. His firm, Anderson Clayton & Co., was the foremost cotton-merchandising concern in the world. Anderson wanted Dr. G. to take charge of The University of Texas M.D. Anderson Hospital and Tumor Institute. But Dr. G. did not feel he could leave his responsibilities at Valmora. Patients traveled from all over the country to see the man they called Dr. G. The main source of patients was derived from those who had been treated at Valmora for TB and from Dr. G.'s country practice. Throughout the years, Dr. G. was frequently the only full-time doctor living and practicing in Mora County.

In 1957 the Valmora Medical Center activities continued to flow despite the fact that TB had been conquered. A total of 5,223 patients were seen in the outpatient clinic, the heart and chest clinic, the baby clinic, the Wagon Mound Health Center, the Montezuma Seminary for priests from Mexico, and the Santa Fe Railroad Hospital Association.[22]

When sanatoria all over the country were closing their doors, Valmora remained a non-profit corporation under the laws of the state of Illinois. The Chicago corporations which initially started Valmora realized that the institution had served its purpose. When chemotherapy made sanatorium treatment unnecessary, the land and buildings of Valmora were turned over to Dr. Gellenthien in appreciation for his years of service. He had been paid a salary of $125.00 a month as Director and had never allowed the Corporation to increase his salary. He had stayed on and kept the doors open. "We didn't close," Dr. G. explained, "except by attrition. Valmora Industrial Sanatorium, Inc., is not defunct. Our doors are open today just as they were 80 years ago."[23]

Many TB patients decided to put down roots in New Mexico since the climate agreed with them. Most were young, just starting to carve out their careers, and the State welcomed new blood. A survey indicated that 85 percent of the practicing physicians in the west came "because of their own health or that of some member of their family."[24] The reasons they stayed were many. One explanation was written by Vivian B. Johnson, "Johnnie" who came to Valmora from Chicago and later became Valmora's secretary. In a letter written December 6, 1937, she explained why she chose to remain in New Mexico rather than return to the east. She felt that an article on tuberculosis was incorrect in stating that the great majority of patients were lonely or unhappy in their western and southwestern sanatoria environments.

> I refer to the unhappiness and loneliness which we supposedly encounter...In the past few years, I have been in contact with tubercular people all over the Southwest, as well as in the Middle West. There is no comparison in the morale of the patients in the two localities. My first two years of "chasing the cure" took place in a sanatorium in the Middle West. It was bearable, for I happen to have the happy faculty of adapting myself wherever I am placed, but I did feel morbid a big part of the time. There were two chief reasons for this.
>
> First, the deadly sympathy bestowed upon me by friends and relatives. To one who hasn't experienced spending a long time in a sanatorium, it would probably be surprising to know that many patients come West to get away from friends and relatives. Because of the great number of people who have "cured" out here, everyone, including those who have never been ill, is understanding and extremely kind. I am sure the majority of patients who have come to the Southwest would rather stay here and settle, then go back East, if it were possible for them to become situated here. I have been here three years and have been fortunate enough to make arrangements to stay indefinitely.
>
> Second, the climate was depressing back East. It is impossible to stay cheerful and comfortable when the weather is cloudy and damp so much of the time. About 350 days out of the year are bright, warm and sunshiny here at Valmora. The cloudy days are so few and scattered that one hardly notices them. There can be no doubt that all of

this is conducive to one's frame of mind, and so to recovery. [25]

Carl Gellenthien, too, was one of those who made arrangements to stay indefinitely after his recovery. It was not that he didn't wish to return to Chicago, but he had found his mission in life at Valmora — to try to conquer the disease that had taken the lives of so many and had threatened his own, to help the people of Mora County and surrounding areas who needed his professional and dedicated service. He was spared, it seemed, to become one of the "movers and shakers" of the world. How he crossed the line from the death row of tuberculosis to the victory parade of its conquerors is a fascinating saga of courage, faith and love.

Walt Whitman expressed his admiration for a person who fought against such great odds as did Gellenthien and others stricken with TB. He wrote:

O joy of suffering!
To struggle against great odds! to meet
  enemies undaunted!
To be entirely alone with them! to find
  how much one can stand!
To look strife, torture, prison, popular
  odium, death, face to face!
To mount the scaffold! to advance to the
  muzzles of guns
To be indeed a god! [26]

At the time the struggle against TB did not appear to be a battle of such noble description. It took great self-discipline and sacrifice. But this self-discipline developed during the struggle with TB and carried over afterwards. It was commonly stated by wise physicians of the day: "If you want to live a long time, get tuberculosis and then take care of it." Many TB patients learned to maintain their health and to pace themselves in a way that encouraged longevity. For the general population, especially in cities, such was seldom the case.

Living conditions before the mid-1900s were conducive to the spread of disease. A man born in 1909 had a life expectancy of 49 years. Hundreds of thousands of children under the age of 12 worked 10 hours a day in factories, mines and farms. For the indigent old there was the poor house. For the parentless there was the orphanage. In 1908 there were 120,000 horses in New York City alone. The prime mover of people and freight created the major task of removal of dung from streets and the decaying bodies of dead horses. Flies contributed to epidemics of typhoid, cholera, dysentery and infant diarrhea. Each year in New York City, some 15,000 carcasses had to be hauled off the streets. An average of 20,000 New Yorkers died each year from diseases spawned by horse manure and spread by flies.[27]

Chicago was no better. When Carl Gellenthien was growing up there, an open sewer running under the sidewalk was part of the normal environment. The children were afraid of falling into it. Many houses had no indoor plumbing, and homes were crowded together in overpopulated areas. Privies had to be cleaned out by hand when they became full because, unlike the wide-open spaces inhabited by country people, in the city there was not enough room to fill in one hole and dig out another. The men who cleaned the outdoor toilets and carried off the human waste were called "honey dippers" and they always worked early in the morning before the general population was up and about.[28]

The city water, too, had not yet been subjected to sanitation laws. It was not uncommon for a small fish to come out of the water tap. Swimming in Lake Michigan was not much better than swimming in a sewer. Carl once saw a rooster walk on water across Bubbly Creek behind the Union Stock Yards. The river was so thickly congested with the grease and fat, "offal," from the meat packing houses that the rooster was able to cross the top of the solid fat covering with no trouble at all.

The city was endless concrete and steel. The horizon was blackened with tall buildings and the dense air of belching factories and steel mills. In the summer time Chicago was so hot the people would sprinkle water onto the walls to try to cool their houses, but that only made the humidity worse. And winters were severely cold, with dense humidity from the lake and frigid winds. The wind off the lake would sweep the inner city with its "marrow bite."

After coming through the flat grass lands of the plains on his first trip to Valmora, Gellenthien began to feel the freedom of the "wide open spaces." But when he saw the breath-taking mountains of northern New Mexico and the clear, blue skies above tall pines, he began to feel what so many Valmora-bound patients have felt: a flutter of renewed hope. He was to live among the wonders of the high Sangre de Cristo Mountains with its crystal streams, ponderosa pines, spruce, juniper, cedar, piñon and sage. Snow-kissed breezes from the blue mountains carried pungent scents through the deep canyons of Valmora; and clear-flowing streams from snow-laden peaks were near by.

Three factors contributed to Gellenthien's recovery: heredity, environment and motivation. His heredity gave him strength, endurance, determination and courage. His early environment prepared him for the battle. It moded his character and taught him to survive. His later Valmora environment gave him an atmosphere conducive to healing, providing comfort, hope, and cheer. His strong will to live was supported by the divine motivation of faith, his desire to achieve, and the romantic motivation of love.

Perhaps it was because of his great desire to achieve that Carl Gellenthien did not give up. He had a conviction of a mission to fill and that gave him a tremendous will to live. He conquered the fear of death with a positive mental attitude, determined to fight his foe and win back his health.

Norman Cousins provided an answer as to why some people recover from "incurable" illnesses. He himself was told by specialists that his particular disease was progressive and incurable. His chances of survival were 500 to 1. Yet he was convinced that he could beat the odds. He was not unmindful of the seriousness of his illness, but he was determined to recover. "Since I didn't accept the verdict, I wasn't trapped in the cycle of fear, depression, and panic that frequently accompany a supposedly incurable illness."[29] Like Cousins, Gellenthien did not accept the death verdict of his doctors.

Cousins stated that the body's defense against infection depends largely on the mechanism of humoral and cellular immunity but that these mechanisms themselves are influenced by the mental state. This is exemplified by the effect of hypnosis on the Mantoux test which consists of the intradermal injection of tuberculin, an extract of tubercle bacilli. The test is used to evaluate the likely response of the body to tuberculous infection. It has been established that hypnotic suggestion can obliterate the vascular manifestations of the Mantoux test, "as near a proof as one could wish of the influence that the mind exerts over the body."[30]

> The tuberculin Mantoux reaction pertains to the kind of body response that immunologists designated "cell-mediated immunity." Since this form of the immune response plays an essential role in resistance to important infectious diseases such as tuberculosis, and probably also in resistance to cancer, there is good reason to believe that the patient's state of mind can effect the course of all pathological processes that involve immunological reactions. [31]

A positive state of mind helped Gellenthien's body build up its defenses. Cousins wrote, "I became convinced that creativity, the will to live, hope, faith, and love have biochemical significance and contribute strongly to healing and well-being. The positive emotions are life-giving experiences."[32]

Dr. Walter H. James, President of Trudeau in 1924, stated:

> This disease (TB) consists of a struggle, an almost equal battle, between the invading germs and a man's body and extending over many

months or even years. The tuberculosis bacilli feed less willingly and
eagerly on cheerful, happy than upon depressed and gloomy tissues. [33]

Cousins found evidence that laughter had a definite curative value, as have other researchers. The writer of *Proverbs* stated earlier, "A merry heart doeth good like a medicine; but a broken spirit drieth the bones." [34]

Dr. Gellenthien would explain to his patients that the cure for TB depended largely upon the patient's own attitude. He would tell them, "We don't know exactly what resistance is. We can't see it, smell it, taste it, or feel it. But it will help you overcome TB. My job is to help you spend it wisely and not waste it. Think of me as your coach." [35] Over-taxing the body or exposing it to excessive stresses would so over-extend the resistance that it could not adequately fight the greater enemy. Thus, rest and good diet, as well as a positive, cheerful attitude, gave the body the help it needed.

The temperament, or mental characteristics, and disposition of the patient are important. On the positive side, these characteristics include: amenity to advice; an orderly but not lethargic temperament, in which there is no compromise, but only literal adherence to the right; a bright and cheerful dispostion; a love for the out-of-doors; and lastly, intelligence. [36]

Dr. G. explained that negative traits include a stubborn disposition, a lack of self-control, indiscretion in the use of exertion, resistance to sanatorium restrictions and routine, a lack of imagination or foresight, and a lack of faith in the doctor. [37]

Regardless of the physical characteristics, the presence of resistance and type of patient are the most important factors in determining the final outcome of any case. Resistance is not man-made. Without it one cannot get well. The new patient who presents himself at Valmora brings a definite amount of this intangible "resistance." We physicians are unable give him a greater amount of it, but we can husband it and help him to spend judiciously what resistance he possesses. [38]

Gellenthien spoke with the authority of one who had been there himself; he understood what his patients were going through. He, too, had learned to keep a cheerful attitude. He looked for a laugh every day, and found it.

The power of faith, too, has been demonstrated many times. A testimony of this power was given by Evangelist Oral Roberts who discovered that he had tuberculosis at the age of 17 when he collapsed during a basketball game, hemorrhaging. Roberts was 6'1¼" tall and weighed 160 pounds, but after lying bedfast for 163 days, his weight dropped to 120 pounds. His brother Elmer borrowed a car and spent his last 35 cents for gasoline to go to Ada, Oklahoma where a preacher was praying for the sick.

I can still hear the music and the sermon. As I sat in that old rocking chair with pillows stuffed around me, waiting for the preacher to pray for me, I thought his sermon was just for me.

But when he laid his hands on me and prayed, God began to heal me from the crown of my head to the soles of my feet...and the tuberculosis left my lungs. [39]

Roberts contended that it was his positive attitude and faith that brought about his healing. When he released his faith, God responded. Gellenthien, too, had faith that God would heal him. His faith in the healing hand of God dispelled his fears. And his positive attitude gave his body's resistance the edge it needed. Along with the beauty of the Valmora environment, there was human compassion and concern, comfort and care, good food, and clear, spring water. Most important, he was surrounded by a powerful Force that drew him away from death.

The mysterious Power that helped Gellenthien recover was an intangible Force which cannot be measured. Yet plants respond to it. Animals thrive on it. Babies die without it. Lacking it, Keats languished in Rome and died. Having it, Elizabeth Barrett Browning eluded death. Poets have described it best, though they, like scientists, have found the Force elusive. Though it remains an enigma, this Force was the one ingredient, added to all the others, that turned the tide in Gellenthien's illness, that thwarted the enemy, that stayed the hand of the executioner.

The Force turned many such "world-losers and world-forsakers" in similar circumstances into world "movers and shakers." It has been the theme of folklore and fairy tales of every culture and every time. It is found in the first kiss that brought Sleeping Beauty from her hundred-year coma and woke Snow White from her death-like trance. It is found in the marriage vow of Beauty, transforming the beast into a prince in "Beauty and the Beast." Adults may smile at such tales, yet these stories are based on the reality of this powerful Force. The changes it brings about in the real world are not always as sudden or dramatic as in the folk tales woven by men, but they are there. The Force of those changes results in health and life. It was that same Force that took the submissive lamb of God, Jesus, to the cross. The English language is pitifully impoverished in its ability to identify or label that Force. Yet the word which describes it best is "Love."

Gellenthien once remarked, "If God didn't want me to go to India why didn't He just tell me — instead of letting me get TB? I'd have come to New Mexico if He'd told me to." [40] But it was that divine

Love which brought him to Valmora. He would not have understood what the TB patient was going through if he himself had not been stricken. He would not have been able to offer his patients the encouragement and testimony of his own recovery.

Albert Schweitzer, the medical missionary, wrote in his autobiography that his own illness gave him a greater understanding of what a patient goes through. In his *Out of My Life and Thought* Schweitzer wrote that when we personally experience pain and anxiety, we no longer belong to ourselves alone. We become the brother of all who suffer. He stated that it is on the brotherhood of those who bear the mark of pain that the duty of medical work lies. It is work for humanity's sake. [41]

This ability to empathize is an invaluable asset. Dr. Gellenthien was able to tell his patients, "I went through what you're going through and I recovered. You can too."

Speaking to the American Medical Association in 1963, the Most Reverend Fulton J. Sheen said that *compassion* means to suffer with someone, to experience what he has experienced. He pointed out that too often those who serve others live on the second floor, while those on the first floor live in misery. It is not enough to go down to them occasionally to relieve the misery and then go back to the comfort of the second story. He said there is such a thing as crossing a line and never coming back, which is what Jesus did when He came down to make Himself one with sinners. It was the essence of Redemption. He said that sometimes people do not have compassion until they suffer. If a physician himself has had an operation, he can empathize with the patient who is about to have one. [42]

Twenty years after Bishop Sheen's address to the AMA, the President of the American Medical Association in 1982, William Y. Rial, M.D., delivered his farewell address to the House of Delegates with much the same concern about the personal relationship of patient and doctor. Dr. Rial expressed the hope that physicians and patients would build long-term relationships of trust, understanding, and confidence and that the patient might not become just another case number. He hoped that the patient/physician relationship has not outlived its usefulness in a modern world where everything is prepackaged, frozen or microwaved and where people in a single trip to the shopping center can buy plastic garbage bags, get their kids new shoes, and get somebody to look at dad's earache in some storefront urgent care center, free-standing surgicenter or other kind of walk-in medical clinic. He feared the concept of strangers treating strangers, where the doctor works for the hospital and not for the patient. "Physicians might man those centers giving technically good but impersonal care to the people who came in."[43] Rial feared the day when no physician would be able to say that mother, father, children and grandchildren are all his patients or when no patient would be able to answer the question, "Who's your doctor?"[44]

Carl Gellenthien's kind of medical practice was the sort Dr. Rial hoped would continue to be available in the future. In 1985, Dr. Gellenthien, in his 58th year of medical practice, continued to practice the personal family care Rial so highly valued. Gellenthien's family practice encompassed five generations. He developed that rare trait of compassion and empathy because, perhaps, of his own bout with the disease that he had ultimately helped to conquer.

The fact that Dr. Gellenthien had developed an understanding and empathy out of his own personal acquaintance with the disease he was now trying to overcome is evident in an account written by a patient and printed in a booklet entitled, "I've Been to Valmora." The patient described his first impression of Dr. Gellenthien.

> The door opened. I turned from the window. In the center of the room stood a young, sandy-haired man who smilingly introduced himself as Dr.—. So cheerful, so altogether human. His manner was totally unlike that heavy, professional cloak worn by so many successful doctors.
>
> I liked him at once and, when I learned he had come to Valmora because ill health had forced him to come, I hailed him as a friend. Here was one who would understand. He did understand. His own "cure" had been bitterly fought for, and knowing that, brought such a wave of pure hope that I felt weak with exultant relief. Those who have secure life feel no need to take stock of their possession, but to him who had been condemned to possible death, reprieve is so sweet it is almost pain.
>
> The knowledge and skill of Dr.— has placed him high in the ranks of medical specialists in this country, but his place in his profession is nothing compared with his place in the hearts of those whom he has helped to "cure."[45]

Dr. Gellenthien, too, had known the sweet painfulness of reprieve so aptly described by his grateful patient. Most patients had the same high regard for the man they called "Dr. G." or sometimes simply "Doc." The Gellenthien name was difficult to pronounce and spell, so Dr. Gellenthien became known as "Dr. G." to everyone throughout the country. An example of how well-known he was by the name "Dr. G." was told by Dr. Lora Shields who worked on research projects with the doctor's assistance for many years while she was Chair of the Biology Department at New Mexico Highlands University in Las Vegas. She had a student with a medical problem and referred the student to Dr. Gellenthien. The student, who was from the local area, insisted he had never heard of this doctor.

"Why he's been at Valmora for years," Dr. Shields said. "Are you sure you've never heard of Dr. Gellenthien?"

"I never have," the student replied.

"I thought everyone in the country knew Dr. G.," replied Dr. Shields, puzzled.

"Oh, *Dr. G.!* Of course! Everyone knows Dr. G."[46]

Dr. Gellenthien attained the respect of his patients by a long, steady climb that led him from death's door to a place as one of several of the nation's recognized specialists in diseases of the chest. He was, in fact, one of the founders of the American College of Chest Physicians in the early 1930s, an organization which now has hundreds of members all over the world.

"I remember when a small group of us worked up the constitution for the new organization," Dr. Gellenthien recalled. "We worked most of the night in a room at the Palmer House in Chicago. I remember looking out the window around one o'clock in the morning. There was a blizzard outside and the wind was that icy, bone-chilling cold that comes off the lake. I was glad to be inside the building where it was warm. And doing this work, starting this new organization that was so badly needed — that gave me a warm feeling inside."[47]

Dr. G. could not have achieved such accomplishments had it not been for the mysterious Force alluded to before, the Power that began to work quietly, persistently, and steadily in his life as a patient at Valmora. In Room #8 he became aware of his strength gradually returning. The moon which shone down on him may have been a pale one, but he still held it in his sights, and he still wanted a fence around it. He may have been only dimly aware of the mysterious Force working in and around and through him, the Force called "Love." Later, as a physician advising his TB patients, Dr. G. would be able to give back some of what he had received, for love is never self-contained.

Harold Walters, a patient at Valmora in 1940, returned to New Mexico in July of 1983 to visit Valmora for the first time since leaving in 1941. He wanted to see Dr. G. again and to thank him for saving his life. He said of Dr. G.:

> He had a good sense of humor...which was healthy for me, but most of all I liked his seriousness, too, for his profession; for he took his profession very, very seriously and yet he was very practical about his instructions. Well, he's a man that you just...to know him is to love him...that's about the truth of it, and he leaves a lasting impression

on you for your entire lifetime — and you have that loving attitude. [48]

Love, like any element, does not exist in a vacuum. The catalyst of the powerful force affecting young Gellenthien's life came in the form of a lovely woman named Alice Brown.

The darkness of Gellenthien's disease had almost totally enveloped him when a small light appeared. The light grew as he reached out and nourished it with hope. As it grew larger and brighter, it dispelled the darkness of despair. After a while the darkness became a dim memory as the the beauty of Alice Brown loomed larger and brighter. Gradually the pale moon, upon which the young man had his sights, began to grow brighter until at last it was a rich, golden glow of dazzling light. Divine Love had responded to Carl's faith. And romantic love followed, responding to his life. Oscar Wilde summed it up best when he said that the mystery of love is greater than the mystery of death.

NOTES

1. "Famous 'T.B.'s'", *The Buzzer*, n.p.,n.d., in Scrapbook 3, Valmora Library, Valmora, New Mexico, p. 71.
2. Enzo Orlandi, ed., *The Life & Times of Chopin*, trans. C.J. Richards (Philadelphia: The Curtis Publishing Company and Arnoldo Mondadori Editore, 1967), p. 64.
3. William Ober, M.D., "Did Chopin Really Die of TB? Diagnosis Reconsidered," *Diagnosis*, 3 (November, 1981), pp. 15-16.
4. *Ibid.*, p. 15.
5. Mooney, *op. cit.*, p. 9.
6. *Ibid.*, p. 79.
7. *Ibid.*, p. 68.
8. *Ibid.*, p. 57.
9. *Ibid.*, p. 51.
10. C.H. Gellenthien, "Adios Amigos, Dios Valla Con Ustedes," *The Valmora Sun*, June, 1939, p. 8, in Scrapbook 3, Valmora Library, Valmora, New Mexico, p. 33.
11. *Ibid.*
12. *Ibid.*
13. **Ibid.**
14. Mooney, *op. cit.*, p. 160.
15. *Ibid.*, p. 9.
16. Benny Valdez, interview at Valmora, April 15, 1983.
17. Arthur O'Shaughnessy, "Ode," quoted in Ralph L. Woods, ed., *A Treasury of the Familiar* (N.Y.: The Macmillan Company, 1943), p. 269.
18. "Statistical Report Tells Graphic Story," *The Valmora Sun, op. cit.*
19. *Ibid.*
20. Eric Diehl, "Valmora: Tonic for Tuberculosis," unpublished manuscript winning first place in New Mexico's Calvin Horn Scholarship Contest, selected by the Committee of the New Mexico Historical Society, April, 1981, Las Vegas Robertson High School, Las Vegas, New Mexico, p. 7.
21. *Ibid.*
22. Carl and Alice Gellenthien, "1957 – For Alice and Me," Valmora, New Mexico, December, 1957, p. 1 in Scrapbook 4, Valmora Library, Valmora, New Mexico, P. 25.
23. Carl H. Gellenthien, interview, Valmora, New Mexico, June 5, 1984.
24. "Sunshine Often Difference Between Life and Death in TB Treatment,

Says Gellenthien," n.t., n.d., newspaper clipping in Scrapbook 1, Valmora Library, Valmora, New Mexico, p. 110.

25. Vivian B. Johnson, Letter to the editors of *Life Magazine*, written at Valmora Sanatorium, Valmora, New Mexico, December 6, 1937, in Scrapbook 2 belonging to Carl H. Gellenthien, Valmora Library, Valmora, New Mexico, p. 71.

26. Walt Whitman, quoted in Lillian Eichler Watson, ed., *Light From Many Lamps* (N.Y. Simon and Schuster, 1951) p. 87.

27. S.I. Hayakawa. "The Good Old Days — You Can Have Them," *The Saturday Evening Post* (Vol. 246, No. 1) January/February, 1974, p. 42.

28. Irma Meyer, interview at Valmora, New Mexico, June 10, 1981.

29. Norman Cousins, *Anatomy of an Illness as Perceived by the Patient* (N.Y.: W.W. Norton & Compnay, 1979), p. 45.

30. *Ibid.*, p. 19.

31. *Ibid.*

32. *Ibid.*, p. 86.

33. Mooney, *op. cit.*, p. 35.

34. Proverbs 17:22, *The Holy Bible* (Nashville, Tennessee: Crusade Bible Publishers, Inc., 1975), p. 577.

35. Carl H. Gellenthien, interview at Valmora, New Mexico, July 24, 1983.

36. C.H. Gellenthien, "Factors Bearing on Prognosis Are Many and Sundry," *The Valmora Sun*, March, 1939, p. 6., in Scrapbook 3, Valmora Library, Valmora, New Mexico, p. 27.

37. *Ibid.*

38. *Ibid.*

39. Oral Roberts, *May Newsletter*, Tulsa, Oklahoma, May, 1982, pp. 1-2.

40. Carl H. Gellenthien, interview at Valmora, New Mexico, March 2, 1983.

41. Albert Schweitzer, *Out of My Life and Thought* (New York: Henry Holt and Company, 1949), pp. 193-194.

42. Fulton J. Sheen, "The Physician, the Clergy, the Patient," Speech delivered to the American Medical Association's Annual Convention, Atlantic City, New Jersey, June 17, 1963, pp. 32-33.

43. William Y. Rial, "Who's Your Doctor?" Speech delivered to the American Medical Association's Annual Convention, Chicago, Illinois, June 19, 1983.

44. *Ibid.*

45. B.D.J., "I've Been to Valmora," printed booklet, n.d., Valmora Sanatorium, Valmora, New Mexico, pp. 3-4, in Scrapbook 2, Valmora, Library, Valmora, New Mexico, p. 12.

46. Lora Shields, telephone interview, November 28, 1982.

47. Carl H. Gellenthien, interview at Valmora, Valmora, New Mexico, June 30, 1983.

48. Harold Walters, interview in Santa Fe, New Mexico, June 17, 1983.

CHAPTER IV

A Balm in Gilead

There were nearly 75 patients at Valmora when Carl Gellenthien arrived in November of 1924. He was met at the train and taken up to his hospital room at the top of the stairs, to the left. Alice Brown watched the new arrivals from a window. She did not imagine that the thin, hollow-eyed young man approaching the hospital door was to be a future Director of Valmora Tuberculosis Sanatorium, nor did she guess that she was seeing her future husband!

Georgie Claiborne, the nurse who served for twenty-five years until she retired in 1952, nearly always stood at the window to watch the new arrivals, sizing them up in her astute mind. Sometimes she had an uncanny way of predicting the outcome of a patient's treatment. She seemed to know which patients would die, which would be undisciplined, or which would be the "trouble-makers." For the patients who cooperated, she would go the extra mile. She would even "spoil" them. But for those who were determined to break the rules, she was as hard as nails. She had no patience for alcoholics or for patients who would not try to help themselves. Had Georgie seen Carl Gellenthien that first day, she might have guessed that he would survive, in spite of his doctors' dire predictions. Georgie didn't have an M.D. degree but she knew people. And she knew a survivor when she saw one.

From the moment Carl Gellenthien stepped off the train, he felt the welcoming acceptance so many patients have experienced throughout the years at Valmora. It was like the Biblical Gilead which was supposed to offer comfort for the sick: "Is there no balm in Gilead: is there no physician there? Why then is not the health of the daughter of my people recovered?"[1] Though there are few Biblical references to Gilead, apparently it was a place of healing. But like Xanadu, Shangri La, El Dorado or the Seven Cities of Cibola, no one has ever been quite sure Gilead actually existed. Valmora valley came as close to the Biblical description as any place could.

The area around Valmora has been a fascinating site for historians, geologists, naturalists, and archeologists. With its latitude at 35-48° and longitude at 104-55°, Valmora is an excellent place for a comfortable climate all year round. Geologists have determined that it took Coyote Creek 135 million years to cut Valmora and Shoemaker canyons. Dakota sandstone forms the steep cliffs which rim the Valmora valley. There is a small exposure of Jurassic rock cut into by the Mora River. The interface between these two units is approximately 135,000,000 years old. [2]

The area around Valmora was once the meeting place of several Indian trails which converged at Lajunta, (now Watrous) about four miles from Valmora. The valley where Pueblo Indians had hunted and built their camp fires later became the campsite of Spanish conquistadores and the hope of gold miners who prospected in the hills surrounding Valmora.

Valmora is practically on the old Santa Fe Trail. The ruts of the trail cut their saga deep into the red earth of the plateau, leaving scars that can still be seen as of the date of this writing. On a high rocky point south and east of the Valmora station is a place called Monte Oro, and from its top one can see to the northwest the ruins of Old Fort Union, the historic army post abandoned in 1891. The old fort played a significant role in the Civil War and post-Civil War periods of the United States. [3]

Located in Mora County at an elevation of 6,200 feet, Valmora lies twenty-four miles northeast of Las Vegas. "The Valley of the Mora" lies on the main line of the Santa Fe railway at the point where Coyote Creek empties its clear waters into the Mora River. The sanatorium was built upon the left bank of the Creek, high enough away from its bed to avoid another devastation should flood waters rise as they did in 1904. The tract of 1,100 acres is rich in vegetation and wild life. The valley, enclosed by sandstone cliffs, is six miles away from the crater of an extinct volcano. [4]

The closest mountains are the Turkey Mountains, not visible from the sanatorium grounds. The range seen from the west porches of the hospital is the Sangre de Cristo range, approximately thirty miles distant. High mesa country above the valley lies under blue skies and is permeated with the scents of piñon, sage, and juniper.

The hospital was constructed architecturally in a combination of California and New Mexican styles. It contained twenty-six patient rooms, nurses' quarters, consultation rooms, offices for the doctors, a complete medical library, a library for the patients, X-ray laboratory, clinical and research laboratory, nose and throat room, and sun porch. There were also rooms for ultra-violet light and physiotherapy treatments. The kitchen and dining hall were also housed in the large building which was constructed around a grassy patio. The cottages were built in neat rows on three sides of the hospital, each having a screened porch and private bath. They served as models for the construction of cottages in sanatoria elsewhere in North America and in Australia because of the excellent pattern.[5] The home of the superintendent, the home of the medical director, the combined store and post office, and the quarters for the staff and workers were in close proximity. The dairy barn, stables for horses, and the vegetable farm were all located in the valley.

The park with its beautiful fountain was centrally located. Lilacs surrounded the central buildings, and flowers of all types bloomed during the warm season. Patients who were well enough could walk a mile on a path that took them in a circle to the railroad tracks, across the creek and then back. Coyote Creek made its way through the far west end of the grounds where the picnic areas were popular and cookouts were frequently held. In the summer time the swimming hole attracted visitors. In winter time, sufficient ice was taken from the pond to provide for the sanatorium's needs.

For those who were nearly recovered, further exploration of the forests and cliffs and mesas was in order. Some climbed the cliffs to see the old gold mines. Some looked for arrowheads and other Indian relics. And some found comfortable ledges along the rim overlooking Valmora where they enjoyed sunbathing.

According to records kept by Dr. Brown, in 1923 there were 24 member patients and 83 non-member patients, a total of 107 patients. The average patient load was 37. The average "days of stay" for 1922 was 238. In 1924, Valmora's assets were $115,872 and the cost of maintenance was $58,771 in that same year.[6] The figures varied from year to year, of course, but Valmora was never in debt. Even during the Depression of the 1930s, Valmora fared well due to its self-sufficiency. At the height of the demand for excellent sanatoria, Valmora was filled almost beyond capacity, with every hospital room, every cottage, every available space filled. As soon as one patient left, another came to take his place.

Gellenthien's initial determination to recover was strengthened by the divine call of God. He did not indulge in self-pity, and he had no intention of becoming a life-long invalid. He met the challenge to turn adversity into advantage. He knew he was not alone. There was the divine help, immeasurable and intanglible, that can be seen with the eyes of faith, that never fails to inspire and guide the believer.

Many have felt that same divine strength when they were at their lowest, and those who did not give up felt the touch of divine inspiration. So, too, Gellenthien felt that the Big Boss was the One to make the decisions. He believed he should live his life in such a way that he was prepared to die at any time. He determined to enjoy each day to the fullest.

Gellenthien found the most important motivating force of his recovery, indeed, of his life, at Valmora. He discovered the power of love. Little did he realize as he made his way from the train stop to the hospital that his future wife was watching him from the window. From that moment on, Dr. Brown's daughter continued to keep a close watch on him. Carl soon learned to recognize her step in the hall. As the hospital's dietitian, she prepared Carl's meals every day. Friendship soon developed into romance. Carl fell in love not only with New Mexico and Valmora — he also fell in love with Alice Brown.

Two well-known love stories provide a study in contrasts of the power of love and its influence on the invalid: the story of John Keats and Fanny Brawne and that of Elizabeth Barrett and Robert Browning.

Keats did not realize the serious nature of his illness, though he had studied medicine. One evening in February, 1820, he returned from a trip, chilled and feverish, and he coughed up blood. He stared for a long time at the spot on the handkerchief and said to his friend Charles Brown, "That drop of blood is my death-warrant."[7] He did not give up hope, however. In his letters to Fanny he expressed his need for her: "I cannot breathe without you."[8]

Doctors told Keats another winter in England would be fatal. He said the thought of leaving Miss Brawne

is beyond everything horrible — the sense of darkness coming over me
— I eternally see her figure eternally vanishing...Is there another life?
There must be — we cannot be created for this sort of suffering.[9]

But Keats had hopes of recovering, motivated by the belief that he would be with Fanny thereafter.

God alone knows whether I am destined to taste of happiness with you: at all events I myself know this much, that I consider it no mean Happiness to have lov'd you thus far — if it is to be no further I shall not be unthankful — if I am to recover, the day of my recovery shall see me by your side from which nothing shall separate me. If well you are the only medicine that can keep me so.[10]

Keats felt that Fanny did not return his love and he may have been right. He wrote that if he had to go to Italy, he was certain he would not recover if he was to be so long separated from Fanny.

Keats, accompanied to Rome by his friend, the artist Joseph Severn, never saw Fanny again. She did not visit him during his critical illness. Of her, he wrote, "I should have had her when I was in health, and should have remained well."[11] He described his feelings with his usual poetic accuracy: "I have coals of fire in my breast. It surprises me that the human heart is capable of so much misery."[12] His doctor could hardly bear to see Keats' pathetic expression, his great eyes "burning with a sad and piercing unearthly brightness in his wasted cheeks."[13] He might have been comforted by the love of his sweetheart and fought to live. Instead, he was thrown into a state of despair because Fanny continued to see other men, to flirt with his best friend while he was away, and to leave him alone when he begged for her. His letters were a cry for help that was, apparently, unanswered. He wrote to her telling her that his whole existence depended upon her, yet she failed to respond. Keats was treated by frequent bleeding and was kept on a starvation diet as part of his doctor's efforts to arrest the progress of the disease. Hemorrhage followed hemorrhage, however, and Keats besought Severn to let him have opium to end it all, not for fear of pain, but so that he might spare his friend the trials which his illness caused. His habitual question to the doctor was, "When will this posthumous life of mine come to an end?"[14] Keats' letters communicate a deep depression as his disease progressed until near the very end when the euphoria characteristic of TB patients was displayed. In one of his last letters to Fanny, his optimism born of that euphoria was evident. He wrote that he had slept well the night before.

> Day by day if I am not deceived I get a more unrestrain'd use of my chest. The nearer a racer gets to the Goal the more his anxiety becomes, so I lingering upon the borders of health feel my impatience increase...how horrid was the chance of slipping into the ground instead of into your arms — the difference is amazing Love. Death must come at last...but before that is my fate I feign would try what more pleasures than you have given, so sweet a creature as you can give.[15]

His was a typical manifestation of the last stages of the disease, believing he was recovering and making plans for the future. He was happily engaged in such planning even as he slipped away into death. Dr. Gellenthien saw many such patients who believed, like Keats, that they lingered upon the borders of health while in reality they were dying. A person can live with only 1/30th of one lung.[16] But Keats had almost nothing left. Only at the last moment did Keats realize the truth. Fanny did not come and it was his friend Severn who sat at Keats' death bed on February 23, 1821, to hear his dying words: "Severn—I—lift me up—I am dying—I shall die easy; don't be frightened—be firm and thank God it has come."[17]

By contrast, Elizabeth Barrett was spared the agony and despair Keats experienced. Her story is a tribute to the power of love, for she rallied, eloped with Robert Browning, and lived 15 more years. When death came, she died in her husband's arms and smiled, "It is beautiful."[18] Browning's love, apparently, gave Elizabeth those added years, for in her *Sonnets From the Portuguese* she repeats the wonder of discovering that she had found love instead of her anticipated death. She had believed that her life was over until Browning came into her world and brought her love. On its strength she fought her enemy victoriously.

The contrast between Elizabeth Barrett and John Keats shows that the invalid who received love thrived, while the one without it weakened and died. Naturally, there are many other variables to be considered. Elizabeth may not have been as ill as Keats.

Still, the question of whether the death of Keats would have been averted if Fanny had responded to his love is an interesting one. His mental attitude was definitely affected by his separation from her; and his despair that she was seeing other men, that she did not return his love, drove Keats into deep depression. There are many letters to Fanny expressing his love. But there are few letters from Fanny to Keats on record.

When one is in love and is loved, there is a great will to live. There is no room for fear or despair. When the love between Alice Brown and Carl Gellenthien began to blossom, something happened to any fear he might have had of dying; something happened to dispel any doubt of his recovery. Like Elizabeth Barrett, he found, "Not death, but Love."[19]

The negative thoughts were crowded out by the powerful, healthy thoughts and emotions of hope, courage, faith, and love. Carl was no longer hindered by his illness, though he still had to live with it. Epictetus wrote:

> Sickness is a hindrance to the body, but not to the will, unless the will consent. Lameness is a hindrance to the leg, but not to the will. Say this to yourself at each event that happens, for you shall find that though it hinders something else it will not hinder you.[20]

The writer of *Proverbs* expressed the same idea: "The spirit of a man will sustain his infirmity."[21]

Carl made plans. Though he might be temporarily hindered by his infirmity, his will was to accomplish his goals. He had a lovely lady now to help him. Slowly the infirmity of his body began to disappear. Perhaps, then, the most crucial factor in Carl's recovery was the way Alice Brown loved him and responded to his love. Had she met his love with apathy, Carl might have given up and succumbed as Keats did. But the love between Alice and Carl was reciprocal and strong, as it was between Elizabeth and Robert Browning.

There were four nurses to care for about 75 patients at Valmora in 1924. The same day Carl arrived, Alice came to his room to take his order for his first meal. Little did Dr. Brown realize that it was his dietitian, his own daughter, who did so much to encourage the patient in Room #8. Little did the nurses realize that Carl listened for Alice's step in the hall. Soon Carl asked Alice to marry him. The engagement gave Carl the greatest purpose for living he had ever known. They were engaged four years while Carl recovered from his illness and finished medical school.

Alice Brown was told by professors from the University of Illinois Medical School, Carl's doctors, that her fiancé would be dead by 1930; but she said she'd settle for even two years with him. They were married April 12, 1928. They had two children, Editha and Carl William. Alice died December 27, 1973. The two years she had hoped for had become 47 long and happy ones. Even a marriage like the Brownings, one of the greatest in the world of romantic literature and of reality, could hardly rival it.

Little did Carl know that when he was sent to Valmora to recover if he could, or to die if he couldn't, that he was to become one of the chosen, one of those who would live long enough to witness the modern golden age of medicine that conquered a multitude of diseases. Many physicians in previous years would have given anything to witness the miracles of the 20th century. The Queen of Sheba made a long journey to visit King Solomon to ascertain if what she had heard about him was true, and she marvelled to find that "the half was not told me; thy wisdom and prosperity exceedeth the fame which I heard."[22] So Carl Gellenthien could not foresee the half of what lay in the decades ahead, for he, too, would walk with the financial and medical kings of this nation and he too, would see and hear the marvels of the golden age of this generation. He would, in fact, become a part of it.

Carl Gellenthien was to become a doctor whose practice would span over half a century. He would see dozens of modern discoveries, many miracles. He would hear the echo of the words of Jesus speaking to His disciples:

> Blessed are the eyes which see the things that ye see: For I tell you that many prophets and kings have desired to see those things which ye see, and have not seen them; and to hear those things which ye hear, and have not heard them. [23]

Carl's journey began when he boarded the train for Valmora on

October 30, 1924. The train left Chicago's Dearborn Station at 10:30 p.m. arriving at Watrous at 12:30 noon the second day, a run of 37 hours. Carl had probably received an informative booklet from Dr. W. T. Brown explaining various matters to prospective patients:

> Buy your ticket to Watrous, N. Mex., notify the Conductor to stop the train at Valmora, wire us in advance and our automobile will be at the train to meet you, no charge for this service. This will save you a five mile drive back from Watrous, the charge for which is $2.00. Unless you notify the Conductor to stop at Valmora you will be carried through to Watrous, as Valmora is only a flag station. [24]

The rates at Valmora in 1916 were $13.00 per week to employees of member companies and $15.00 a week to others. Bed patients were charged fifty cents per day extra. [25] Railway fare, Chicago to Watrous, was $29.00 for a Pullman Sleeper and $7.40 for a Tourist Sleeper. Harvey meals enroute were $3.75 at that time. [26] The rates had probably not changed much by 1924 when Carl began his ride to destiny.

Carl Gellenthien found his balm in Gilead at Valmora where the contrast between the congested, urban world of concrete canyons he had known and the spacious Rocky Mountain wilderness of Valmora's sunny canyons renewed his hope.

After he was able to leave Valmora, Gellenthien received his B.S. degree in 1923 and his M.D. in 1927, both from the University of Illinois. His internship was completed at St. Luke's Hospital in Denver in 1927. He then completed a residency at Agnes Memorial (Phipps) Sanatorium in Denver (now Lowery Air Force Base.) Then he studied at Trudeau School of Tuberculosis in Saranac Lake, New York and attended Harvard University in Boston for further training in Internal Medicine. Thus, Gellenthien's plans to go to India as a missionary were changed, but his mission was no less significant. He went to Valmora as a patient, arriving November 1, 1924, but returned on September 14, 1927 as a doctor. If becoming Valmora's Medical Director were not triumph enough, he married the boss's daughter!

Valmora, then, was a Balm in Gilead. It gave Carl Gellenthien the environment he needed to regain his health. It reinforced his positive thinking. It gave him solitude in which to meditate and feel the healing hand of God. And it gave him the woman of his life to love and to cherish while attaining the goals of service to mankind he had so desired. Little did Carl realize that day when he found out that he had tuberculosis what the future held. When Carl crossed over the bridge that fateful day in Chicago and looked down at the Chicago River, he did not understand that he was crossing a bridge in his life which would lead to his destiny, his life's work, and to the woman he would marry. At Valmora Carl crossed a kind of bridge, too, one that led him back into the land of the living as he reached out for love. His fears and doubts left him as his positive attitude grew stronger, for "There is no fear in love; but perfect love casteth out fear."[27] Carl was made perfect in love as every passing day at Valmora brought more joy and confidence in Alice's love for him and as his love for her grew. His fear of death was gone, and his faith in God grew stronger as he felt His healing love. Had Carl chosen suicide that day he crossed the Chicago river, the lives of thousands would have been deprived of the help he had to offer. But he chose to live, and he found the bridge that leads from death to life. It was at Valmora that he found "not death — but love."

NOTES

1. Jeremiah 8:22, *The Holy Bible, op. cit.,* p. 656.
2. Report notes in Scrapbook 5, Valmora Library, Valmora, New Mexico, p. 34.
3. Carl H. Gellenthien, *The Valmora Guide,* Booklet 5, n.d., p. 43, in Scrapbook 1, Valmora Library, Valmora, New Mexico, p. 32.
4. Paul Wright, "Valmora, The Wilderness Retreat," *New Mexico Highway Journal,* May, 1931, p. 18.
5 *Ibid.,* p. 20.
6. Emerick, *op. cit.,* Appendix IV, p. 79.
7. Foreman, *op. cit.,* p. xviii.
8. Trilling, *op. cit.,* p. 248.
9. Foreman, *op. cit.,* p. xix.
10. Trilling, *op. cit.,* p. 255.
11. Sontag, *op. cit.,* p. 22.
12. Foreman, *op. cit.,* p. xx.
13. *Ibid.*
14. *Ibid.*
15. Trilling, *op. cit.,* p. 259.
16. Carl H. Gellenthien, interview at Valmora Clinic, July 24 1983.
17. Foreman, *op. cit.*
18. Lillian Eichler Watson, ed., *Light From Many Lamps, op. cit.,* p. 58.
19. Elizabeth Barrett Browning, *Sonnets From the Portuguese* (N.Y.: Harper & Row, Publishers, n.d.), p. 7.
20. Epictetus, quoted in Lillian Eichler Watson, ed., *Light From Many Lamps, op. cit.,* p. 93.
21. Proverbs 18:14, *The Holy Bible, op. cit.,* p. 578.
22. I Kings 10:7, *The Holy Bible, op. cit.,* p. 330.
23. Luke 10: 23-24, *The Holy Bible, op. cit.,* p. 889.
24. W.T. Brown, *Valmora Sanatorium,* Booklet 7, Valmora Sanatorium, n.d., p. 1, in Scrapbook 1, Valmora Library, Valmora, New Mexico, p. 2.
25. *Valmora Sanatorium: An Invitation,* Booklet 1, Valmora, New Mexico, 1916, p. 6, in Scrapbook 5, Valmora Library, Valmora, New Mexico, p. 60.
26. *Ibid.,* p. 18.
27. 1 John 4:18, *The Holy Bible, op. cit.,* p. 1058.

CHAPTER
V

"Gelly" vs. Bain – et. al.

The nurses on the third floor of St. Luke's Hospital in Denver had seen angry young interns before, but they had never seen righteous anger explode in front of the nurses' station like it did the night young Dr. Gellenthien vented his fury in a stormy wrath that assured everyone he would never see graduation day.

It happened one evening when a 10-year-old girl was admitted about 11 p.m. with respiratory trouble. Dr. Ralph Bain,[1] the attending physician, said the girl had a foreign body in her bronchus. He instructed Gellenthien to locate the object with a bronchoscope and remove it. Then he went home.

Bain had been left in charge while the regular supervisor, T.E. Carmody, was out of the country. Gellenthien had almost completed his internship at St. Luke's where he'd come just after being pronounced "apparently arrested" and able to leave Valmora. As an intern he received $15.00 a month plus room and board along with his white uniforms and laundry expenses. The student nurses received no salary at all. Gellenthien considered himself lucky because, although the hospitals solicited interns who were an excellent source of cheap labor, a student still had to have an outstanding academic record to be accepted. No one had bothered to check on his health history or he would have been turned down in favor of someone who had never had TB. But as long as he could keep up with the strenuous work load, no one cared.

After examining the patient, Gellenthien found no evidence of a foreign body. Indeed, he found that the girl had pneumonia. She was very ill, so Gellenthien called Bain at home to tell him what he had found and how sick the girl was. Bain, who had been drinking heavily, cursed Gellenthien and instructed him to do a tracheotomy. Realizing that such a surgical procedure would be a useless, unnecessary risk to a patient already in critical condition, Gellenthien refused.

"Are you refusing to carry out my orders?" Bain roared through the phone.

Gellenthien affirmed that he was.

After a barrage of threats, Bain stormed down to the hospital, thoroughly intoxicated. The patient was unconscious. Bain cursed Gellenthien in front of the patient's family, declaring that if the girl died, it would be Gellenthien's fault. His reasoning dulled by liquor, Bain was determined to carry out the tracheotomy. He continued his barrage of obscene name-calling, a stream of vulgarities directed at Gellenthien, this time in front of the nurses' station. Then he ordered the nurses to get the instruments necessary to perform the tracheotomy.

Gellenthien objected, telling the nurses — and attempting to persuade Bain — that the tracheotomy was unnecessary. When Bain insisted he would do the tracheotomy in spite of Gellenthien's objections — punctuating his remarks with more obscenities directed at Gellenthien — the young intern suddenly punched Bain and knocked him out in a single blow.

The nurses behind the desk were horrified, momentarily frozen. Appalled at the drama they had just witnessed, they were certain this outburst meant the end of young Gellenthien's career. All of the nurses liked him and affectionately called him "Gelly." It was too bad, they thought, that such a promising young intern would never practice medicine. They realized that Gelly might have been right about the patient, but no one ever crossed a staff member. And this young intern had physically attacked his superior! What a pity. Graduation day was so close at hand.

Graduation had never come easy for Carl Gellenthien. He was a good student, but he had a way of getting into trouble just before commencement. Prior to high school graduation his physical education teacher gave the entire class so many demerits they were sure they wouldn't graduate. In fact, the teacher told them they wouldn't. Later, he admitted it had been a mere threat. But young Carl and his classmates sweated out the last few days before commencement.

Then, after three years of medical school, it seemed certain that Gellenthien would never graduate from the University of Illinois after his TB was discovered. No one expected him to return from Valmora to graduate. His classmates like Earl Ewert graduated ahead of him, but they were there to congratulate him when he received his diploma.

Prior to Gellenthien's rendezvous with Valmora, he had been ill with pleurisy but his doctors did not suspect that he also had tuberculosis. His doctors at the University of Illinois had tapped his chest and drained off a sterile, straw-colored liquid. They told him he had "wet" pleurisy and he dismissed any thought of a more serious illness. That summer of 1924 at the YMCA Summer Boys' Camp at Lac du Flambeau in northern Wisconsin, young Gellenthien enjoyed the beauty of nature and performed his first unassisted surgery. It was unassisted, not so much because of Gellenthien's competence as a surgeon, but because the patient was singularly unpopular. The patient was a skunk.

The young campers had trapped the polecat and asked their resident medical student to perform an operation to remove the scent glands so the young creature could be tamed. Gellenthien donned rubber gloves, wrapped his head in a towel and wore a clown suit, the closest thing to a surgical gown he could find. A barrel with boards placed across the top served as an operating table. The operating room was the middle of the baseball field. The camp's citizens wanted to give the surgeon plenty of working space. The young doctor's surgery was successful. The skunk became a loveable pet. But the surgeon was ostracized for some time afterwards.

Gellenthien decided that if he was old enough to be the camp doctor, he should look the part. He grew a mustache that summer. When he returned home at the end of the summer sporting a mustache, his family was appalled. They all agreed that he should shave it off. He never did.

Starting his senior year of classes, Gellenthien noticed he felt tired most of the time. He had fever and chills. He woke up with night sweats. His grades began to suffer. It seemed his pleurisy was returning. Finally the unhappy day when he discovered his TB arrived, and by November 1, he was out of school and confined to the grounds of Valmora. It was a happy time when he finally arrived back on campus to finish up his senior year.

Yet, after all his trouble and delay, it seemed that again graduation eluded him. Prior to graduation from medical school there was a problem in Gellenthien's obstetric's class. Two students were caught cheating on the final exam. The class was told they'd all have to take the exam over because they had undoubtedly all cheated. There was a cupola on the ceiling where the professors would monitor tests, using opera glasses. Gellenthien was sitting in the front center. He was insulted at being called a cheater along with the rest of the class when only two students, apparently, were guilty. He stood up in class and challenged his professor. He stated that since the professor had been down the street shooting pool during the exam, he could hardly have observed anyone cheating. And if he had not been there to observe, he had no right to accuse anyone, much less the entire class. Gellenthien thus became the spokesman for the class. He and two others went before Dr. D.J. Davis, Dean of the Medical School, who sympathized with them but told them they would have to see Dean Tommy Arcle Clark who would then make the decision. After Clark heard the students, only the two caught cheating had to re-take the exam. In fact, what Gellenthien called the "sneak and peek" system was changed to the honor system after that. As Gellenthien received his diploma on the long-awaited graduation day, the President of the University, to everyone's surprise, called out, "Congratulations, Gellenthien!"

Thus, history repeated itself as the day of Gellenthien's graduation from St. Luke's approached. Again, commencement seemed beyond his reach. This time the situation was more ominous than ever, and Gellenthein feared he would not pass his internship. He would not, therefore, obtain his M.D. degree from the University of Illinois.

Since officials at St. Luke's did not know that Gellenthien had been a victim of tuberculosis, they had no idea what a strain the young intern had been under. When they admitted him, they did not check his health record; they were interested only in his transcript, which was impressive. Gellenthien's roomate, however, could not help noticing that his friend was not well, and Gellenthien admitted that he had come to Denver after being declared "apparently cured" of TB, meaning that the disease was no longer dangerously active. The roomate, H.T.S. Bonesteel, known to his friends as "Bud," was a great help. He concealed the secret of Gellenthien's prior confinement and did his best to make Gelly's free time restful. Like all TB victims, Gellenthien had learned to pace himself carefully to avoid a relapse. He rested as much as possible. Still, the rigid schedule of his work kept him on the brink of a relapse. It is ironic that Gellenthien, who might have died of TB at any time, lived, while Bud contracted polio from a patient a few years later and died when he was still very young.

Gellenthien planned his schedule carefully when he entered the program at St. Luke's, saving surgery until last because it was supposed to be the most taxing, physically. He had heard that obstetrics was the easiest, but after three days and nights of delivering babies — with very little sleep in between — he decided it wasn't. The baby boom hit on the Fourth of July weekend. After it was over, Gellenthien declared, "If July 4th is this bad, what is Labor Day going to be like?"

Now, as the end of his internship approached, the situation which jeopardized his graduation arose, putting Gellenthien under heavy stress. Dr. T. E. Carmody, on the Medical Board and Staff at St. Luke's, had gone to the Mediterranean, leaving his assistant, Dr. Ralph Bain, in charge. As an intern, Gellenthien was subordinate to Bain and was supposed to follow his orders without question. With graduation just around the corner, Gellenthien realized he was really in trouble this time: he had hit his boss in front of witnesses, not only hit him, but knocked him out.

When Bain regained consciousness, he was hasty to apologize to Gellenthien. Nursing his black eye, he assured Gellenthien that these misunderstandings happen, that he would not hold the incident against him. Gellenthien accepted the apology, thinking that Bain wanted to be reasonable. They shook hands.

Later, around one a.m., the night supervisor of nurses who had been at the desk during the incident, called Gellenthien.

"Gelly, you didn't believe Dr. Bain when he apologized and said he'd forget the whole thing, did you?"

Gellenthien said that he believed Bain had been sincere.

The nurse replied, "Oh, no, Gelly. don't trust him!" she warned. "After you left, Gelly, Dr. Bain said, 'I'll get that s.o.b. if it's the last thing I ever do!'"

Forewarned, Gellenthien went to see the Superintendent, Mr. Charles A. Wordell, at seven o'clock the next morning. Wordell was a friend who listened sympathetically to Gellenthien's story, but he told the intern it was beyond him to be able to help. He could offer little encouragement.

"Gelly," Wordell said, calling him by his nickname, "I'll do what I can. But this is serious. It's in the hands of the Board." The Chairman of the Hospital's Board of Trustees was Dr. W. W. Grant who was quite renowned among his colleagues. It was said that he had performed the first appendectomy west of the Mississippi River. Gellenthien would be called before the Board and the decision affecting the young intern's future would be up to them.

The Board met shortly thereafter. Dr. Bain was called in first. Gellenthien knew he would make his side of the story good. Besides, he was supported by a cablegram from Egypt, a statement from Dr. Carmody saying that he backed up his assistant in this matter, one hundred percent. After Bain had finished his statement, he was sent out of the room and Gellenthien was summoned.

It was an extremely tense moment. Gellenthien walked into the room and saw the solemn faces of his judges, the members of the Board. Gellenthien was not asked to sit down. He stood facing those severe expressions and was asked to make his statement.

Gellenthien hesitated for a moment. In addition to the Board members, he saw Miss Nichols, Secretary of the Hospital Superintendent, who was there to record the proceedings. Seeing the lady there, Gellenthien asked if he should tell exactly what happened, using the exact language that had been used. He was told he must do so, even though Miss Nichols was present.

Gellenthien told the series of events that had led to his striking Dr. Bain. He described Bain's intoxicated state, the patient's condition, and the language Bain had used. He explained the danger Bain had placed his patient in, unreasonably insisting on performing an unnecessary operation. He described his anger at being "cussed out" in front of the girl's parents and in front of the nurses. He told the group that he had concluded the only way to stop this incompetent doctor from harming the patient was to hit him, so he did.

Gellenthien's entire career hung in the balance. The decision made at that moment would determine the events of the rest of his life.

After a few moments of silence, Dr. Grant asked, "Dr. Gellenthien, did you hit Dr. Bain *at the nurses' station?*"

"Yes, Sir," the intern responded.

"And did you hit him *with your bare fist?*" he asked, emphasizing the word "fist."

"Yes, Sir," Gellenthien replied honestly.

Then Dr. Grant asked the final question. It was a rhetorical one. "Why didn't you hit him with a *club?*"

The Board agreed that Dr. Bain had been incompetent that night. Consequently, Bain was removed from the staff. Furthermore, Dr. Gellenthien's diagnosis proved correct. The patient did, indeed have pneumonia, not a foreign body in her throat. She recovered.

Carl's parents and grandparents were proud on Carl's graduation day. They had helped him financially as much as they could. Carl's grandfather believed in education but didn't quite understand the American system of specialized education. Once a gas line broke at their home. Grandpa Gellenthien said, "When Carl comes home, he can fix it." His wife explained that Carl didn't know how to do things like that. The grandfather was exasperated. "You mean he's been going to school all these years and he can't fix a pipe?"

In spite of Carl's ignorance of the plumbing business, he understood the anatomy of human plumbing as well as human psychology by the time he finished his internship. He learned through grueling, exhausting, sometimes unpleasant work. Once the nurses called Gellenthien to try to calm a maniacal patient. When

Gellenthien opened the door of the patient's room, he got a full bed pan thrown in his face.

In spite of such incidents, Gellenthien was pleased with his internship. On June 6, 1927, he wrote to Dr. D. J. Davis at the University of Illinois College of Medicine:

> I have been well pleased with my work here (at St. Luke's) and feel that the past year has been a worthwhile investment of my time.
>
> The Superintendent of the Hospital, Mr. Wordell, who used to be Superintendent at St. Luke's in Chicago, realizes the purpose and wants of an internship, and has made an honest effort all year to fulfill these wants. He is a hard taskmaster, but I have always found him impartial and fair.
>
> The attending men, as a whole, have the teaching idea and are willing to turn the case over to the intern, as soon as they were sure he could be relied upon...
>
> The only major weak point that I have been able to see is that one's input equals one's output. That is, one could go through the entire year without learning much. But that is true of most hospitals, and after being in the Grant and Lutheran Memorial Hospitals in Chicago, and knowing what the size hospital has to offer, I am enthusiastic and feel that I can unconditionally recommend St. Luke's Hospital here in Denver for a twelve month's internship.
>
> Last fall I wrote (scored) second place in the Colorado State Board examination and my plans for the future are to spend three or four months in the different tubercular sanatoria around Colorado in an effort to learn the methods and routine of the different institutions before locating at Valmora. [2]

He did spend some time in Colorado before returning to Valmora where Alice was wearing his fraternity ring as a token of their engagement. He borrowed $15.00 from his father to buy her wedding ring. In later years, he bought Alice a more expensive diamond ring, but she always preferred wearing the original one. Alice and Carl were married and he began work at Valmora. But his real education was only beginning. Dr. Brown taught him as much or more than he had learned in his formal education. His father-in-law became his teacher, his friend, and his mentor.

NOTES

1. a pseudonym.
2. Carl H. Gellenthien, letter to D. J. Davis, June 6, 1927, in Scrapbook 11, Valmora Library, Valmora, New Mexico, p. 3.

CHAPTER
VI
Valmora – Home of Santa

Until 1938 Santa Claus lived at Valmora — or so the children of northeastern New Mexico's Mora and San Miguel Counties believed. And in a way he did. He was Dr. William Townsend Brown who played the role of good Saint Nicholas every year, giving out thousands of gifts and goodies to the area's children. Moreover, he made the spirit of Christmas live year-round through his contribution to humanity, for he was the founder of Valmora Industrial Sanatorium. He would have been the perfect prototype of the man Charles Dickens honored, one who "knew how to keep Christmas well."

Year after year Dr. Brown prepared Christmas gifts for the children of the two counties. In 1931 he delighted 400 pupils of the Mora public schools and nearly 600 children from adjacent rural districts when they assembled about a huge lighted Christmas tree in front of the public shcool building in Mora. The next day he played a similar role at the Manuelitas rural school for students of four districts.

> The big-hearted, and physically huge superintendent of the tuber-culosis sanatorium will not don a Santa Claus costume this year in handing out the gifts but through his generosity, thousands of toys, a half ton of candy and usable gifts of clothing are to be parceled out to every child in the county in the two celebrations tomorrow and in in-dividual distribution already made or to be made by Dr. Brown, his daughters and the staff at Valmora.[1]

Each youngster received two or more gifts as well as candy. The gifts included toy garden tools, tennis rackets with balls, marbles, trucks, dolls, trains, books, rubber balls, popguns, and clothes. All were in perfect condition and were from first class gift stock from some of Chicago's finest stores. The tons of items received at

Valmora for distribution were brought in with freight paid by the Santa Fe railroad, but the costs of distributing them were borne by Dr. Brown.

Previously Dr. Brown has played Santa Claus in each individual school district of the central and western part of the county but this year the burden was found too great and a few central celebrations are to be had for the distribution. Dr. Brown's Christmas charity has become widely known and he is perhaps ranked with the nation's most noted Christmas givers. Certainly few if any other bears the distinction of playing Santa Claus to the school children of a whole community. [2]

Dr. Brown was lauded as an ambassador for the state of New Mexico in an article appearing in the Las Vegan in 1932. It was noted that he had told thousands of people about the State's beauties, natural resources, and its healthful, invigorating climate. He was labeled, "New Mexico's friend and champion."[3] But he was especially commended for his role of Santa and the generosity he displayed in accepting such an awesome responsibility. He entertained 5,000 children at community Christmas trees in Mora, Cleveland, Holman, Guadalupita, Ocate, Le Doux, Rainsville, Watrous, Nolan, Wagon Mound, Levy, Gascon, Rociada, "and wherever there are enough children to warrant a community tree."[4]

He is a regular Santa Claus for that entire section of the state. He has a lot of assistants. He gets many of his gifts from Chicago corporations who support the sanatorium. He accumulates thousands of toys, great quantities of candy and edibles. He has been doing this for nine years and the task is growing heavier each year. But he gets as much satisfaction out of it as do the children. He's the king of volunteer Kris Kringles in the state. [5]

An interesting item entitled, "Weelum Enjoyed the Valmora Banquet," was written by "our Scotch contributor" who attended the dinner in support of Valmora in December 9, 1931 in Detroit. He wrote, "Do ye ken why Gude made some men sae big — weel, it's because ye canna' pit a great big heart like Doctor Broon's intil a 'wee bit maun. He had tae find out a sax an' a half footer for that heart."[6]

This community has probably the largest Santa Claus in the whole United States in the person of Dr. W.T. Brown, superintendent of Valmora Sanatorium. Not only is Dr. Brown a big man physically, but he is big in other ways. Kind-hearted, progressive and a lover of children...He likes to see the little tots happy, especially at Christmas time, and in order to bring joy into the lives of as many of the children in this vicinity as possible, he is this year again playing Santa Claus to *thousands of them.*

Children who receive gifts from his hand will never forget the big Santa Claus from Valmora. His kindness and influence for making children happy will live after him in the memory of those he takes such pride in making happy now. Old Kris Kringle with all his wealth of toys and dolls at the North Pole never took more pride in his storehouse of delights for children than does Dr. Brown as he sees load after load of gifts leave Valmora for the kiddies of the schools of Mora and San Miguel counties. [7]

Brown went to Chicago every year where Sears, Roebuck and other stores gave him their surplus toys. Sometimes they would give him defective toys and then he and his helpers, including Alice and her sister Margaret, would get them in shape for distribution. Santa and his helpers had a big job preparing to distribute hundreds of dollars worth of Christmas trees, toys, candy, musical instruments and toys. One editor said that if Dr. Brown were not Santa Claus himself, he certainly must be that old saint's right hand man, "not the rotund, squat person you and I have been asked to believe in as children, but a man of large stature, one who attracts attention because of his manly figure, tall and strong. [8]

Again this year Doctor Brown has procured toys and candy which are being distributed among children in forty schools and other groups in Mora County and beyond. These gifts are the only evidence of Christmas that the greater number of these children in the scattered mountain settlements have.

The work of sorting and mending the toys, packing the boxes, etc., was in charge (sic) of Margaret Brown. She was ably assisted by Mrs. Tipton, Mr. Kesterson and Ted Rehnquist. Santa Claus in his northland establishment is popularly supposed to be assisted by a host of little brownies. Well, it can't be said there is anything little about his crew of helpers in this southwestern agency! [9]

Born in Maryborough, Queens County, Ireland on January 2, 1870, Brown grew up in England. He moved to Grant County in Wisconsin when he was 15 and lived with an older brother, Harry, who was an attorney. He drove livery between Fennimore and Bescobel, and it was said that no man would get a passenger there quicker than he. He also worked for the Hinn Merchandise Company, gathering cream from 14 creameries owned by the Hinn Brothers.

...as there were no trucks in those days he drove horses and a wagon; seldom came home at night with the team he started out with; would stop a farmer any place in the road and trade horses. Well, this young man developed into an organizer or a promoter. [10]

After receiving his medical education at Hahnemann Medical School in Philadelphia, Brown set up his first office in Ripon, Wisconsin as a general practitioner and eye, nose and throat specialist. Soon thereafter he met Editha M. Hassell, daughter of Samuel Hassell, a medical doctor. On April 28, 1897 William T. Brown and Editha Hassell were married at Lancaster, Wisconsin. The Browns had two daughters, Alice born January 7, 1901, and Margaret, born three years later.

Brown first came to New Mexico in the early 1900s when the Atchison Topeka and Santa Fe Railroad was conducting excursion tours. He was searching for a place where consumptives could go to recuperate — an ideal place. From Wisconsin to Texas to Wyoming, Brown searched.

> In 1904, Dr. Brown came to New Mexico and settled at Romeroville. Immediately he saw the possibilities of this section from a health standpoint and in 1905 established Valmora Sanatorium, specializing in the treatment of tuberculosis and chronic diseases. After five years of private operation Dr. Brown interested a score of Chicago's larger business firms and the sanatorium was enlarged to its present capacity. [11]

For a short time Brown established a practice at Romeroville, just south of Las Vegas. He continued to look for an ideal site for a Sanatorium. The Valmora site had been chosen by Ashley Pond II as a school for asthmatic boys the year before, but shortly thereafter the school was flooded out by the unusually heavy rains received in late September. On October 1, 1904, residents of the Mora valley, including the Ponds, had to flee for their lives as the Mora river became a raging torrent, thundering like Niagra Falls, carrying away cottonwood trees, livestock, houses, bridges, and iron rails from the Santa Fe Railway.

"It was perhaps the worst single natural disaster in New Mexico history. The death toll reached at least 30 and damage was in the millions of dollars." [12]

Pond consequently sold the Valmora acreage to Dr. Brown and went on to establish his boys' school at Los Alamos which later became the scientific laboratory that gave birth to the atomic bomb. Brown built the hospital and cabins at Valmora on a hillside to assure future safety from flood waters.

The site was the answer to Brown's dreams. He had been looking for a location accessible by the railroad from the east, one which was isolated from nearby settlements while still reasonably close to a community. He also needed a place with an abundant water supply. Valmora was located four miles from the village of Watrous and about 20 miles from the small city of Las Vegas. The tracks of the Santa Fe Railroad came down the Mora valley and passed through the sanatorium grounds. A spring located in the rimrock of the canyon wall provided abundant water which was piped down the hillside into tanks and brought from there into the buildings at a flow rate of 22,000 gallons a day.

Brown originally planned a private sanatorium for 21 patients and put up ten structures that first year. The initial staff included a nurse, maintenance man, and cook. Patients were accepted the next year. [13]

In 1908 Brown built a new home for his family to the west of the old ranch house they had lived in at first. The original ranch house was then used for patients. During a Chicago visit in 1910, Brown talked with physician friends about the need for treatment facilities for patients of moderate means, and the idea of an industrial sanatorium evolved. [14]

The need for a sanatorium was evident. The loss of workers to tuberculosis was increasing annually. Working in crowded conditions in offices and factories, workers were vulnerable to the disease. When the National Tuberculosis Association was formed in 1904, there were about one hundred sanatoria and hospitals in the United States, not enough to accomodate the needs of so many TB victims. National corporations were suffering from the terrible toll tuberculosis took on their employees every year. Workers could not afford hospital care, and many died.

Dr. Brown felt that both employee and employer were the losers to the ravages of TB. Employees had no place to go if they became ill and no job future if they recovered sufficiently to return to work. Brown thought it would be to the advantage of the businessmen to provide for the health and security of their workers by providing a place where the stricken could go with the knowledge that, upon recovery, a job would be waiting.

Marshall Field & Company, with more than five thousand employees, was one of the first supporters of Valmora. After hearing Dr. Brown's plan, they realized that supporting a sanatorium would be a wise investment. Their workers could recover and then return to work. The savings in the cost of training new workers was in itself a great benefit they would reap from that investment. Some companies like International Harvester saw the wisdom of Dr. Brown's plan and guaranteed their workers a job to return to, paid their transportation to and from Valmora, continued to pay their salaries, and helped care for their families. Thus, the sick employee did not have to worry about his family back home while he was recovering and probably recovered more quickly.

Brown presented his plan for a tuberculosis sanatorium to prominent physicians and businessmen in Chiciago and St. Louis. At first the sanatorium with only 75 beds seemed little more than a lonely ranch in the badlands of New Mexico to the Chicago doctors, inadequate to handle the needs. But Brown sold them on the idea. An account of the meeting of Brown with promient physicians in Chicago was related in an article by a physician in *The Valmora Sun:*

> I am reminded of an incident which occurred at a meeting of these men when the creation of Valmora was being considered. They were considering the size institution Valmora was to be and had decided upon a small one, about seventy-five bed capacity, so that the patient would never lose his individuality and become known as a number, and the relationship between the doctor and patient would be a personal one.
>
> The renowned Dr. Frank Billings, Dean of Rush Medical College, arrived late at the meeting and when he was told the bed capacity would be seventy-five, he felt that the whole project was too small and not enough people would be benefited; that it would be better to institute a large, wide-scale anti-tuberculosis educational campaign.
>
> To Dr. W.T. Brown, this was most discouraging and probably meant that Valmora would die aborning for Dr. Billings was recognized as the leader of the medical profession of that time. As soon as he could, Dr. Brown arose and said, 'Dr. Billings, you live on the North side of Chicago, and I know you walk along the lake shore to your office almost every morning. Suppose as you walked along this morning you saw a man drowning. Would you have said, Too bad. We must start a wide educational swimming campaign so this won't happen again? No. I am sure you would have been among the first to tear off your coat and try to save that drowning man.' Dr. Billings laughed, capitulated, and the plans for Valmora's organization went ahead. [15]

That was really the beginning of Valmora Industrial Sanatorium.

In 1910, thirty-five of the largest industrial organizations in Chicago and St. Louis offered financial support for the sanatorium to provide care for their stricken workers. Valmora was incorporated under the laws of Illinois as a non-profit corporation with no capital stock. Fifteen men listed as incorporators in the record of the corporations' filing in New Mexico were: E. Fletcher Ingals, Joseph E. Otis, J.H. McDuffee, Edward M. Skinner, Philip L. James, John M. Glenn, A.A. Sprague II, Frank Billings, Charles Louis Mix, John M. Dodson, James M. Blazer, A.M. Corwin, William T. Brown, Edwin B. Teteur and Frederick Tice. [16]   The first Board of Directors consisted of Ingals, President; John T. Pirie, Jr., Vice President; Harry E.

Mock, Secretary; Otis, Treasurer; E.D. Raynolds, Assistant Treasurer; and Julius Rosenwald, Tice, John F. Wolff, James Simpson Sprague, Teteur, Marvin B. Pool, and Blazer, Counsel; W.G. Hibbard, Jr., Dodson and Corwin.[17]

The first Medical Board consisted of Robert H. Babcock, Billings, Brown, Corwin, N.S. Davis, Dodson, Arthur R. Edwards, Henry B. Favill, O.T. Freer, Ingals, Mix, Mock, John R. Murphy, A.J. Ochsner, John A. Ribison, W.F. Scott, Otto L. Schmidt, George H Simmons, Tice, Teteur and George W. Webster.[18]

Initial subscribers to the Valmora Industrial Sanatorium, Inc., were from Chicago, except where otherwise indicated, as follows:

> Boston Store; Butler Brothers; Carson, Pirie, Scott and Co.; Chalmers Motor Co., (Detroit); Chicago Daily News; Continental and Commercial National Bank; Corn Exchange National Bank; Richard T. Crane; The Fair; John V. Farwell Co.; First National Bank; Dr. A.E. Freer; F.A. Hardy and Co.; Hibbard Spencer Bartlett and Co.; Hiberian Banking Association; Illinois Trust and Savings Bank; Mary E. Ingals; International Harvester Co.; Mandel Brothers; Marshall Field and Co.; Morris and Co.; National Bank of the Republic,; National City Bank; Northern Trust Co.; Peoples Gas, Light and Coke Co.; Ripon Anti-Tuberculosis Society (Wisconsin); Rothschild and Co.; J.T. Ryerson and Son; Dr. Otto L. Schmidt; Sears Roebuck and Co.; Sels Schwab and Co.; Siegel Cooper and Co.; Sprague, Warner and Co.; Charles A. Stevens and Brothers; Union Trust Co.; Western Trust and Savings Bank; John F. Wolff.[19]

The total amount given by these subscribers was $29,097 in the period of 1909-1910. Later contributors were:

> American Radiator Co.; Armour and Co.; Automatic Electric Co.; Carleton-Ferguson Dry Goods Co. (St. Louis); Central Republican Bank; Central Trust Co.; Chicago Telephone Co. (Later Illinois Bell Co.); Continental Illinois Bank and Trust Co.; Ely Walker Co. (St. Louis); Hamilton Brown Shoe Co. (St. Louis); John E. Hardin; Holabird and Roache; Lamson Brothers and Co.; Harry Lobel; Merchants Loan and Trust Co.; Morris and Co.; National Bank of the Republic; Rice, Stix Dry Goods Co.; Rosenthal Sloan Millinery Co. (St. Louis); Seigel, Cooper and Co.; Simmons Hardware Co. (St. Louis); Charles Stevens and Brothers; W.A. Wieboldt and Co.; Wilson and Co.; William Wrigley Jr.; Swift and Co.[20]

In later years there were numerous other additions to the group of supporters, including United Airlines.

Victor F. Lawson, an editor and publisher of the Chicago Daily News, helped Dr. Brown in the founding of Valmora, as did many other influential people who believed Valmora's fresh air, sunshine,

Carl H. Gellenthien, Chicago, about 1904.

Charles and Bertha Gellenthien on their wedding day in 1899.

Carl Gellenthien (left) with his brother Henry about 1907.

Carl H. Gellenthien at graduation from Crane Junior College, Chicago, June 17, 1921.

Carl H. Gellenthien, graduate of the University of Illinois College of Medicine, June 11, 1926. Commencement exercises were held at Ashland Auditorium, 32 South Ashland Blvd., Chicago.

Carl Gellenthien, about 1930.

Valmora valley.

Above: *One of Dr. Brown's early photos of patients on the porch at Valmora, about 1918.*
Below: *One of Dr. Brown's early photos of a patient in front of her cabin at Valmora, about 1918.*

Dr. Carl H. Gellenthien,
Medical Director,
Valmora Industrial
Sanatorium, 1933.

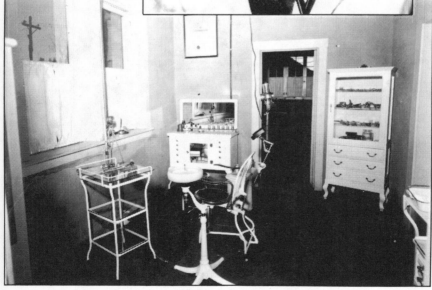

One of the examining rooms at Valmora Clinic — "Ear, nose and throat room,"
about 1938.

Above: *Dr. William T. Brown, about 1930.*
Below: *Halloween Party at Valmora Sanatorium, October, 1930. Dr. Brown, back row, fourth from the right and in the center of the group, is surrounded by patients in a variety of costumes.*

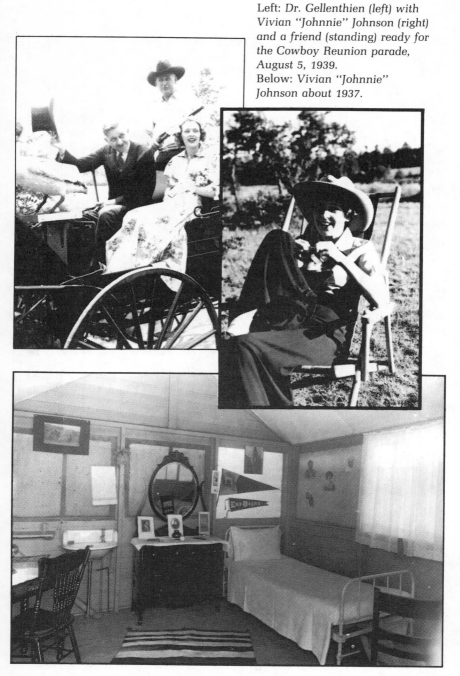

Left: *Dr. Gellenthien (left) with Vivian "Johnnie" Johnson (right) and a friend (standing) ready for the Cowboy Reunion parade, August 5, 1939.*
Below: *Vivian "Johnnie" Johnson about 1937.*

A typical Valmora cottage room. The cottages were reserved for patients who were well enough to leave the hospital rooms and usually accommodated two patients.

high altitude, dry climate, and quiet atmosphere would contribute to the recovery of TB victims — and it did.

From 1905 to 1931 over 5,000 patients received treatment at Valmora. The longest stay was 7 years, the average was 2. Valmora had the lowest death rate in the United States and the highest percentage of cures of all the registered TB hospitals. Patients came from all over the world.

> The thirty year statistical report revealed the treatment and discharge of 2,561 hospital patients from forty-four states of the Union and fifteen foreign countries — China, England, Ireland, France, Norway, Finland, Cuba, Colombia, Bolivia, Argentina, Brazil, Panama, El Salvador, Canada, Mexico and the Canal Zone. [21]

A map on the wall of the waiting room at Valmora Clinic presents an impressive picture of the homes of patients. A red dot marks each city or country. The United States is blotted with red where nearly every state is represented. In addition to the countries mentioned, red dots indicate patients from Brussels, Belgium, and various countries in Central America.

Valmora began to grow immediately after it was instituted. In his first annual report, March 31, 1912, Dr. Brown listed 43 patients in residence at Valmora Industrial Sanatorium. During the previous year, 96 had been admitted altogether. The average length of stay had been 160 days. [22] A coal house had been built, a poultry plant was added, a calf shed with corral was constructed, a room was added to the laundry, and the dairy herd was in good condition. Six calves were raised, as well as 450 chickens and various other poultry including ducks, geese, and turkey. Bees were also kept. Vegetables were grown. And 120 tons of ice were put up, cut from Coyote Creek and stored in the ice house. [23]

By 1914, sleeping porches, 10' by 12' in size, were added to fourteen of the 12-foot square cottages. Also, a 40' by 120' kitchen and dining hall had been built. A rock and cement reservoir for conserving the spring water had been constructed. [24] The dairy, consisting of 32 cows and calves, had produced over 15,000 gallons of milk at a cost of 16 cents a gallon. Dr. Brown was proud of his dairy herd, for he believed it was largely responsible for the very satisfactory weight gains of his patients. [25]

In the spring of 1915, tragedy struck at Valmora. Dr. Brown was leaving for one of his frequent business trips to Chicago. Mrs. Brown took the girls, Alice who was 14 years of age and her younger sister Margaret, to see their father off on the train. The creek was high that day after heavy rains had flooded the valley, and the regular foot bridge was washed out. On the way back home, they had to cross over the high railroad bridge which spanned the river canyon. They were familiar with the train schedules and had no fear of a train coming at that time.

Suddenly an unscheduled freight train approached them from the rear. The rushing water deafened the little trio to the sound behind them. When Editha Brown glanced behind her, she saw the engine bearing down upon them, just yards away. She called out to Margaret to jump down to the bank, for the girl was near the end of the bridge. Then Mrs. Brown managed to reach Alice, who was directly in front of her. She pushed her off the bridge onto the bank below, the momentum of the shove sending Alice sprawling to safety. But Editha Brown was unable to save herself and was killed upon impact.

Dr. Brown was notified of the tragedy and turned back home. What sorrow awaited him! He and his two grief-stricken daughters sorrowfully watched while Editha Brown was buried on a hillside above Valmora. Only one thought comforted him. She had died a noble death, fulfilling the highest aspiration of all of life. She had preserved the lives of her progeny though it meant giving up her own. She had been true to her God-given mother instinct.

In the early 1920s, Dr. Brown married again. The new Mrs. Brown had been a TB patient — Frances McFarland of Chicago. But she died within three years, never having conquered the disease.[26] She was buried at Gascon Ranch.

In spite of life's sorrows, progress continued to be made at Valmora. In 1918 bathrooms were added to each of the cottages. Now, instead of a bath house, each patient would have a private bath. That same year, 15 acres of land were broken, a dam and irrigation system were installed, and patient facilities were expanded.

In 1919 Dr. Brown planted a huge orchard. Hail destroyed most of the trees in the following years, and those violent storms taught Dr. Brown never to use anything except a tin roof on his home. The loss of the orchard disheartened him so that he never planted another. There are yet a few apple trees remaining.

That same year, a twenty-five horse power International Harvester engine and ten Kilowatt General Electric generator were installed. Wiring to the various buildings was nearly completed. The most significant event of the year was the letting of a contract for the new hospital in the amount of $18,210, not to include the heating plant, plumbing, and finishing of the offices.[27]

It was also in 1919 that Dr. Brown purchased the old Gascon Ranch at the head of the beautiful valley 50 miles farther north and 2000 feet higher than Valmora. The 4000 acre ranch property adjoins the Pecos Wilderness, 30 miles northwest of Las Vegas. It was located at the end of the old Indian trail across the mountains and was purchased from the widow of Richard Dunn. She was the daughter of Jean Pendaries, an early French settler. Dr. Brown hoped to raise beef for the sanatorium and to provide a recreation area for his family and friends.

As one of New Mexico's earliest promoters, Dr. Brown excelled in public relations work. An annual banquet at the Stevens Hotel, the largest in Chicago (the present-day Hilton Hotel) was held to promote Valmora. As many as 1100 doctors attended at a time. In 1939 more than fourteen hundred people attended, including supporters, directors, and former patients.

Each year Dr. Brown saw that the best in entertainment and food was provided. There would be native Indian songs by his friend, Princess Tsianina, cowboy and Spanish songs by Miss Gladys Anderson, and music by other distinguished visitors. Brown would show slides of New Mexico. Navajo blankets were raffled off. At the 1930 banquet, flags of New Mexico were draped along the balcony, ribbon festoons in red and yellow were hung from the chandeliers, and cactus plants adorned the tables. Cowboys colorfully dressed in native garb escorted guests to their tables.

The menu always included native New Mexican dishes such as enchiladas, frijoles, and piñon nuts. Dessert might be ice cream shaped and colored like little adobe houses topped by cake-like cactus plants.

As part of the entertainment in 1930, Princess Tsianina, the famous Cherokee mezzo-soprano, attired in Indian costume, presented a group of Indian songs, and Mrs. Gladys Anderson, clad in vivid Spanish costume, sang old Spanish songs. The menu that year featured wild turkey with all the trimmings, apples, wild honey and piñon nuts.[28] Dr. Gellenthien spoke to the audience of several hundred physicians and supporters of the Sanatorium.

> Whereas the valuable rays of the sun seldom can penetrate Chicago's pall of smoke during winter months, there were only six days last year when the sun was not visible at Valmora. In the 21 years of its existence, since its establishment by Chicago businessmen, not one case of pneumonia has developed at Valmora, Gellenthien said.[29]

The fact that patients never developed pneumonia and seldom caught colds was pointed out when the wisdom of their sleeping on screened-in porches in the winter time was questioned. A common belief that night air was bad still persisted. Doctors attempted to persuade patients that windows should be opened at night regardless of the season. Gellenthien informed the audience that at Valmora windows were kept open at night no matter what the weather, with no ill-effects.

Brown's banquets, featuring menus which included enchiladas and frijoles, espangnole, and other New Mexican dishes, became so famous in Chicago that in October of 1931, the city of Detroit induced him to put one on there.[30] The annual banquet idea was conceived to acquaint Chicago backers of Valmora with the work the sanatorium was doing. It was so successful it was carried on until Brown's death in 1935.

Brown was the subject of many newspaper articles. One Wisconsin editor wrote:

> He is so well and favorably known in New Mexico that the postmaster told me that he had had mail directed to Dr. Brown, New Mexico, and it found him. This boy is a product of Grant County and they should be very proud of him.[31]

An Albuquerque reporter also lauded his fame:

> Another thing for which Dr. Brown is famous in his home section is the annual Christmas party he puts on for the school children of Mora county and a few in San Miguel county. At his Christmas party this year, he had 4,000 children, school teachers from practically all the districts in his territory bringing in their children for miles, in automobiles and wagons. It has grown to be quite a big undertaking, but he arranges to provide toys and candy for all, partly through the assistance of the Chicago firms in his association from whom he buys the supplies at greatly reduced prices. The **Journal** recently said he gave away a ton of candy this year, but he says to be accurate it was only a half a ton.[32]

Years later when Dr. Gellenthien made house calls around the county, he would sometimes see a toy perched up on the mantle above the fireplace or in some other strategic area. He would learn that it had been given to some occupant of the household years ago and had been kept new and intact, a tribute to Dr. Brown. The carefully displayed treasures, toys from Santa Brown's gift bag one Christmas long ago, were kept through the years for sentimental reasons, out of respect for the man who gave them so generously. A doll stands on a shelf in her original box, a toy drum adorns a fireplace mantle, a little violin is tucked away in a china cabinet, a teddy bear occupies a special corner, a little horn hangs from the ceiling. They are mementos of happy days gone by, childhood treasures grown old with their owners. Dr. Brown had won his place in the hearts of many children. It was the greatest honor a man could earn.

Dr. Brown knew he would need a strong successor. After Carl married Alice and had served as Medical Director for several years, Brown turned over most of the responsibility of Valmora to his son-in-law. Although Gellenthien's philosophy was basically the same as his mentor's, there was a difference in approach. Gellenthien believed Brown was too authoritarian in his methods and that patients often rebelled against such strict insistence that rules be followed to the letter. Gellenthien wanted patients to develop self-discipline, to be motivated from within. Thus, Gellenthien approached patients with the idea that he was only their coach, and that they had to take responsibility for their own progress.

Dr. Brown's first set of rules was entitled, "Patients Upon Entering the Institution, Subscribe to the Following Rules and Regulations." There were 14 of them. Patients were not to leave the Sanatorium grounds without permission, were not to smoke, use stimulants or drugs except those prescribed, and were not to use profane or obscene language. They were to be in bed with lights out before 9:00 p.m. and were not allowed to rise earlier than half an hour before the rising bell. Rest periods were to be kept between 10:00 a.m. and 11:00 a.m. and between 1:00 p.m. and 3:00 p.m. Patients were to avoid talking to each other about their symptoms. Patients were to cover the mouth when coughing or "turn away so that the droplets will not strike anyone."[33] Patients were required to have with them at all times boxes to use for expectoration or a sanitary pocket cuspidor. "Spitting upon the floor, in the washbasins, sinks, closets, baths or on the grounds or walks about the building is strictly prohibited."[34] Rule #8 regarding "visiting" stated:

> Wholesome social intercourse between patients is desirable, but private association of men and women is strictly forbidden. Men are forbidden to enter the cottages occupied by any woman, and vice versa, excepting by special permission.[35]

Finally, patients were held responsible for their own personal property and were to avoid damage to any property of the Institution. Complaints were to be made to the Superintendent or his associate, and patients were required to give the Superintendent one week's notice before departure. Patients were expected to sign a statement at the bottom of the page of rules as follows: "I have read and understand the rules, a copy of which has been given to me, and I cheerfully agree to conform to them and to such other regulations as may be made during my residence at the Sanatorium."[36]

If Dr. Brown's rules seemed strict, it should be noted that anywhere "lungers" were found, there were firm rules intended to prevent the spread of disease. Spitting on the public streets was strictly forbidden in most places. At Saranac, a $50.00 fine was imposed and strictly enforced for spitting in the public streets. [37]

Gellenthien emphasized the positive cooperation between doctor and patient. The patient had paid to be given the best possible care. If he violated the rules, he was just throwing his money away and hurting himself. "Don't break training," he advised. "It's your choice. but if you die, the rest of the world will go on without you." Gellenthien wrote:

> There are two ways in which a sanatorium may be conducted. In one, the doctor is an autocratic director. It is for him to give orders and for the patients to obey promptly and not to ask why he should or should not do certain things. When the patient who has been under this sort of regime leaves the santorium, he is very apt to feel that now he is liberated from this despotic doctor, he can do as he pleases. A relapse frequently follows. The other way, the one we use at Valmora, is for the doctor to be a coach or advisor to the individual patient. As soon as our study of the new patient's case has been completed, he is called into the office and told honestly and frankly what his condition is, what his chances for recovery are, what he should do to get well, and how he can do it.
>
> The result is that our patients have an intelligent conception of what they are trying to do, and understand why they should do what we ask of them. They are less apt to break training while in the sanatorium, and are less likely to break down after they leave the sanatorium, because they know better how to take care of themselves. [38]

Gellenthien was praised by patients for this attitude. He introduced educational and social activities to help patients better understand and cope with the enemy. He wrote articles for the Valmora newspaper and gave frequent lectures. Anyone with a question about TB could deposit it in a question box inside the dining room door. Then the questions were answered every Friday at 6:55 p.m. in the dining room by Dr. G. All patients were expected to be present for the lectures during their first two months of residence and after that attendance was optional. [39]

A booklet prepared for patients when Dr. Brown was Superintendent and Dr. Gellenthien was Medical Director stated the necessity for rules:

> Unlike a home or boarding house, an institution housing many people is obliged to issue certain rules, in order that all shall conduct themselves in a way not only to promote their own welfare, but also to interfere as little as possible with their neighbors' comfort. [40]

The rules were about the same as the earlier ones with a few additions. No gambling was permitted and it was forbidden to have alcoholic stimulants in one's possession. Drinking and smoking were strictly discouraged. Since Valmora was a state game reserve, no killing of wildlife was permitted. No pets were allowed in any of the cottages. Patients were forbidden to go into the kitchens and were expected to leave the dining room if they had to cough while at the table. Conversations between patients as to their diseases, symptoms, or "any subject relating to illness, is forbidden during meals and is discouraged at all times as it frequently leads to considerable mental depression."[41] Patients were expected to keep the place neat and to protect the furniture and other property from injury. They were not to throw rubbish on the grounds, not to cut boughs or shrubbery or peel bark on the grounds. They were not to drive nails or tacks or "otherwise deface" the walls.[42] The use of electric current for other than lighting purposes was to be reported by the patient to the office. And no electrical appliances or radio sets interfering with radio reception were to be permitted. "Such appliances will be confiscated if found, as non-interfering appliances may now be readily obtained."[43]

There were also rules for bathing, clothing, rest, exercise, and amusements. Special rules for patients suffering with hemorrhage from the lungs were listed. Under personal hygiene numerous rules were given. Patients were advised to cover the mouth with a handkerchief when coughing but to expectorate into squares of bleached cotton or crepe paper which could be burned rather than using the handkerchief.

> Do not throw your toothpicks, gum, apple cores, or fruit skins on the ground. They are as dangerous to others as your sputum. Dispose in your sputum boxes.
>
> Kiss no one.
>
> Children are very susceptible to tuberculosis and you should never kiss or fondle a little child.
>
> Remember that anything that has touched your lips may be a carrier of tuberculosis germs.
>
> We can teach you when, how and where to "chase the cure," but we cannot do it for you. [44]

Some of the rules were necessary to protect others. However, some of the rules would be considered too strict by today's standards.

> Visiting inside the cottages between men and women is forbidden and may be followed by dismissal.
>
> General sociability among the patients is, of course, expected but the practice of "pairing off" will not be tolerated. [45]

It was further stated that any patient whose behavior "is obnoxious to others, or who, in any way violates the rules of the institution may be discharged at any time when in the opinion of the Resident Physician or Superintendent his further stay is no longer advisable."[46]

Dr. Brown's rules covered just about anything and everything. He was kind but firm. Inevitably patients would try to skirt the rules, but Dr. Brown was usually one step ahead of them. A couple of youths decided to go duck hunting one day, although they knew it was forbidden. They went out to one of the ponds away from the grounds and shot several ducks. They hid them carefully when they brought them back to cook for supper. While the ducks were roasting, they anticipated the delicious meal they were going to have, a rare delicacy never found in the usual hospital fare. As they were smugly congratulating themselves, Dr. Brown suddenly appeared on the scene, taking them totally by surprise. He had smelled the cooking fowl and had sniffed out the source of the suspicious odor. The fellows were soundly scolded. They had not only broken the rule regarding the slaughtering of wildlife in the place, but they had broken the health rules related to overexertion. They argued that since the deed had been done, they should at least be allowed to eat their dinner. They could not undo the deed. But Dr. Brown declared that they had killed "his" ducks and he would eat them. And he did — all of them, with the disheartened boys watching hungrily.

Dr. Brown believed that self-discipline was necessary for the benefit of the patient and those around him. Gellenthien agreed but was willing to make exceptions when he felt the spirit of the law was more important than the letter of the law or when an individual case required special consideration. It was useless to try to enforce many of the rules. For instance, a man would visit a woman's cottage, standing with one foot outside the door, claiming that he was not "inside" the cottage and therefore not violating the rule forbidding visits to the cottages of members of the opposite sex. Basically, Gellenthien and Brown were in agreement about the rules, and gradually the rules became more flexible for the benefit of the patients. As Gellenthien assumed more of the responsibility at Valmora, Brown, who was a stronger leader, promoter, and teacher, was able to devote more of his time to promotional purposes. He spent time lecturing and writing promotional booklets to encourage people to discover the benefits of Valmora and New Mexico. A booklet published in the early 1920s exemplifies Brown's writing:

> Valmora Sanatorium, with its 1100 acres, is located in the beautiful valley of the Coyote, four and one-half miles from Watrous, New Mexico, and twenty miles from Las Vegas. The altitude, 5900 feet; the pure dry and bracing air; the mild winters and comfortable summers; the bright sunshine and absence of excessive rainfall, all combine to make

a climate ideal for the treatment of tuberculosis.

Abundant and nourishing food and, especially, the pure rich milk and cream which we obtain from our herd of twenty-four Jersey cows, are as important as the climate in effecting a cure. The entire herd was tested by the State Live Stock Inspector and pronounced free from tuberculosis...

A big feature at Valmora is its unsurpassed water supply. A beautiful spring, pure and cold, is located about two hundred yards north of the Administration building at an elevation of about fifty feet, with a flow of 22,000 gallons a day. Water is piped from the spring directly to the buildings and each cottage. [47]

Such promotional material attracted the sick and offered them the hope of recovery in a pleasant environment.

Suddenly, all the responsibility of Valmora fell upon Carl Gellenthien's shoulders. On August 30, 1935, William Brown died quietly in his sleep at the age of 65 from an apparent heart attack. He had been out horseback riding with his friend, Dr. Volney S. Cheney, Chief Surgeon of Armour and Company, at his beloved Gascon Ranch. He had enjoyed a good dinner and a pleasant evening.

It was a rainy day when Dr. Brown was buried, his huge casket carried up the steep hill to the final resting place beside Editha Brown's grave. It was not unlike the final act in Thornton Wilder's *Our Town.*

Damon Runyon wrote a story about a town doctor, "Doc Brackett" who never turned anyone away in his forty years of dedicated practice, not even on the day he was to marry. On his wedding day he got a call to go out into the country to see a sick Mexican child. His fiancée never forgave him. She called the wedding off. The doctor never married. Doc's office was upstairs over a store, and a sign at the foot of the stairs directed patients: "DR. BRACKETT, OFFICE UPSTAIRS." When he died, the townspeople wanted to get a beautiful monument for his grave. Before they got around to it, the grateful parents of the child he had saved, having no money to purchase a stone, took the sign from the foot of the stairs and stuck it over his grave: "DR. BRACKETT, OFFICE UPSTAIRS." [48] This same kind of love was expressed by many of the people of the Valmora area whose caring hands toiled most persistently to overlay the graves of Dr. Brown and Editha with stones placed in cement. There is no inscription. But Brown's lasting monument is Valmora itself and the lasting legacy of its service to mankind. With Brown's death, the dream of Valmora did not fade.

The tuberculosis bacillus chose its victims impartially. And so Valmora took them all in and gave them Dr. Brown's legacy, impartially, and remembered — especially at Christmas time — how he came nearer to being Santa Claus than any other man had ever been.

NOTES

1. "Plays Santa Claus For All Mora County's Children in School Tomorrow Afternoon: Dr. W.T. Brown of Valmora Is Presenting Gifts to Over 1,000 Little Folks," n.t., newspaper clipping from Las Vegas, New Mexico, December, 1931, in Scrapbook 1, Valmora Library, Valmora, New Mexico, p. 25.
2. *Ibid.*
3. "A Real Santa Claus," *The Las Vegan*, Las Vegas, New Mexico, 1932, newspaper clipping in Scrapbook 1, Valmora Library, Valmora, New Mexico, p. 42.
4. n.t., n.d., newspaper clipping in Scrapbook 1, Valmora, Library, Valmora, New Mexico, p. 42.
5. *Ibid.*
6. "Weelum," "Weelum Enjoyed the Valmora Banquet," n.t., n.d., newspaper clipping in Scrapbook 1, Valmora Library, Valmora, New Mexico, p. 17.
7. "A Real Santa Claus," *op. cit.*
8. "Helping Santa Claus," *The Spirit of Valmora*, December, 1930, p. 3., in Scrapbook 3, *op. cit.*, p. 41.
9. *Ibid.*
10. W.E.D., "The Old-Timers' Column," *The Boscobel Dial*, June 21, 1933, newspaper clipping in Scrapbook 1, Valmora Library, Valmora, New Mexico, p. 84.
11. "Valmora Resort Widely Known," *The Valmora Sun*, Valmora, New Mexico, 1938, p. 1, in Scrapbook 3, Valmora Library, Valmora, New Mexico, p. 19.
12. Fritz Thompson, "The Flood," *Impact / Albuquerque Journal Magazine* (Albuquerque, New Mexico) March 15, 1983, p.4.
13. Emerick, *op. cit.*, p. 10.
14. *Ibid.*, p. 11.
15. V.S. Cheney, "Early History of Valmora Reveals Pioneer Effort," *The Valmora Sun*, Valmora, New Mexico, June, 1939, p. 10, in Scrapbook 3, Valmora Library, Valmora, New Mexico, p. 33.
16. *Valmora, An Invitation, op. cit.*, Scrapbook 5, Valmora Library, Valmora, New Mexico, p. 60.
17. V.S. Cheney, *op. cit.*
18. *Ibid.*

19. Emerick, *op. cit.*, pp. 73-77.
20. *Ibid.*
21. Carl H. Gellenthien and Alice Gellenthien, "1957 — For Alice and Me," *op. cit.*
22. Emerick, *op. cit.*, p. 24.
23. *Ibid.*, p. 18.
24. Emerick, *op. cit.*, p. 22.
25. *Ibid.*, p. 24.
26. *Ibid.*, p. 31.
27. *Ibid.*, pp. 25-26.
28. "Stopping at the Stevens," Stevens Hotel Company, Chicago, Illinois, November, 1930, p. 3., in Scrapbook 1, Valmora Library, Valmora, New Mexico, p. 35.
29. "Chicagoans at Dinner to Boost Sanitarium for the Tubercular," n.t., October 1, 1931, in Scrapbook 1, Valmora Library, Valmora, New Mexico, p. 35.
30. "Today in Albuquerque," n.t., December 31, 1931, in Scrapbook 1, Valmora Library, Valmora, New Mexico, p. 21.
31. W.E.G., "The Old-Timers' Column," *op. cit.*
32. "Today in Albuquerque," *op. cit.*
33. W.T. Brown, *Valmora Industrial Sanatorium, Valmora, New Mexico: Patients Upon Entering the Institution, Subscribe to the Following Rules and Regulations*, Booklet 2, Valmora, New Mexico, n.d., m.p., in Scrapbook 5, Valmora Library, Valmora, New Mexico, p. 53.
34. *Ibid.*
35. *Ibid.*
36. *Ibid.*
37. Mooney, *op. cit.*, p. 81.
38. C.H. Gellenthien, "Dr. Gellenthien Inaugurates Series of Health Articles: Stresses an Intelligent Cooperation Between Doctor and Patient," *The Valmora Sun*, November, 1938, p. 5., in Scrapbook 3, Valmora Library, Valmora, New Mexico, p. 19.
39. Valmora Sanatorium, *Valmora, New Mexico*, Booklet 4, *op. cit.*, p. 28.
40. *Ibid.*
41. *Ibid.*, p. 29.
42. *Ibid.*, p. 39.
43. *Ibid.*
44. *Ibid.*, p. 10.
45. *Ibid.*, p. 29.
46. *Ibid.*
47. William T. Brown, *Valmora Sanatorium*, Booklet 7, *op. cit.*, pp. 1-2.
48. Damon Runyon, "Doc Brackett," quoted in Audrey Stone Morries, ed., *One Thousand Inspirational Things* (Chicago: Peoples Book Club, 1958), pp. 38-39.

CHAPTER
VII

She Ain't Heavy: She's My Patient

On a special day in 1941 Carl and Alice Gellenthien boarded a train in Las Vegas to attend the wedding of a former patient in Santa Fe. Kay Bandelier had come to Valmora as a young girl, stricken with TB but not with despair. She kept her spirits up and was able to leave with a bright future. Forty-two years later she wrote:

> To me, Dr. G. was not only a great friend, but held a very special place in my life. He not only saved my life (literally) but was "best man" when I married Frank (Gorsline) at the Presbyterian Church in Santa Fe on March 21, 1941. He and Alice started out from Valmora by car but were stopped by a blinding snow storm in Las Vegas — just as The Chief was pulling into the station for a five minute stop. They raced aboard with Phoebe Crocker (another old friend and patient, now gone) and made it over the mountains to Santa Fe — and to the wedding "on time."[1]

The Gellenthiens took three patients with them who were able to travel, including Marjorie Shea and Phoebe Crocker, close friends of the engaged couple.

Phoebe had arrived at Valmora at the age of 17 on June 15, 1938. She had stayed in Room 17 of the hospital until she had recovered sufficiently to be placed in one of the cottages. Though she was not yet well enough to leave Valmora as Kay had, she was well enough for some travel.

It was a wonderfully happy day in spite of the threatening clouds and the big snowflakes that fell, first gently, then furiously. That afternoon a freezing wind came up. By the time the train pulled to a stop at Valmora, there was at least a foot of snow on the ground. The road from the railroad stop to the cabins was barely visible through the blinding blizzard.

They had prepared for the possiblity of a storm that morning.

Before leaving the train, the little party donned warm coats, hats, gloves and boots. Gellenthein feared that the three patients would have difficulty making the walk through the snow. Even for Alice and Carl, who were in good health, the walk would be somewhat exerting. The distance from the train stop to the cottages was over three-fourths of a mile.

Phoebe was the most fragile of the group. The travel and excitement of the day had taken its toll on her fragile body, and though she was not seriously ill, she was already fatigued. The doctor feared a walk through the blizzard would exhaust her.

Phoebe made a valiant effort to fight the icy wind and stinging snow, plodding through the deep drifts, trying to keep up with the others. She paused, fighting the wind, thinking she would surely fall, exhausted. At that precise moment she felt strong arms around her and to her surprise, she was suddenly being carried.

"Doctor, what are you doing?"

"I'm carrying you, of course," her physician replied calmly.

"But Dr. G., I'm too heavy!" she protested.

"Nonsense! You're as light as a reed. I won't allow you to walk. You're not strong enough. Relax. We'll make it all right."

And they did. The doctor carried his young patient over a quarter of a mile to her cabin. His progress was slow as he fought the wind and blowing snow. Though Phoebe weighed less than 100 pounds, her added weight slowed down the doctor's steps considerably. Yet if Dr. G.'s own 5'10", 150 pound body protested his task, no one ever heard about it. The former TB patient was now a doctor and he was doing what any good doctor would do. She wasn't heavy; she was his patient.

Those who remember the Boy's Town, Nebraska slogan, "He ain't heavy; he's my brother" can appreciate the significance of the slogan. The Christmas seals depicting a youth carrying a tot on his shoulders spoke a message that if you care enough for someone, it is no burden to help. It was with this attitude that Dr. G. treated each patient. He thought nothing unusual about carrying a patient through a blizzard. She was his responsibility. She was exhausted. He was her doctor, and nothing could be more natural than to take the burden on himself.

Phoebe suffered no ill effects from her day out, nor did the others. It was a day Phoebe would always treasure in her heart, for her best friend had recovered, left Valmora, and married. And she herself had been allowed to attend the wedding. In time, Phoebe's story, too, had just such a happy ending. She married a fellow patient, William Guinn, who became a successful writer.

When William Guinn came to Valmora, his lungs were almost gone. His X-ray showed one lung completely obliterated — white on the film. Only about a fourth of the other lung appared black on the X-ray, and even it was pitted with white nodules. But while he lay in his bed, he quietly planned to write a novel. As his lungs healed, he took up his pen and paper and began to write. After he left Valmora, he published *Death Lies Deep*, a novel written at Valmora with the language and color of the old west. In fact, the character of the doctor in his novel was inspired by Dr. Gellenthien. Guinn described his Doc Freeman as "...a young man, no more than forty, but a young man with a well-established reputation." Doc Freeman's manner of speaking to the patient in the novel is typical of Gellenthien's own. When a fellow is shot in the story, Doc Freeman hurries to his side as soon as he is summoned:

> Doc handed his lantern to George Crenshaw and dropped down on one knee beside McCann. "I understand we've had a little dry-gulching going on," he said, opening his bag and getting out a pair of surgical shears. "Mind if I cut your shirt a little, fellow? It seems to have a couple of holes in it already..."
>
> The shock from his wound was beginning to wear off, leaving him grunting out his pain. "I don't have to be carried," he (McCann) protested. "I can walk."
>
> Doc put a hand on McCann's good shoulder to keep him from rising. "I know you can, Grandfather. But you'd better let us carry you. That hole is too close to a tombstone to give us a margin for Spartanism."
>
> McCann relaxed and offered no further objection, and Doc and Clyde Marshall eased him carefully forward and onto the door. When they had him ready to go, four men spaced themselves around the door and lifted him gently and carried him back across the street to the Marshall home. [2]

Guinn consulted with Dr. G., in writing about his doctor, for technical advice in the medical details of his stories. Guinn's character, like many of the doctors of the old west, was referred to as "Doc." Dr. Gellenthien, too, soon learned to drop the formalities of the customs of "back east" and adapted to the western lifestyle, the more relaxed and easy dress, language, and pace. Thus, he, too, answered to the name of "Doc" though more often he was called "Dr. G." After his book was published, Guinn wrote a note of appreciation to Dr. G. in the copy he gave the doctor:

> Dear Doc:
>
> My doctor comes in on pages 77 and 81. If I handled your advice wrong, just call me a damn quack and don't admit to ever knowing me.
>
> Bill. [3]

118

The character of the dedicated doctor in the novel was inspired by Dr. G. whose kindness was demonstrated on many occasions when he acted "beyond the call of duty" — such as carrying a patient through a blizzard.

Gellenthien would sometimes sit up nights with his patients. One Christmas eve during World War II, Dr. G. left the comfort of his home to sit up with a woman who lay in the hospital seriously ill with TB. He found her weeping in despair for fear her husband would never return from overseas where he was fighting for his country. As Dr. G. sat at her bedside, trying to comfort her, he promised he would try to get her husband home. He gave her hope to cling to that night, and it was not false hope. Through the Red Cross, Dr. G. was able to bring the man home from the battlefront due to his wife's critical condition. The woman fought to live because Dr. G. gave her a vision of the future. But her troubles were not over. When her child was very small, he, too, developed tuberculosis. He was dying of spinal tuberculosis when he was brought to Dr. G. in a coma. Dr. G. decided to administer a new drug, streptomycin. It had been introduced in 1944 and was the first drug known to be effective against TB, although it had to be used judiciously because of possible side effects. Dr. G. didn't know whether it would work. He thought it might be too late to save his young patient, but the boy recovered fully.

Tony Iacomini, a patient in 1943, stated that he and other patients marvelled at everything Dr. G. accomplished.[4] As Medical Director, Dr. G. had the responsiblity of each patient's welfare, of the staff and maintenance of the hospital and its grounds, and of its administration. Of course, he had good helpers or he could not have succeeded as he did. The business manager, "Hoff", was very efficient, as was the secretary Vivian "Johnnie" Johnson. The nurses were equally efficient, and Georgie Claiborne's energy was unceasing. Each member of the Valmora staff "family" worked to make the operation a success. But in the final analysis, it was Dr. G. who was responsible for Valmora.

In addition to his regular duties at the sanatorium, Dr. Gellenthien was always active in other areas. He was a member of various professional and civic organizations. He also had his outpatients and made house calls all over the country. Additionally, he was a consultant for numerous other places such as the State TB Sanatorium in Socorro, the sanatorium at Fort Stanton, about 75 miles from the Socorro institution, and the sanatorium at Fort Bayard near Silver City. He was also a consultant for diseases of the chest at Bruns Army Hospital in Santa Fe. At the same time he was consultant for the Montezuma Seminary for Roman Catholic Priests of Old Mexico near Las Vegas. He was also Surgeon for the Santa Fe Railroad Hospital Association. Looking back, Dr. G. stated that he had good help, delegated authority where he could, and set his priorities to accomplish the most he could with his time; however, his family life suffered. He could never attend school activities or parties with his children and seldom was able to take Alice to a social event. He admitted that he was a poor father because he was unable to spend much time at home.

Dr. G. left the household affairs up to Alice. He paid little attention to such things as cooking and baking. Although Alice was a gourmet cook, Carl was an easy man to please. He did not live to eat; he ate to live. He was happy with anything set before him. Sometimes, however, he wasn't sure what he was eating.

One night Dr. G. came home late after making a house call. Alice was asleep and he was hungry, so he went to the refrigerator and found a bowl marked "Stew" and ate it. He thought it was the worst stew he'd ever eaten, so the next day he asked Alice about it. She was mortified to learn that he had eaten the dog food she had saved. She had forgotten to remove the label on the bowl she had previously used for stew.

A doctor lives intimately with life and death and learns to show little surprise at death's approach. It was important for Roman Catholic patients to be given extreme unction, and Dr. G. always made sure it was done. He learned the ceremony of baptism for the newborn which he could perform when no priest was available. Naturally, he preferred the priest to be on hand. He almost always knew when a patient was going to die. He had learned to recognize the signs. "Coming events foreshadow themselves," he often stated. Of course, at times a patient surprised him and recovered in spite of the odds. Dr. G. never gave up on a patient. He always believed that only God could determine the time a person was to die.

Once in Room 14 a patient, a newspaper editor, began hemorrhaging severely. Dr. G. called for the priest. While the priest was performing the last rites, the doctor was working with the patient, collapsing the lung. He was able to get the lung collapsed and stop the bleeding. The patient lived to write about his experience. He recovered, left Valmora, and returned to work in Chicago.

An instance of Dr. G.'s persistence in attempting to save a life is evidenced in a newspaper appeal for blood donors in about 1932.

> Blood suitable for transfusion to save the life of a Valmora Sanatarium patient is being sought by Dr. C.H. Gellenthien, medical director of the famous sanatarium in the Mora River Valley, near Watrous. [5]

The patient who was from Chicago was suffering "with both lungs collapsed, an unusual development in tuberculosis, is bleeding steadily from the lungs and requires a transfusion of blood in order to survive."[6] The item concluded by stating that the sanatorium offered $25.00 per pint to blood donors "who may apply to Dr. Gellenthien."[7] Blood transfusions in those days were uncommon and people were not accustomed to donating. The blood drives of today were unheard of. In fact, this incident was one of the factors in Dr. G.'s involvement in an early blood donor program, the Southwest Blood Bank in Phoenix, Arizona.

One of the most talented patients was Harold D. Walters from Bloomington, Illinois. He played the role of Jesus of Nazareth in The American Passion Play, an annual production sponsored by the Scottish Rite in Bloomington. The cast included over 250 men, women, and children. Additionally there were about 20 stage hands, 20 musicians, and numerous others in wardrobe, make-up, and so on. There were 12 performances a year, usually on weekends, starting in late March or early April and running through the end of May. The play was a four-hour production on the life and works of Jesus. The speaking lines of Jesus alone consisted of one and a half hours of talk altogether.

Walters, a Methodist minister, first played the role of Christ in 1938. He was a big man, 6'4" in height, with a deep, baritone voice. On March 30, 1940, just two days before his final performance of the season, Walters learned he had tuberculosis. He had gone to his family doctor, been referred to a chest specialist, and a diagnosis had been made. Only two people in the theatre, including the director, were told. The doctors strongly advised Walters not to perform, telling him that such exertion could be fatal. But Walters had no understudy, and he felt he must go through with his role.

Forty-five minutes before curtain time, as Walters' make-up artist was putting on the crepe beard, Walters coughed and hemorrhaged. The make-up man called for the house doctor who examined Walters and strongly advised him not to go on with his performance, warning him that it could be his last. But Walters felt he must go on.

He put a rubber pouch under his white robe so he could spit into it if he coughed up more blood. It was fortunate that he had it. He had to use it several times, discreetly hiding his actions from the audience. About a third of the way through the play, Walters finally stopped hemorrhaging. But he was extremely weak. There were 1,400 people in the audience that night watching a weak and bleeding Jesus hanging from the cross in the final act. None suspected just how weak the actor was or how much blood he had

121

lost. Walters, weak from loss of blood and sick with tuberculosis, made it through the performance so well that none of the audience suspected the actor had hemorrhaged throughout the show. If anyone saw a sign of blood, he must have assumed that it was stage blood and that "Jesus" was playing his role very realistically.

Through his doctor, Walters arranged to go to Valmora. Dr. Paul Kionka knew Dr. G. and told Walters that if he stayed in Illinois he would be flat on his back for 12 months but at Valmora there was hope for a faster "cure." Also, in New Mexico, he would be able to carry on his insurance business by "remote control." He could write, bring his records up to date, and so on at intervals. Walters did so and lost only one account while at Valmora. He stayed seven months.

Walters did not realize how sick he was, how dangerous his condition was that night he went on stage in spite of his hemorrhaging. In fact, when he left Illinois to go west, he took a couple of friends to Colorado Springs on his way to Valmora. He decided to climb to the top of Pike's Peak before continuing on to Valmora. He had no idea how dangerous such an endeavor was at the time. Wondering why the new patient was late, Dr. G. called his doctors in Illinois, but all they could say was that Walters was on his way. Walters never heard the end of his detour by way of Pike's Peak. After he arrived at Valmora, Dr. G. would not even let him bend over to put on his own slippers. Nor did he attend many of the social functions for he was kept in bed to prevent hemorrhaging.

Dr. G. called him "Wally". He must have trusted the big, gentle man who played the role of Jesus so convincingly, because after his arrival at Valmora, Dr. G. asked Wally to take a very special patient to the rodeo. The patient was Dr. G.'s secretary, "Johnnie."

The Cowboy's Reunion and Rodeo came to Las Vegas on August 2, 1940. Teddy Roosevelt's Rough Riders' Reunion was the big event of the year in Las Vegas. Vivian "Johnnie" Johnson had come to Valmora dying of tuberculosis in 1934 but had been "arrested" and had stayed on as Dr. Brown's secretary. After Dr. Brown's death she worked efficiently as Dr. G.'s secretary, but she never conquered the disease and she was sinking fast. Dr. G. feared this would be her last rodeo. It was.

Later Harold Walters was glad that he had been chosen to take Johnnie to her last rodeo. There was a parade with the remaining rough riders in it and a big rodeo where men like world-champion bull dogger Dee Bibb competed for prizes. Dr. G. wanted Johnnie to go and couldn't take her himself. But he knew she would be in good hands with Harold Walters. And she was.

Wally was at Valmora from July 10, 1940 to January, 1941. He would have left in December of 1940, but it was in December that Johnnie died and in her letter of last request she stated that she wanted Wally to assist in the final arrangements, the scattering of her ashes. As the representative of the clergy, Wally performed the last ceremony while Dr. G. scattered the ashes.

When Wally left Valmora he was ready to follow Dr. G.'s advice. The doctor had made an impression on him about guarding his health. Harold Walters made a return trip to New Mexico in 1983 and stopped to see Dr. G. "He hasn't changed," Wally commented, "'except he jokes with me more freely now. Before, he was afraid he'd make me laugh too hard and cause me to hemorrhage."[8]

He stated that Dr. G. taught him how to live carefully so that he would not have a relapse. He felt he owed his life and well-being to Dr. G. Wally returned to his home in 1941 and continued his work as an insurance agent and an actor in the self-supporting American Passion Play. He played Christ for 24 consecutive years and was director for 6 years thereafter. He never missed a performance of the play. Walters was also active in the Masons and became a third degree Mason.

When Wally returned to New Mexico in 1983, he, his wife Margaret, and a colleague, Barbara J. Griffith, met with Dr. G. in Santa Fe for breakfast. Barbara had played the role of Mary Magdalene and Herodous in the Passion Play and was writing Walters' biography. Dr. G. said he felt privileged to have been able to live so long to see a patient living such a happy, successful life. Not many doctors live long enough to have such a God-given privilege, Dr. Gellenthein said. Afterwards, Dr. G. told friends he had gone to Santa Fe that morning "to have breakfast with Mary Magdalene and Jesus Christ."

Many other grateful patients have returned years later to thank Dr. G. A patient who was a child in the 1950s returned in 1982 to give Dr. G. a Norman Rockwell print of "The Doctor and the Doll." The picture of the little girl holding her doll up for the doctor to examine reminded her of herself when she was his patient. She had been brought in just before Christmas with rheumatic fever. She needed penicillin. Because her mother had no money, she had been unable to purchase medicine in the city. Dr. G. saw the 5-year-old girl and gave her mother the medicine. Ellen, the nurse, was giving the mother some pills along with a few final instructions. The mother opened her purse.

Dr. G. came out of his office and asked the mother now much money she would have left for Christmas after paying her bill. She told him she would have two dollars left.

Dr. G. turned to Ellen and said, "I don't want that money, do you?"

"No," Ellen replied.

"Spend it for Christmas," Dr. G. ordered. It was a good prescription for both mother and child. The little girl never forgot her Christmas that year as she recovered her health and treasured the little gifts her mother was able to buy.

It took strength to carry on in spite of grief, especially when tragedy struck close to home, and it did, more than once.

One Christmas Eve Dr. G. had to leave his family to assist the victims of a car accident near Valmora. As he rushed to the scene, he regretted leaving his wife and two children alone on Christmas Eve; but as soon as he arrived he had no more regrets. The victims were lying about moaning and calling his name. "Dr. G.! Dr. G.!" they cried. He realized he was their last desperate hope as they hung on to life in their pain and agony.

In February 1982 tragedy struck when Dr. G.'s receptionist, Lucinda, lost her home in a fire. Then, about a month later, her husband was killed in a one-vehicle accident. Dr. G. felt the helpless frustration of being unable to assist except to try to comfort the bereaved family.

Since Dr. G. usually knew when a patient's last hours had arrived, he would send a telegram to the family, send for the clergy, and remain nearby. He always said no patient at Valmora would ever die alone, and none did. Most patients died easily, sleeping away, often in the characteristic euphoria. TB literally consumed its victim; the fast pulse rate betrayed the heart which was on a race course for death under the stress of the disease. The heart literally raced itself to death.

In his "Farewell Advice" to patients well enough to leave Valmora in 1939, Dr. G. wrote:

> Too often I have had to scold them (the Valmora Staff) when, at three or four o'clock in the morning, I found them shamelessly crying after we had lost a hopeless, but desperate and dramatic fight against death. We learn to know you all so well that your success or failure in your fight for life takes much out of each one of us. We realize only too well our repsonsibilities and the fact that we have to live for you until you again are strong enough to carry on for yourselves. [9]

It took a special kind of compassion to carry the patients' burdens for them until they were well enough to take them up again. Sometimes this required physical and literal strength as when Phoebe was carried through the blizzard. Sometimes the task took great emotional strength, endurance and courage. It was Dr. G.'s assiduity that un-

124

doubtedly inspired the poem written by Fay B. Edsall, describing her feelings in leaving her son in Dr. G.'s care:

A smile enigmatic
A word most emphatic,
A twist of the lips, a raise of the brow,
A soul most congenial,
A friend to each menial;
A dean in his world, a man who knows how
To still the wild heart throbs
To calm fear that oft robs
One of slumber in the darkness of night.
Undaunted and fearless
I can go now, and tearless,
As the eyes of his seeing has given me sight.
So into his keeping
I give without weeping
The manchild I cared for and held to my heart.
Knowing care that is best
Putting him to the test
Of manhood, — which will be playing his part. [10]

Besides physical and emotional burdens, there were the heavy burdens of the soul that only those who sacrifice their time for others can truly comprehend. More than once Dr. G. carried such a burden for someone.

One of those people was Johnnie. She had been sent to Valmora after the director of the Chicago Municipal Sanatorium told her they "needed the bed for someone who is going to live." Like many patients who ended up at Valmora, she was dying of pulmonary tuberculosis. Yet she lived to become one of the most colorful personalities at Valmora.

Born in Minnesota of Swedish parentage, Johnnie had worked in Chicago as a secretary until she became ill. She had a friend who was head nurse at International Harvester, one of Valmora's most avid supporters. This friend may have had influence in getting Johnnie to Valmora. At any rate, Johnnie came to Valmora in 1934 and lived several more years. She was so efficient at taking dictation and typing that Dr. Brown never knew she couldn't take shorthand. He wouldn't have hired her if he had known. But her typing was so fast he never knew the difference. Only Dr. G. knew, and he wasn't about to tell.

Johnnie was in a state of arrest for several years and then her TB flared up again. She inspired another poem by Fay B. Edsall:

Gleaming teeth and sparkling eyes,

Her atmosphere a paradise;
All about she spreads her glamor;
She bewitched us by her manner.
Lives she in a world selected,
Till she has us all affected
By her air that's always sunny,
Wholesome, lovely, little "Johnnie." [11]

Indeed, Johnnie always cheered everyone up. She accompanied Dr. G. on various journeys, had her picture taken with Governor John E. Miles and was a great public relations personality. As a receptionist, she was tops. She made people feel good just to be in her presence. "Wholesome, lovely, little Johnnie" was an accurate description. She was fun to be around, and her friends would tease her with the popular song, "Oh, Johnny, Oh, Johnny, Oh!" Although the song was written for a man and sung by a woman, it was sung in gaiety more than once for Johnnie by her friends. Photographs taken by friends show her enjoying life in many ways. She is dressed up for a parade, enjoying a picnic with friends, sitting on a swing in the patio, or working at a desk in Dr. Gellenthien's office. Wherever she was, she had a happy smile for everyone around her.

Johnnie was one of Valmora's most vivacious workers after she was well enough to become secretary to Dr. Brown. She was described in *The Valmora Sun's* "Who's Who" as follows:

Miss Vivian Johnson — Secretary to Dr. Gellenthien. Her phenomenal spirit and energy, sheer power of will, sense of humor and love of the immensities of life have made her struggle for health legend among friends of Valmora. Interesting because she is interested; loyal, considerate, and sincere. Rates her friends by "he's a peach." Likes letters, John Erskine, peanut-brittle, curls. Adores bunny-buttoned caps. Dislikes unfriendliness and "snobs." Is preparing a brochure on Valmora. [12]

Johnnie, as loyal and faithful secretary, guarded the office and Dr. G.'s interests assiduously. But she knew she didn't have long to live. Once she turned from her work in the office and told Dr. G. that when she died, she wanted to be cremated and have her ashes scattered.

"Johnnie, you shouldn't think about dying," Dr. G. admonished her gently. Johnnie was still very young, in her early 30s.

"Well, I just want you to promise me you'll carry out my wishes," she replied. "Knowing you, you'd probably just take my ashes and flush them down the toilet. I won't have you doing that to me!" She knew how to balance her sorrow with laughter and make the best of things.

Johnnie often remarked how, after a shower, the rainbow always seemed to end on the hillside across the railroad tracks where the old gold mine was located near the top. "Look Georgie," she'd say, or, "Look, Dr. G.," pointing to the rainbow. "The end of the rainbow's right there at the old gold mine!"

Johnnie was so faithful that she refused to give up her office keys until the very end. Her frail body grew thinner and thinner. Finally she was about to "burn out." Johnnie knew her time was short. Mooney was convinced that victims of TB know when the fight becomes too uneven, when they struggle in too deep a bog in spite of all the bright and encouraging words of others. "I think there comes a time in a terminal disease when the ill unplug themselves from life, detach their minds — when they look inward and see that it is time to let go." [13] It must have been so with Johnnie. Five minutes before she died, she finally handed over the office keys to Dr. G. It wasn't easy for him to take the keys from her her because it meant that she had finally admitted the battle was over and had given up her valiant struggle. She told Dr. G. about the letter she had written and put in his desk drawer, her final instructions. He promised he would carry them out.

In her letter of last request, Johnnie asked that no one except Dr. G. be allowed to see her body, that she be cremated, and that her ashes be scattered "at the end of the rainbow" at the entrance of the gold mine.

After Johnnie died, Dr. G. carried out each of her last wishes. He accompanied the emaciated body and watched its cremation. He was going the second mile; he would not have done this for anyone else because he had an almost violent revulsion of death. He would avoid being with a patient at the very moment of death if he could. When he knew all help was useless, he would turn the patient over to the nurse and the priest and leave. He would do what he could to comfort the survivors but he didn't want to see a patient die. He would pronounce the patient dead when summoned, sign the death certificate, and leave, as quickly as possible. He didn't want to examine the body unless an autopsy had to be performed. Then he would carry out his duty. But he would often turn away and vomit in the sink, then courageously return to his work.

Georgie accused him of being a coward, shirking his duty to the patient. But she did not understand what a blow every death is to a doctor. Death is the doctor's enemy. He does all he can to delay its entry into the patient's life. But in the end, he knows he will lose the battle. Each time a patient died, Dr. G. was reminded that his victories were only temporary. He had won a battle, perhaps, but he would not win the war. Death would conquer all at last. Only One

Man had ever succeeded in overcoming death. The empty tomb of Jesus Christ attested to His victory. And though faith in Him gives life to the believer, at the moment of death, the doctor felt like Martha when she cried, "Lord, if thou hadst been here, my brother had not died."[14]

Dr. G., Alice, and Harold Walters rode horseback as far as they could go up the rim. Riding along the sheer ridge on loose shale and rock through dangerously rough terrain in the brisk January air was not a burden, for the little party knew they were doing the last thing possible for Johnnie.

Wally had never carried out a ceremony like this before in his experience as a Methodist minister. His deep baritone voice, used so often in his role of Jesus Christ in the American Passion Play, echoed from one side of the canyon wall to the other. There was no organ music to accompany his reading of the scripture, no choir and no stained glass windows. But nature herself provided both backdrop and sound effect. Johnnie would have been pleased.

As Dr. G. scattered the ashes, perhaps they remembered how Johnnie's eyes had sparkled at the words of the song: "Oh, Johnny, Oh, Johnny, Oh!" Now, years later, after a rain, those who still remember look up at the hill where the rainbow ends and they remember Johnnie the way she wanted to be remembered. Maybe they think of Judy Garland's famous "Over the Rainbow" rendition. Whatever they think of, they think of Johnnie.

When a patient like Johnnie needed him in the final moments of life, Dr. G. graciously, though reluctantly, accepted even that burden, giving up his grief to a higher law. No, she wasn't heavy; she was his patient.

NOTES

1. Kay Gorsline, letter written to Dorothy Beimer, from Chicago, Illinois, November 27, 1982.
2. William Guinn, *Death Lies Deep* (N.Y.: Gold Medal Books, 1955), pp. 77-78.
3. *Ibid.*, front inside cover of copy belonging to Carl Gellenthien.
4. Tony Iacomini, personal interview at Valmora, October 24, 1981.
5. "Need Blood to Save Sick Man at Sanatarium," n.t., n.d., n.p., newspaper clipping in Scrapbook 1, Valmora Library, Valmora, New Mexico, p. 43.
6. *Ibid.*
7. *Ibid.*
8. Harold Walters, personal interview in Santa Fe, New Mexico, June 17, 1983.
9. Carl H. Gellenthien, "Adios Amigos, Dios Valla Con Ustedes: The Doctor's Farewell Message and Parting Medical Counsel to Graduates," *op. cit.*, p. 3.
10. Fay B. Edsall, "The Doctor," *Impressions of Valmora*, July, 1937, n.p., in Scrapbook 1, Valmora Library, Valmora, New Mexico, p. 81.
11. Fay B. Edsall, "Johnny," *Impressions of Valmora*, July, 1937, poem in Scrapbook 1, Valmora Library, Valmora, New Mexico, p. 81.
12. "Who's Who at Valmora — Past and Present," *The Valmora Sun*, December, 1938, p. 4., in Scrapbook 3, Valmora Library, Valmora, New Mexico, p. 21.
13. Mooney, *op. cit.*, p. 183.
14. John 11:21, *The Holy Bible, op. cit.*, p. 922.

CHAPTER VIII

Fishing Lessons

"Well, good-by, Dr. G." With those words an elderly TB patient put a pistol to his head, determined to take his own life.

Dr. G. acted on instinct. "Go ahead," he said. "If you're such a loser, the world is probably better off without you anyway. You're no good to anyone if you're so set on dying. You'll just depress the other patients. Go on then, do it!"

Inwardly, Dr. G. quavered. If his gamble failed, his words might merely quicken the man's trigger finger.

But the patient put the gun down.

The man was a retired employee of Western Union and was very ill. Confined to a cabin, believing he had nothing left to live for, he slipped into a deep depression and decided to end it all.

After Dr. G. had confiscated the gun, he sat down and had a long talk with the man. It seemed the patient had lost interest in life and could see no future for himself at all.

"What have I got left, Doc? All I know is telegraph. Western Union won't take me back even if I get better. They've got me on disability. That's all I've ever done; it was my whole life."

After some probing, Dr. G. discovered that the man's desire to continue to work in his area of interest was the incentive he needed to live. It was then that Dr. G. suggested setting up telegraph equipment in the patient's cabin. It was done, and after that the old man was happily engaged in listening and sending out messages. He made himself quite useful to the little community. There were no radios at that time so he served as a communication life line. When the World Series was playing, he would find out the score over the wire and then tell the folks outside the cabin who was winning. He did the same thing when elections were taking place. He became contented with his life after he discovered how to use his ability in a new way.

Dr. G. was summoned to another cabin one evening after a beautiful young patient slashed her wrists. Examination showed that the cuts were superficial. The girl had not really intended to die. After Dr. G. bandaged her wrists, he gave her a lecture. Suicide attempts always tried the doctor's patience and wit. He never knew for sure what approach would work best. What would snap one patient out of his depression and determination to die might plunge another one into deeper despair. This time Dr. G. repsonded with a pep talk that did the trick. The young lady never again tried suicide and recovered well, both physically and emotonally.

Another time Dr. G. saw a mentally deranged neighbor sitting on the railroad track. He refused to move, saying that he wanted to die.

"You can't make me move," he told the doctor defiantly.

"I don't have to," Dr. G. replied. "I'll stop the train." And he did. He went up the track and flagged the train down, telling the engineer there was a man sitting on the track ahead. Naturally when they arrived at that point, the man was gone. He had decided not to stick around for one of Dr. G.'s lectures.

Most TB patients did not become depressed to the point of suicide. They were not in pain for the most part. They experienced the euphoria peculiar to the disease. There were some exceptions, however. One man saved up his sleeping pills and took them. Dr G. got to him in time, pumped out his stomach, and saved his life. His was not a hopeless case, and there was reason to believe he would recover fully from his disease. When the patient opened his eyes and saw Dr. G. leaning over him, he realized, Dr. G. said, "he wasn't where he wanted to be, and I got the cussing out of my life for saving him."[1]

The staff worked hard to keep morale up. Sometimes it was the clergy's assistance which made the difference. Dr. G. got along with Catholics and Protestants equally well. When Father Frank Byrne of the Wagon Mound Parish found out that his brother Edward, also a priest, had TB, he sent for him to come to Valmora. The brother then made the trip from Ireland and became Dr. G.'s patient and friend. When he recovered, he took the parish at Wagon Mound after his brother left. Then he became chaplain at St. Vincent Hospital in Santa Fe.

Dr. G. worked closely with the clergy to give the patients incentive to go on living. A poet once concluded that both blessing and curse took place when Jesus resurrected Lazarus from the tomb. Though he was raised to new life, Lazarus would have to die again. When TB patients were declared well enough to return to their homes, it was as though they had been restored to the land of the living once again. But consumptives knew they could have a relapse at any time. Even if they maintained their health, many could never again return to their previous occupations. While an artist or a writer might return to his old vocation with little adjustment, a carpenter, brick layer or laborer of any kind could not go back to his former strenuous work, nor could anyone who had worked with the public. A school teacher or librarian could never again return to their previous jobs. No one wanted a tubercular contaminating the children or exposing the public to a potential hazard. Such fears were well grounded. There was one case in Minnesota where the school teacher's undetected tuberculosis had resulted in contamination of every child in the entire one-room school. About 22 pupils in all, developed TB. It was well known that once a person had TB, he was never entirely free of the disease. He might have a relapse and die at any time. He harbored the deadly bacilli and was a menace to society. Thus, there was the physical restriction that kept the consumptive from exertion, and there was the social stigma that kept him away from the public.

So it was with the patient who left Valmora. Though his life had been restored to him, he could not return to his former life, with rare exceptions. As the impending departure drew near, the patient became anxious about his occupation. The long anticipated freedom from the sanatorium grounds began to look less inviting when the patient had no job to return to. The lucky ones were those sent by companies guaranteeing them jobs when they returned. Most of the Chicago firms which supported Valmora had such agreements. But for others, the patients who came to Valmora independently like Harold Walters, the future was dim unless they, like Walters, already had an established occupation that could be carried on.

Patients would turn to Dr. G. and ask, "What am I to do?"

Taking the cure put a lifelong stamp on you. The pace became ingrained, the push of life elsewhere looked frighteningly brisk... many of the old jobs were too demanding and suggested too many possibilities of relapse, the old fear of cured tuberculars. With their old life in shambles, many recovered patients stayed on having nothing to go back to or preferred what they had. [2]

Many patients remained in the Valmora area if they were able to find a satisfying occupation. One man established a business as a photographer and opened a studio in Las Vegas after leaving Valmora. When Johnnie stayed on as Valmora's secretary, she knew she had a job where she could pace herself in an environment where she could survive.

Ivan Hilton moved to Las Vegas after his stay at Valmora. He had a thriving business and had a lease in the Merchandise Mart Building in Chicago, the largest business office building in the world at that time. Dr. G. helped him get out of his lease so that he could remain in New Mexico where he became a successful Las Vegas businessman and banker.

There were some patients who were fortunate to be able to carry on their usual occupations. One was John Wylie, an architect and artist. He was able to continue his work while a patient at Valmora and never had to change vocations.

When a patient asked Dr. G., "What shall I do now?" he tried to help them find answers. But he knew he could not wait until the day of departure to help a patient find the resources to prepare for the rest of his life. Thus, deeply ingrained in the program at Valmora was a two-fold plan. It was an educational plan sometimes called "occupational therapy" today. Although the term was not used at Valmora in those days, it was that and more. It was a method of keeping the patient busy and happily occupied so that he might recover speedily and pleasantly. At the same time it was a plan to help the patient discover hidden talents and new interests that could be developed into permanent vocations in the future.

An ancient Chinese proverb came to mind as Dr. G. sat in his office and planned his strategy for making life more meaningful for patients at Valmora: "Give a man a fish and he will live for a day. Teach a man to fish and he will live for a lifetime." It was Dr. G.'s hope to teach his patients to change their lifestyles, to adapt to the demands of the consumptive body, to learn to live with tuberculosis and still have a fulfilling life. He realized that it was not an easy task.

For one thing, TB was a disease of the young. It caught a person in the middle of his initial plans for the future or in the beginning of his early career, at a time when his social and personal relationships were intensely important to him. For another thing, it was a painless disease for the most part. The lungs have no nerves and thus could not warn the body that they were being attacked and eaten away by TB. Only after the disease had largely advanced and destroyed much tissue did it become evident that something was wrong. Often the victim would not realize anything was amiss until, like Keats, he coughed up blood.

The doctor's task was to first make the patient realize how serious his illness was and to discipline himself for the rest and routine necessary to overcome the enemy. He had to pace himself in order to avoid future relapses. Secondly, once recovery was begun, the task was to help the patient keep up his spirits and occupy his time. The patient must be taught that he could not resume the fast pace of his previous life. He must adjust his routine to meet the demands of strict discipline.

As Dr. G. wondered how to teach his patients to live with TB and yet live productively, he thought of the elements necessary for learning. First, there must be a willing learner and an able teacher. Next, there must be an environment conducive to learning. Proper facilities and materials must be provided. And progress must be rewarded at every step. Finally, the future must be visualized in a realistic and optimistic fashion so that the patient could carry on his self-directed learning after he had left the sheltered walls of the santorium.

The first consideration was the attitude of the patient.

In no other disease is the cooperation of the patient as important as it is in tuberculosis. If we could only imbue a patient with the "will to be well," if we could teach him from the start to obey strictly the rules and follow the routine of the "cure," half the battle would be won.

I frequently tell my patients that the trouble they have below the neck is often not as important as the trouble they may have above the neck. [3]

Dr. G. often thought, "To be successful in the treatment of TB, one must treat first, the patient, second, the disease." [4]

The intelligence of the patient is one of the most important factors in the successful treatment of pulmonary tuberculosis, just as it is in other chronic diseases. "An intelligent patient with little resistance will do better than an unintelligent one gifted with even greater resistance," Gellenthien stated. [5]

The fortunate patients are those who recognize their limitations and learn to live within them.

Disciplinary routine is not complicated, but because of its very simplicity, patients are not always impressed with the necessity of following it. Naturally, it is easier for patients to learn the importance of such routine in company with others who are working toward the same end.

At home, and in the general hospital, group education is not possible; consequently, sanatorium life is particularly advantageous. The patient lives in an environment especially designed to educate him in the principles of the treatment which will lead him to recovery. He observes, at first hand, the penalty exacted by Nature when such principles are violated, and, at the same time, he sees other patients reaping the reward of faithful observance of the rules. The sanatorium facilities, along with the doctors and nurses in attendance, constitute an educational organization which is of unique value to the majority of patients. [6]

The ultimate goal was to teach patients to understand why they should continue to practice the advice they had been taught at the sanatorium. Then they should learn to carry on after leaving the sanatorium to avoid a future break down. They should learn to take care of themselves so well that they could continue to live productive lives within the limitations of the disease.

Educating a patient for future living was like teaching a man to fish. He would not live for just a little while but would have the necessary abilities to survive for a lifetime.

> *Modern treatment in but a few cases can directly influence the disease in the lungs. In the vast majority of cases we cannot reach into the lung. We can only regulate the life of the patient in an effort to bring his entire system into a more nearly normal condition. The general improvement then will enable the body forces to react upon the local disease...Each year, there are many unnecessary deaths because the patients disregard medical advice.* [7]

When Dr. G. took over as Director in 1927, he tried to create a free atmosphere instead of a dictatorial policy. His attitude was, "It's your life and if you die, it won't affect the others. It's up to you if you want to get well." Naturally, some rules had to be strictly enforced such as "no hunting on the grounds," for Valmora was a State Game Reserve. And more than once Dr. G. had to break up card games played by candlelight after the "lights out" time. He expected patients to work just as assiduously as he did in fighting TB. Patients were expected to help by keeping a daily temperature chart, recording their temperatures at specified intervals. Some would write the whole chart up at once when it was due at the end of the week, making up anything within reason. They could never understand how Dr. G. could always tell when they'd faked it.

"I was always forgetting to take my temperature," Tony Iacomini stated, recalling those days. "I thought it was a simple matter to just fill in the chart at the end of the week. But I never could get away with it! Dr. G. always knew what I'd done!" [8]

Patients were taken on various outings to lift their spirits and give them a better perspective, a sense of freedom. There were special occasions, too. Once a year there was Valmora Day in Las Vegas when those who were able were taken to the movies and given various treats in town. Any time a party from Valmora went to Las Vegas, they always met at Murphey's Drug Store for a soda before returning to Valmora.

Dr. G. loved a good joke. He would take patients on their first excursion to Las Vegas, showing them the country as he drove along.

When he reached Onava, which is about half way between Valmora and Las Vegas, he would stop. There were only a few houses in the tiny village. Then Dr. G. would say, "Well here we are in Las Vegas. Enjoy the big city!" The little group was always astonished until they caught on to his joke.[9]

In the summer time there were picnics at the far end of the Valmora grounds. Dr. G. wanted patients to get out of sight of the buildings so they would feel they had "vacationed" away from the institution and consequently feel less confined.

Dr. Ray C. Armstrong, who was a classmate of Dr. Gellenthien at the University of Illinois, was a patient at Valmora in 1938. While he recovered from TB, he studied the mechanism of drafts in fireplaces and put the results of his conclusions to practical use by building the outdoor oven and fireplace in Coyote Canyon where picnics were held. "No picnic was complete without "Doc" frying the potatoes."[10] But J.C. Bohannon, a patient affectionately known as "Bo," also liked to cook and volunteered his services quite often. The patients were urged to put on weight, so rich foods were not discouraged. Butter and cream, produced at Valmora's dairy, were readily available. Thus, Bohannon generously cooked a frying pan full of chicken using an entire pound of fresh butter. It was delicious and added needed calories to the consumptives' diets.[11]

A description of one such picnic was given in the December, 1938 *Valmora Sun:*

> One afternoon during the month of November a group from Valmora set out for the picnic grounds. Everyone made himself useful in preparing this delectable lunch. As we all know it simply is not a picnic without some music — of which there was Quantity but we don't mention the Quality. Among the more gifted musicians were Dr. Gellenthien with his accordion, Curt Brink with his guitar, Ernie Stephenson with the ukulele and Herb Miller with his "flute." Everyone joined in the vocals.[12]

Dr. G. was kidded about his accordion nearly as much as Jack Benny was kidded about his violin in his famous comedies. It was always said that Dr. G. would take any request, but it always came out sounding like "Home on the Range," the only song he could play! It is no wonder that when a group tried to run him for Governor of New Mexico, they chose "Home on the Range" for his theme song! Dr. G. refused to run, but his theme song stayed with him thereafter.

A description of a party in November, 1938's *Valmora Sun* is one of many references to Dr. G.'s famous song:

> The party got under way about 7:00 p.m. and during dinner we were entertained by Curt Brink, his guitar...We were also serenaded

by a professional guitarist who obliged with "Home on the Range" in
which he competed and lost to Dr. G., and "El Rancho Grande" with
which he came in an easy first. [13]

Another reference to Dr. G.'s playing was made in a report of a Christmas party in 1938. Dinner was served to 64 persons in the dining hall and an annual program was presented. Dr. G. and his family were hosts to the visitors and residents "most of whom were able to attend the dinner and program, which they had anticipated as a brief respite from their usual routine." [14] Mrs. C.L. Miller played several Christmas carols, leading the audience in singing. Mr. Jim Tomsic of Cannonsberg, Pennsylvania was then asked to play the accordion.

He readily consented to play, throwing off his coat on the way to the
stage, commenting while he fastened the straps over his shoulders:
"Dr. G. has got the keys all messed up playing 'Home on the Range.'"
He was loudly applauded for an encore. [15]

Entertainment had always been an important part of the routine at Valmora. Twice a week in the early days orthophonic Victrola concerts were held. Later, movies were shown Sunday nights and a newsreel on Wednesdays.

Radio Station KFUN had a Valmora Hour each week and played special requests for patients. Dr. G. had good rapport with the station's owner and manager who brought the station to Las Vegas. Ernest Thwaites and his wife Dorothy opened with their first broadcast on December 25, 1941. Dr. G. telegraphed from Valmora that Thwaites' first announcements sounded good — but it was too bad his false teeth whistled so loudly. Fortunately, Thwaites, too, had a sense of humor. He and his wife owned and operated KFUN until his death when his small plane crashed as he flew alone into a thunderstorm one night.

It was Dr. G.'s sense of humor and concern for others that made him so popular. He wanted his patients to follow his advice, but he didn't want them to feel that they were being forced. The patients needed plenty of rest and sleep. They knew the rules. He told them that if he saw a light on after 9:00 p.m., he knew it meant that someone was sick and needed help. He would come right over to the cabin to offer assistance. He was not trying to "catch" someone breaking the rules. To him a light on after hours was most certainly a cry for help. Dr. G. hoped to make patients want to obey the rules for their own benefit, not because someone told them they must.

Infractions of the rules usually rated a lecture from the doctor, however. He insisted that patients should care enough about themselves to follow advice, not to "break training." Dr. G. had help in seeing that patients did everything necessary to recover. There were several exceptionally good nurses throughout the years, including those who were called "the three musketeers." They were Mrs. Louella Kendrick, affectionately called "Ken," Miss Alma Engestrom, and Georgie "Smitty" Claiborne. It should be noted that the patients were often referred to as "guests" or "visitors" rather than "patients" in an effort to make them feel more at home in a ranch setting rather than a hospital or institutional setting. Angeline Tipton, a local girl, was also an excellent nurse, as was another local girl, Ellen Dominguez. The Valmora Sun gave a description of two of the nurses:

> Miss Alma Engstrom — Valmora's capable laboratory technician and X-ray expert. Highly esteemed for her admirable professional manner and ability. Favorite saying: "The doctor has the report." Loves animals, especially Pedro, the cat, and flowers; her pansies inspire her to see expressions in them generally attributed to people. Close observer of people and human nature; generous of human frailties. Electrifies residents with a dry wit; a keen student of current events of which she keeps herself well-informed. Refers to "intruders" on her privacy as "dear enemies." [16]

> Georgie M. Claiborne — Better known as "Smitty," she rates as an outstanding personality at Valmora. Cheerful and pleasant, she imparts a reassuring spirit to the residents. Dislikes "big" babies but idolizes little Billy Gellenthien. Likes gardening and keeps the hospital generously supplied with beautiful flowers in season. Enjoys good eats of which she partakes with zest and gusto as well as blithe disregard for calories and her figure. Generous and kind, her friends are legion. [17]

Not only did Dr. G. have excellent nurses and a competent staff, but he also received help from resident physicians who came to Valmora to assist and to complete their residency requirements before going on to establish their own clinics. Dr. Robert Weaver was assistant physician from May 1936 to December 1936. Dr. Rollin S. Moore was assistant physician from December 1936 to July 1937. After completing his internship at St. Luke's Hospital in Chicago, he began a practice in Streator, Illinois. [18]

One of the early residents was Dr. R. Yale Lyman, a native of Montana. He came from Chicago's Northwestern University School of Medicine and arrived at Valmora on November 2, 1938 to assume his duties as resident physician, planning a return to the Univeristy for post graduate work under a fellowship. He hoped to specialize in X-ray work after his months at Valmora were completed. [19] The

Valmora Sun gave the following description of Dr. Lyman:

> R. Yale Lyman — Resident physician at Valmora Sanatorium; B.Sc. (Montana), M.D., Northwestern University (1936). Studied psychiatry and mental diseases in Providence, Baltimore and Chicago. Student instructor in anatomy; author of articles on Anatomy and physiology for medical journals. Present interest lies in X-ray specialization; has a scientific approach to medicine; solicitous, conscientious to detail. Shows an indomitable spirit and admirable physical courage. An excellent horseman and hunter. Filming of children and birds a passionate avocation. An engaging conversationalist on varied subjects. [20]

Valmora's secretary Johnnie Johnson wrote an interesting account describing a typical morning at Valmora's medical office which was published in *The Valmora Sun* in February, 1939. The article is entitled, "It's All in a Day's Work." The subtitle reads, "Valmora's Boswell Relates the Functions of the Staff As the Day Hums By." It reads as follows:

> With a banging of doors and a clanging of shovels, I awakened with a start and rushed into the living room.
>
> "Buenas dias, mum," grinned Maximo who was building the fire. "Mucho frio, no?" There must have been a mix-up for Louis Dominguez came in, too, to build the fire. He just grinned and said nothing. In spite of the early hour, there was nothing to do but grin with them.
>
> It was a bright morning and it looked as if things were off to a good start. I tripped over to the office, but as one would expect, Miss Engstrom was there ahead of me. We had our usual gab-fest while putting things in order for the day. No time wasted, of course — that would be inefficiency.
>
> Nurse Ken came in with a cheerful smile. She is always the same whether she sleeps the night through, or spends most of her time up trying to keep someone comfortable.
>
> At this point, Dr. Lyman came in with a gay air of bravado which was covering up a pair of drooping eyes from a sleepless night, and heels that were dragging. Suppose he had been digging the stork out of the mud again.
>
> He buzzed around the office for a few minutes, and with a last effort to get those orbs open, he dashed out of the door singing, "Morning never comes to soon. I can face the afternoon, but OH — those lonely nights." He called back to say he was off to make rounds.
>
> By ten o'clock, these and a dozen more interruptions had me feeling rather hopeless, and I decided to go up to the kitchen after the day's menu. Mr. Mann, the chef, and Al, the second cook, extended their

usual warm greetings. Leo Martinez, Sam Gurule, Lee Wasson and Vicente Marquez shouted simultaneously, "Buenas dias, linda." "Como Esta, amigo?" "I'll open the door for you," and a few more remarks in their native tongue which I am sure were nice. As I told them I was "pretty bueno," Slim came in from the dining room promising to test my radio tubes. His generosity never wanes.

When I returned to the office in just exactly five minutes, Dr. G. was waiting anxiously to dictate his letters, and claimed he had been waiting for at least a half hour. He had hardly begun when a peal of laughter and merriment from across the campus attracted our attention. We both went to the window to see what was happening. It was Nurse Smitty regaling an audience of ten or twelve by modeling a funny new hat which one of the girls had just purchased. No sooner had we witnessed this than she was off at a gallop to the next cottage.

Miss Tipton, our Valmora Mother, solicitiously was visiting each cottage to see that everything was in good order and everyone was happy. Ferminia Medina and her sister Marcella, the cottage attendants, were also hustling around busily.

Before we could get settled again, Hoff came strolling in singing, "Morning never comes too soon, I can face the afternoon, but OH — those lonely nights." He had to see Doctor about a few deals, and I left them in the office talking it over.

He finally left. But in another minute Juanita and Nora Medina came in from the laundry with such a loud argument afoot that it was useless to try to carry on. Clemencia, our attendant on the boys' wing in the hospital, interpreted a few of Juanita's words, although we could understand too many ourselves. There seemed to be such glee bubbling within Clemie.

At the same time, Charlotta, our good and faithful attendant on the girls' wing, came in to pick up the mail which as yet had not been written, or even dictated. She had to go on and finish her rounds. In a few minutes, Jess Tipton sent up Ed Connor, our new helper at the store and P.O., to see how much longer it would be before the mail was finished.

Frantically, Dr. G. and I made one last attempt to get that one important letter finished when we heard a loud flapping noise overhead. The doctors grabbed their bags and dashed off, beating the stork, with a baby boy, to the home of Leo and Ester Gentry Martinez.

Oh well, there is always mañana. I put my notebook away and went to my cottage singing "Morning always comes too soon, Think I'll sleep all afternoon, and maybe ta de de."[21]

Johnnie's description of a typical day at Valmora gives a vivid portrait of the cheerful mood, vitality, and atmosphere of the place.

In all the Valmora library and office files, her description is unequalled. There was always activity. Even for a patient who had to remain quiet, there was always something to occupy their thoughts. And as for reading material, there was no scarcity. Not only was there a library for the patients, but there was a wide selection of newspapers and magazines in the daily mail, and all of them were widely circulated.

Years later, patients and staff alike held fond memories of Valmora after going on to future endeavors elsewhere. Some found the future less happy than those memorable days spent at Valmora. Young Dr. Lyman stood on the threshold of a promising career after his residency. A few years later, however, he suffered from chronic ulcerative colitis, a long, painful illness. Morning left too soon; and the lengthening shadows took him into the lonely night long before he should have gone.

Good morale was necessary if the patients' spirits were to be kept up. Dr. G. tried to teach them to make their own fun. Today there are specialists in recreational therapy, but then the Valmora group simply attempted to pass the time creatively in constructive, entertaining ways. Patients produced newspapers, pamphlets, plays, and programs of various types. Much art, music, and literature was created at Valmora. Many patients learned new skills such as weaving and developed interests that turned into vocations afterwards. When a patient had to change his lifestyle to adjust to the less physically taxing life required by the consumptive, a new skill such as photography could be started in the spirit of recreational therapy, and developed into a full time occupation later.

At a Christmas party in 1938, Phoebe Crocker and Leonard Lazar provided a minstrel skit with the script written by Lazar. It was entitled, "Small Fry." [22] Lazar and his brother started the popular Lazar moccasin business. Lazar was highly successful in learning a new lifestyle with a vocation that would fit his needs; and he started when he was bedfast at Valmora.

In spite of many recreational activities, some patients found time heavy on their hands. Tony Iacomini recalled that as a young man at Valmora, he had to fight boredom more than anything. His disease had been diagnosed early and he didn't feel sick. He was only 19 years of age and had been an active youngster. As a single young man, he should have been out enjoying dances and parties, having good times with his friends; instead he found himself confined to an institution. He recalled that Dr. G.'s efforts to provide stimulating activites and programs helped a great deal, but there was still not enough going on to keep an active young man happy. The seriously ill patients confined to the hospital struggled each day just to live, but the patients in the cottages were not critically ill. For them recreation was a high priority. Some of the men would walk the four miles into Watrous to purchase liquor. They hoped to return before their absence was discovered. Usually it was, and they received a sound lecture from Dr. G. and a tongue-lashing from Georgie. Any consumptive who would overexert himself for liquor was beyond her understanding. To break up the time, the men in the cabins would play poker. More than one game was played by kerosene lamp after curfew.[23]

Parties were held not only on special occasions but at any time an excuse for one existed. One Monday morning, October 24, 1938, it was rumored that Dr. G. was available for the evening. "...his very efficient secretary, Johnnie, whipped up a party in true Chicago fashion (none of this *mañana* business). The party and dinner featured guitar music and singing by Curt Brink.[24]

Through the years there were numerous journalistic ventures at Valmora. The first effort was known as *The Val Moran*, a paper issued December 25, 1925. It was a four-page, six by nine inch paper, containing local news, poetry, and jokes. The next paper came out November, 1928, and was called the *Valmora Tattler*. Then came the *Valmora High Ball* in October, 1929. Later it was changed to *The Spirit of Valmora* in December, 1929, and changed again to the *Valmora Chatter* in March of 1931. The papers recorded activities, news, parties, trips and other points of interest.[25]

In November of 1938 the patients initiated *The Valmora Sun*, a monthly publication edited by Ernest Stephenson. Associated editors were May R. Freedman and George Kosatka. Business manager was Marjorie Shea. Advertising manager was Adolph Hornstein and circulation manager was Mildred McDonell. Dr. Gellenthien and Mr. William G. Harrison of Baltimore, Maryland, designed the logo which appeared at the top of the first page, a rider on a horse chasing a steer, his rope ready to fall around the neck of the animal, and the rope itself spelling out "Valmora" as it sails through the air. To the left of the illustration are the words, "In the New Mexico Rockies — where Coyote Creek enters Shoemaker Canyon." The same logo was used on official Valmora stationary, also. The newspaper kept the patients informed about the goings-on within the institution and provided needed stimulation while at the same time giving its staff excellent occupational therapy.

Occupational therapy came into its own during World War I and was a form of treatment using work to help the patient improve. Usually the patient did the work as part of his treatment and did not expect to carry it on later as a means of support. But at Valmora, it often was a means of giving the patient a livelihood after leaving. "Indirectly, it prepares him mentally and physically for whatever he plans to take up later on."[26]

> The first stages of occupational therapy are simple enough. The patient who up to now has had to lie absolutely quiet in bed, with little or no solace except perhaps the radio, or reading aloud by a nurse or friend, is allowed to sit up in bed or to be propped upon pillows and to hold a book and read, or to sew, knit, or write, always for a certain definitely prescribed length of time. After this, progress becomes more rapid. Sketching and painting the surrounding mountains, embroidering leather with beads, weaving on a small hand loom, doing basket and silver work, knitting and various forms of fancy needle work are encouraged. Each patient is told to "keep his hands busy" during the day, outside of rest hours. If the patient will do this, his mind is kept occupied and there is less chance and time for introspection and worry. At the end of the day, he has tangible evidence of his work and also a feeling of having accomplished something.[27]

Since patients needed to find new vocations if they could not return to their former ones, the staff attempted to stimulate new ideas and develop talents and skills among the patients. Some "graduates" of Valmora were especially good at readjusting. William J. Stehle, who came from Armour and Company in Chicago, had been a middle executive with the packing house before being admitted to Valmora in the early 1930s. He realized his lifestyle would have to change. He could not live in his former environment. He was interested in the Navajo Indians who came to Valmora and camped out, selling jewelry and trading their wares. He was so fascinated that after he left Valmora he went to a Navajo Reservation and set up a trading post. He left Valmora on June 1, 1934, and stayed on at the Reservation for the next 30 years, having learned the language and been totally accepted by the natives.

Istvan "Steve" Gladics did not develop a new talent but simply refined the talent he had. Admitted October 28, 1938, Steve entertained himself by reading and composing music. He occupied Room 14 where he spent hours reading music. He had played the flute for the Chicago Symphony Orchestra before coming to Valmora, weighing only 109 pounds upon admittance. After he left Valmora on December 30, 1939, Steve went to work at The Conservatory of Music in Kansas City, Missouri and became the chief flute player for the Kansas City Symphony. There he met his wife, also a musician.

Dr. G. was amazed at Steven's talent. "I would go into his room and find him reading music like anyone else would read a novel. It was hard for me to understand how all those notes on the page could be so meaningful to him. But he 'heard' them with his inner ear."[28]

Some patients became nationally and internationally famous after leaving Valmora. Herbert E. Kleist developed an interest in ornithology as a patient at Valmora when he had nothing to do but watch birds. He became Professor of Ornithology at Harvard University. After leaving Valmora, he wrote:

> There is a great deal of pleasure as well as instruction in observing bird life at close range, especially during the mating season, when events prove that the course of home-building and family-raising runs by no means as smoothly as might be supposed.[29]

Playwright Courtney Savage wrote while at Valmora and had two plays on Broadway while at Valmora.[30] Journalist Leland D. Case, a patient in 1938, was editor of the *Rotarian* and continued to write. He was Paris correspondent for the *New York Herald-Tribune* before coming to Valmora. He had written Lindbergh stories after the epic flight of 1927 and had turned down the invitation to accompany Richard E. Byrd as correspondent on the second antarctic expedition. Stefan Urbanowicz, a dentist, was a patient from September, 1935 to August, 1936. His early love was music. He developed his musical talent and after leavintg Valmora, began teaching choral groups.[31] Paul P. Harris, who founded the Rotary International club in 1905, was a patient at Valmora for a short time in 1928. He lived nearly 20 more years and saw his club expand to more than 70 countries with 293,000 members.[32]

A consulting and construction engineer from Chicago, C.M. Garland, developed a talent and created a unique work of art while at Valmora, a portrait of George Washington. He began by attempting to correct the existing imperfections of Washington portraits by making his portrait conform with the life mask made of Washington by The French sculptor, Jean Antoine Houdon who came to America in 1785 to create the only statue of Washington "made from life." Garland explained to reporters that he became interested in the portraits of Washington while at Valmora and decided to make a study of them. He came to the conclusion that no portrait displayed the true character or personality of Washington.

A critic wrote the following:

> There were no Raphaels to paint Washington. The result is that we have all but lost his dominating personality. From my study of these portraits I found that practically none of them corresponded to the life mask taken by Houdon, but that the portrait by Savage at the Chicago Art Institute possessed certain realistic characteristics, particularly about the eyes and forehead. The body is also unquestionably the best

body ever painted of Washington. [33]

With the Savage portrait as a basis, Garland copied the body and corrected the proportions in the Savage painting to correspoond to the Houdon life mask. Garland was quoted as saying:

> I have produced a likeness of Washington which unquestionably possesses some of the dynamic qualities that Rembrandt Peale sought to produce some twenty years after the death of Washington. As you will remember, Rembrandt Peale regretted the fact that no one had succeeded in reproducing the character of Washington in paint. I believe that my portrait is the most accurate likeness of Washington in existence. [34]

A critic stated that usually attempts of this sort turn out to be "merely a stunt." but in this case, "Mr. Garland has produced a portrait worthy of consideration alongside Rembrandt Peale..." [35]

Frederic Mizen was an artist who visited Valmora and undoubtedly inspired patients there. He was employed by the Santa Fe Railroad to design their popular annual calendars. He asked Ellen to serve as a model for one of his portraits. Few people who hung up the Santa Fe Railroad calendar that year realized that the professional nurse in white uniform was a portrait of Valmora's nurse.

William Guinn, mentioned previously, was another who began a new career at Valmora. Before his illness he was a military man. He knew he could not return to his military career so he developed his writing talent. Guinn and his wife Phoebe, who developed a talent of her own at Valmora, weaving, lived years after leaving Valmora because they had adopted a lifestyle that allowed their bodies to resist the consumption which had nearly destroyed them in their youth. While both eventually died of their tuberculosis, they were given many productive years because they were "arrested" at Valmora and taught how to live, and live productively, with their disease.

Harold Walters, also mentioned previously, did not have to learn a new trade but was able to carry on the work he had just begun in the insurance business. He would lie in bed and carry on his correspondence a little at a time.

"I really believe Dr. G. is responsible for my being here today," Walters said 42 years after leaving Valmora. [36] He explained that it was at Valmora that he learned to live with his illness and to develop a lifestyle that would allow him to work at an easy pace.

The attitudinal change in Walters was more evident than in other patients. He was the man who made a detour on his way to the hospital to climb Pike's Peak. He was the actor who had "gone on with the show" in spite of his doctor's warning. But by the time he left he had learned to recognize his physical limitations and to live with them. Walters explained that when he came to Valmora, he had only $50.00 a month in health insurance. The fee at Valmora was $20.00 a week. He was grateful that he was allowed to carry on his business through correspondence and that afterwards he could buy more insurance. Obtaining insurance was ordinarily a serious problem for anyone with a history of TB. Dr. G. recalled a hospital patient who sent in a card indicating interest in purchasing life insurance. An agent came all the way from Albuquerque to sell him a policy. The salesman was shocked to discover that Valmora was a sanatorium and his interested "customer" was a TB patient! The Valmora Sun commented on such a patient: "Word had been received here of honors soon to be bestowed upon Mr. Harry—— who had the unique record of having turned in a life insurance application to his company for 1000 consecutive weeks." [37]

Patients were grateful for their learning experiences at Valmora. William G. Harrison, who graduated from Johns Hopkins University with a B.A. in architecture, was in San Juan, Puerto Rico to build a convent and install marble works in a cathedral when he lost his health to TB. While at Valmora he kept busy refining his talents. He processed pictures, landscaped walks, painted unique water-colors of scenery on sandpaper, and found time to search for gold. When he left Valmora, he continued to work with greater insight. [38]

Patients who had recovered or were nearly well enjoyed hiking and even horseback riding. "Bo" Bohannon wrote about a trek he and Waldo Davis made up to the old "Volcano" or "Old Baldy." Both men had come to Valmora sick with TB. Finally they were well enough to enjoy a wonderful excursion. After a ten mile ride, they arrived at the rim where they looked down into the bowl of the volcano 500 feet deep and about 300 yards across. To the east, they could see the Mora River 15 miles away, and on the west the Turkey Mountains could be seen. It was an awesome view. [39]

Tony Iacomini, called "The Cicero Kid" because he came from Cicero, Illinois, recalled how the entire staff helped patients adapt to new lifestyles and develop new talents. Patients learned to use the resources at hand to make their lives more pleasant. There was no electricity when he was at Valmora except when the DC generator was turned on for a few hours in the evening or when Doc turned it on during the day to take X-rays. When the patients in the cabins heard the "lunger" come on, they'd yell, "Doc's taking X-rays!" And they'd all turn on their radios to take advantage of the electricity.

Tony remembered the nurses who were at Valmora in 1943. Miss Engestrom was a small woman who commanded attention. "She was Swedish and she was strong! When she spoke, we listened," he recalled. "Ken — Miss Kendrick — was tall and shy. She was sweet. When she asked us to do something, she'd always say 'please.' And Georgie 'Smitty' Claiborne was like a mother hen, staunch, sturdy, and firm. She would scold patients who went out in the sun if they were supposed to stay inside."

"I'm only going to take a photograph," Tony replied when admonished.

"I knew someone once who died just because he went out 'only to take a photograph,'" she replied. That was her standard argument. Someone had once died from doing the very thing you were doing if she didn't approve.[40]

Georgie's strict discipline may have saved many lives for she paid attention to detail. She knew, for instance, that while sun could be used as effective therapy against tuberculosis, improper or excessive exposure could cause death. Yet Ken's gentle requests or imploring manner were equally effective, and some patients responded more quickly to her endearing manner. The different personalities of the nurses complemented each other as they worked in harmony for the benefit of their patients.

Georgie completed twenty-five years of continuous service as nurse at Valmora on June 11, 1952. Georgie Smith had come to New Mexico with her sick husband. He succumbed to his tuberculosis, and she worked for Dr. J.H. Steele in Wagon Mound until she began working at Valmora in 1927. The patients always called her "Smitty," even after she married Ayres M. "Slim" Claiborne, a patient who also eventually succumbed to his TB, leaving her a widow for the second time. Upon her retirement, Dr. G. had a special twenty-five year pin made for her, and she received a letter of praise from Valmora's president, Arthur Dixon, expressing his appreciation. He stated that she had helped in treating over 2300 cases under Dr. Brown and Dr. Gellenthien. She had had the satisfaction of seeing many who arrived sick and discouraged leave as well men and women.[41]

But Georgie did not retire. After moving to Las Vegas, she realized that she could not be happy without working. She did some private care work for a while and then applied for a job at the Las Vegas Hospital. She worked at the Las Vegas Hospital for a number of years.

Through the years, many patients were able to carry on their usual work from long distance. One was a journalist who wrote a daily column for the *Chicago Daily News*, sending his work from Valmora faithfully. On one occasion he described mirages after he had taken a drive over the sandy deserts with Dr. G. He wrote back that one fellow, a visitor to the State, didn't know better than to take a bath in a mirage, and he never knew the difference till he got out to dry himself on a towel. The reporter's success continued after he left Valmora.

For women, the adjustment was sometimes difficult. Dr. Brown was an advocate for women's rights. In one of his first promotional booklets on Valmora he wrote that women are accepted on the same terms as men at Valmora. "We have few printed rules and need few, for the spirit of the whole place is that of a democracy of men and women who are there for the one purpose of getting well."[42]

In the real world of work and social activity, however, women were often treated as second class citizens. Having the stigma of TB made life more difficult than ever. Most women with TB, even after having taken "the cure," were considered "unmarriageable." Tuberculosis ravaged the female body, often rendering it unable to reproduce. Few men wanted to marry a sterile woman with a contagious disease, an illness that might reappear at any time. Thus, Valmora women were urged to prepare for the future. Some developed new talents, others turned hobbies into salable skills, and some arranged to return to school.

One woman, referred to here as Susie, was luckier than most. She became ill when she was very young. On the train headed for Valmora, facing a future of illness and poverty — for she had no money and no family — Susie met a wealthy young man. The few hours the two spent together on the train blossomed into romance and they vowed to spend their lives together. At Valmora Dr. G. tried to get Susie to plan for her future. She had no skills, no great amount of formal education, and would be tagged a "consumptive." How was she to support herself? He urged her to plan for school or to develop some skill. But she insisted that she would marry the rich young man she had met on the train. It seemed unlikely, but Dr. G. said nothing to dash her hopes. Surprisingly enough, after she recovered sufficiently to leave Valmora, Susie and her young man were married. He was a banker in Chicago and Susie lived happily there, free of finanical worries.

For the most part, however, a woman who came to Valmora with TB faced a bleak future unless she was already married or had some means of support or could learn a new trade that would fit into her revised lifestyle. There were some women who hoped to "catch" a husband among their fellow patients, although "pairing off" was discouraged. "The Red Menace" was an attractive young lady who always dressed up in fine robes and gowns even for a short walk to the post office. Her favorite attire was a lacy red robe.

Most of the patients managed to cope adequately after leaving Valmora. Many of them attained outstanding success. In his farewell address to patients in 1939, Dr. G. said:

> Many of you arrived at Valmora, filled with despair, and discouraged because you had to leave your job, your family, friends, and your life's ambitions. It has been pleasant to see how, like a wilted flower, you began to straighten up, flourish and blossom under the warm New Mexico sun. As you mended in body and spirit you began to take on new hope, and to plan to pick up life's threads where you had been forced to drop them. And now you are soon to be discharged. It is a fine tribute to Valmora that as your departure draws near, you hesitate to leave its friendliness and security...Smitty, Ken, Miss Engstrom, Mrs. Tipton and Johnnie, Dr. Lyman and I feel happy and grateful that you have responded to treatment and now are ready to return to your families and homes. But we cannot help feeling sad, for we will miss you as we do the many others who have left before you. How happy we are to receive your good reports after discharge!...But after all, you have won your fight. You are not one of the six percent who failed...All of us on the staff rejoice with you in your good fortune and pray that it may continue. To you as patients and friends, I say: "Adios, amigos, Dios valla con ustedes."[43] (Goodby, friends, God go with you.)

Today there are many words for the kinds of learning that went on at Valmora — "learning styles," "self-directed learning," "recreational therapy," "occupational therapy" and "group therapy." But Dr. G. summed it all up when he said:

> Treatment was a learning style. There was no specific therapy. It was good nutrition, bed rest, and a positive mental attitude. Patients had to learn a new lifestyle, a new attitude. They had to adapt to that new lifestyle in order to survive. Learning and developing new talents and skills was fun, but it was motivated by the need to survive.[44]

NOTES

1. Carl H. Gellenthien, interview at Valmora Clinic, Valmora, New Mexico, December 29, 1980.
2. Mooney, *op. cit.*, p. 56.
3. C.H. Gellenthien, "Dr. Gellenthien Inaugurates Series of Health Articles: Stresses an Intelligent Cooperation Between Doctor and Patient," *op. cit.*, p. 1.
4. *Ibid.*
5. *Ibid.*
6. *Ibid.*
7. *Ibid.*
8. Tony Iacomini, personal interview at Valmora, October 24, 1981.
9. Waldo Davis, personal interview at Las Vegas, October 21, 1983.
10. "Who's Who At Valmora Past and Present," *The Valmora Sun*, January, 1939 p. 4, in Scrapbook 3, Valmora Library, p. 41.
11. Waldo Davis, personal interview, *op. cit.*
12. "Cuff Notes," *The Valmora Sun*, December, 1938, p. 4., in Scrapbook 3, Valmora Library, Valmora, New Mexico, p. 21.
13. "Valmorans Report Frolic at Ricardo's," *The Valmora Sun*, November, 1938, p. 1, in Scrapbook 3, Valmora Library, Valmora, New Mexico, p. 19.
14. "Christmas Week and New Year's Day Joyous Events," *The Valmora Sun*, January, 1939, p. 1., in Scrapbook 3, *op. cit.*, p. 23.
15. *Ibid.*, p. 7.
16. "Who's Who at Valmora Past and Present," *The Valmora Sun*, March, 1939, p. 4., in Scrapbook 3, *op. cit.*, p. 27.
17. "Who's Who At Valmora Past and Present," *The Valmora Sun*, February, 1939, p. 4., in Scrapbook 3, *op. cit.*, p. 25.
18. "Alumni News," *The Valmora Sun*, December, 1938, p. 3., in Scrapbook 3, *op. cit.*, p. 21 and January, 1939, p. 3.
19. "New Resident Physician Arrives," *The Valmora Sun*, November, 1938, p. 3., in Scrapbook 3, *op. cit.*, p. 19.
20. "Who's Who At Valmora Past and Present," *The Valmora Sun*, June, 1939, p. 4., in Scrapbook 3, *op. cit.*, p. 33.
21. Vivian (Johnnie) Johnson, "It's All in the Day's Work," *The Valmora Sun*, February, 1939, p. 7., in Scrapbook 3, Valmora Library, Valmora, New Mexico, p. 25.
22. "More About the Christmas Party," *The Valmora Sun*, January, 1939, p. 8, in Scrapbook 3, Valmora Library, Valmora, New Mexico, p. 23.

23. Tony Iacomini, interview at Valmora, April 10, 1983.

24. "Valmorans Report Frolic at Ricardos," *op. cit.*

25. "Earlier Journalistic Efforts Recounted: Former Papers More Intimate But Less Comprehensive in Scope," *The Valmora Sun*, January, 1939, p. 1, in Scrapbook 3, *op. cit.*, p. 23.

26. C.H. Gellenthien, "Dr. Gellenthien Inaugurates Series of Health Articles," *op. cit.*, p. 5.

27. *Ibid.*

28. Carl H. Gellenthien, interview at Valmora, June 10, 1983.

29. H.E. Kleist, "Bird Home Builders Bravely Overcome Many Difficulties: Life Does Not Always Run Smoothly for Our Feathered Friends," n.t., n.d., n.p., in Scrapbook 1, Valmora Library, Valmora, New Mexico, p. 72.

30. Carl H. Gellenthien, interview at Valmora, December 5, 1983.

31. "Who's Who At Valmora Past and Present," *The Valmora Sun*, December, 1938, p. 4, *op. cit.*

32. "Milestones," *Time* (February 10, 1947) n.p., in Scrapbook 1, Valmora Library, Valmora, New Mexico, p. 133.

33. "Bullet's Artless Comment: George Washington — C.M. Garland," newspaper clipping, February 24, 1934, in Scrapbook 1, Valmora Library, Valmora, New Mexico, p. 57.

34. *Ibid.*

35. *Ibid.*

36. Harold Walters, interview in Santa Fe, New Mexico, July 17, 1983.

37. "Alumni Potpourri," *The Valmora Sun*, April, 1939, p. 3, in Scrapbook 3, Valmora Library, Valmora, New Mexico, p. 29.

38. "Who's Who at Valmora Past and Present," *The Valmora Sun*, January, 1939, p. 4., *op. cit.*

39. "A Volcanic Experience of Mr. Bohannon," *The Valmora Sun*, November, 1938, p. 7, in Scrapbook 3, Valmora Library, Valmora, New Mexico, p. 19.

40. Interview with Tony Iacomini, February 17, 1984, Las Vegas, New Mexico.

41. Arthur Dixon, letter to Mrs. A.M. Claiborne, March 2, 1953, in Scrapbook 5, Valmora Library, p. 50.

42. William T. Brown, *Valmora: An Invitation*, *op. cit.*, p. 13.

43. C.H. Gellenthien, "Farewell Advice," *op. cit.*, p. 8.

44. Carl H. Gellenthien, personal interview, Valmora, New Mexico, August 9, 1983.

CHAPTER
IX

Country Doctor

In the early days of New Mexico Territory a country doctor never went anywhere without his two able assistants: his black medical bag and his gun. The former was to ward off the invisible enemy of disease: the latter was to ward off the visible but equally deadly scourge of human greed, hate, and violence.

Dr. Brown saw New Mexico's transition from Territory to State in 1912, but that momentous date did nothing to change the unscrupulous characters like those of the Silva Gang which had exerted an unchallenged reign of terror around Las Vegas in earlier days. With the advent of the railroad in 1879, Las Vegas exerienced growing pains not unlike that of other boom towns and then settled in to a more-or-less peaceful period of development. But Mora County where Valmora is located kept its reputation as the wildest, most "uncivilized" area of the state for a long time. As the poorest county in New Mexico, Mora's crime rate continued to climb. Watrous, the closest community to Valmora, was dubbed "the toughest town in the west".

After Dr. Brown's death in 1935, Dr. Gellenthien was the only doctor in Mora County, an area of 1,942 square miles. In 1940 the population of the County was 10,387. Until the time of this present writing — 49 years after Dr. Brown's death — Dr. G. has been the only permanent resident physician in the County to remain for any length of time. Others have come and gone, but Dr. G. has been content to stay. It was Dr. Brown who taught his young protégé from Chicago how to survive in the west and how to be a good country doctor.

One of the lessons Dr. Brown taught his son-in-law was how to avoid a shoot-out. At the time Brown had been considering the purchase of the Phoenix Ranch four miles from Watrous. The local population was accustomed to holding their Saturday night dances in the deserted ranch buildings there. Insurance companies refused to insure the buildings against fire as long as the Watrous crowd continued to use the buildings. Consequently, Dr. Brown notified the townspeople that he was going to buy the place and that they could no longer use the location for their dances. He posted "keep off" signs and closed the main gate, indicating that it was private property.

Soon thereafter, Dr. Brown was ambushed as he drove through Watrous. Hearing bullets whiz over the roof of his car, Brown realized that someone was following him, shooting! And the bullets weren't blanks!

Just a week before Brown's experience on the Watrous road, a school board election had been held and a fight broke out at the store in Watrous. A good friend and prominent merchant, Charlie Baxter[1], tried to intervene to break it up. He pushed one of the men aside, but as the fighter fell backwards, he drew his gun. The downed gunman pointed his pistol at his enemy and pulled the trigger. But Charlie was still in the way and the bullet hit him instead. Dr. G. was called immediately. A local rancher said he had never seen the doctor's car fly so fast. Dr. G. rushed to his friend's side, but it was too late. Charlie had died instantly.[2]

It had been just a week since Dr. G. saw Charlie buried. And now Dr. Brown had been shot at. Young Dr. Gellenthien was looking for a fight. His friend Paul Frank recalled how he almost found it.

Paul arrived at the Valmora home one day when his wife Marge was visiting her cousin Alice Gellenthien. As soon as Paul drove up, Carl ran out of the house and told Paul to bring in his gun: he expected trouble. Dr. Brown was on the phone at that moment talking to the Attorney General. Carl and Paul were deputized to go and see if anyone had broken into the Phoenix property. They had two handguns and two shotguns between them.[3]

Alice, pregnant with her first child, was worried and said, "Remember, Carl, you and Paul are only supposed to go and see if there's been any harm done. Stay out of trouble."

"Yes, do hurry back soon," Marge advised.

The two men drove out and found no damage, but Carl insisted on continuing to drive around. They noticed they were being followed. Finally Carl and Paul stopped and got out, guns in hands. The men in the vehicle behind them also stopped and got out, guns in hands. In fact, there were two car loads of men behind the doctor's car — about 15 men in all. Each group pointed guns at the other, but not a word was exchanged. Finally Carl and Paul got back into the car and drove on. The same thing happened five or six times over a period of an hour. Paul suggested they drive back home, but Carl didn't want to give up. At last, however, Carl drove back to Valmora to report that no damage had been done. Due to the ill-will of his gun-toting neighbors, Dr. Brown decided the ranch wasn't worth blood-shed and did not purchase the Phoenix.[4]

There was nothing Dr. G. could do for Charlie Baxter but he could help his widow who was expecting a child; and he did. He saved her life.

When Mrs. Baxter[5] went into labor at the Valmora hospital, she was soon in trouble. The baby was too large. Forceps were useless. In those days a Caesarean section was not possible after dilation of the cervix. Dr. G. had called in an older doctor from Las Vegas. The nurse had kept the patient under ether for hours. The baby was dead. And it appeared that the woman would die soon.

"It's useless," the older doctor finally said as the hours approach-ed daybreak. "I'm going home."

"But this young woman will die. We have to do something," Dr. G. declared. He remembered Charlie and determined not to let his widow die. In desperation, Dr. G. took a surgical saw, called a "gigli," cut the pubic arch open and removed the dead baby. The older doctor protested that the woman would be paralyzed for the rest of her life.

"She'll never walk again," he declared.

"Well, at least she'll be alive," Dr. G. replied, and sewed her up.

Mrs. Baxter was not paralyzed. In fact, she lived to remarry and give birth to three lovely children.

"That was the time I sawed a woman in half," Dr. G. remembered years later. As far as he knows, the technique had never been done before.[6]

One of the most frightening moments in Dr. G.'s career occurred just after his daughter Editha was born. Dr. Gerritt Heusinkveld, head of obstetrics and gynecology at St. Luke's Hospital in Denver, Colorado, and attending gynecologist at the General Hospital there, had flown in to deliver Editha, the Gellenthien's first child, born Oc-tober 25, 1934. Dr. G. was looking forward to spending a quiet Thanksgiving at home with his family when he got a call Thanksgiv-ing morning to go out into the country. The caller was insistent that his daughter was seriously ill, so Dr. G. got his medical bag and went.

When he stepped into the house, Dr. G. felt two guns pushed into his back.

"We're gonna kill you," the two men declared.

Dr. G. realized too late that he had fallen victim to the insanity of two drunken men. He usually carried a gun with him, but this time he didn't have his pistol. The fact that he was unarmed, however, may have saved his life. Desperate to defend himself, Dr. G. saw that there were no weapons in the room except a poker by the fireplace. It would have been useless against the guns. He realized the only thing he could do was to try to talk his way out. He asked the men why they were upset with him.

The men accused the doctor of saying that the daughter of one of them had syphilis. Dr. G. managed to convince them that he had never said such a thing. As it turned out, the woman had told her hair dresser that Dr. G. said that her dandruff was NOT caused by syphilis. The whole story had been distorted. Dr. G. managed to get out of the situation by remaining calm. But he never went on a call without his gun again in those early days. And he found that having a pistol along gave him an edge he otherwise would not have had.

Soon after Dr. Brown's death, the ranch foreman at Gascon, referred to here as Leroy, decided to take over the place. He began to dress in Dr. Brown's clothes, to sleep in his bed, and even to ride the stallion that no one but Alice and her father had ever dared to ride. Dr. G. decided it was time to ask the man to move on. But he feared a fight and decided to get help from the toughest man he knew. Tom Tipton, a neighbor who lived across the river, was an experienced soldier who had fought at Verdun during World War I. After returning home he told Dr. G. that the bodies there were so numerous one could walk the distance from Valmora to Las Vegas — about 20 miles — without ever touching the ground. Tom wasn't afraid of anything, Dr. G. thought, so he asked him to go along to see Leroy at Gascon.

When the two arrived they found Leroy sitting on Dr. Brown's stallion dressed in Brown's clothes.

"Get off that horse and go into the house. I want to talk to you," Dr. G. ordered. Leroy did as he was told.

Then Dr. G. told Leroy to put on his own clothes and leave the ranch. He refused to allow him to take a horse.

"How will I get to town?" Leroy asked.

"You'll walk," Dr. G. commanded.

"All 30 miles?"

"Yes. Now get started!" Dr. G. commanded.

Again, Leroy offered no resistance and did as he was told. But he was not a man to be trusted and Dr. G. feared he might try to ambush them on the way back. They were cautious and nothing happened.

Afterwards, Tipton said, "You didn't need me along. He didn't even offer to put up a fight after you gave your orders. You talked so tough he didn't dare!"

"If he'd wanted to fight, I was ready," Dr. G. said, revealing the pistol he had been carrying under his coat the whole time.

Tipton grinned, "No wonder you were so bold! Nobody's going to argue with that!"

The street wise kid from Chicago's northwest side learned to be a country doctor by the best means possible, not just through formal education, but through association with other country doctors. Not only did he learn from his mentor, Alice's father, but he also learned from Alice's grandfather, Dr. Samuel Hassell, a pioneer doctor from Wisconsin.

"If you're going to be a country doctor, there's one thing you've got to learn, young man," Dr. Hassell declared.

The ink wasn't yet dry on Gellenthien's sheepskin but he thought he'd learned just about all he needed to know to practice medicine. He had even studied obstetrics under the famous authority and author in the field, Dr. Joseph De Lee who sent him and the other young medical students into the ghetto near the University of Chicago to make home deliveries. But Dr. G. found out he was just beginning to learn.

"What's that?" the young man asked.

"You've got to learn to pull teeth," Dr. Hassell told him. "People come to you with a toothache and want a bad tooth out. If you explain that you're not a dentist, they'll just reply, 'Well, you're a doctor, ain't you?'" He explained that any country doctor is expected to take care of all the needs of the people, and that includes dental work if no dentist is available. Indeed, in the remote mountain areas of northern New Mexico few dentists were to be found in those days. So Dr. G. learned to pull teeth and he still has the dental instruments Dr. Hassell gave him. He learned other effective techniques from Alice's grandfather, too. He was able to put one of them into practice when a patient in Watrous had a dislocated shoulder.

Dr. G. went to the man's home and examined him. The man was much bigger than Dr. G., but the doctor knew just what to do. He pulled off his own cowboy boot, set his heel firmly under the patient's armpit, and pulled with all his strength. Doctor and patient "wrestled" on the adobe floor for a while and ended up under the kitchen table; but Gellenthien wouldn't quit until he got the shoulder in place. Other doctors used more subtle techniques but they were more time consuming, more expensive and in the long run, more painful. One Las Vegas doctor at that time kept a patient with a similar dislocation lying on a table with weights hanging down from his arm for hours to try to get a reduction.

Besides Dr. Hassell and Dr. Brown, there were numerous other country doctors who contributed to the education of Dr. Gellenthien.

Dr. G. knew Arthur E. Hertzler, author of *The Horse and Buggy Doctor*, a well-known pioneer physician in Kansas. Hertzler looked like Ichabod Crane — tall, lanky, and disheveled, wearing rumpled clothes. They were listening to a lecture at a medical meeting on an obscure condition of the abdomen in a boy. Hertzler had his long legs wrapped around the chair in front of him while the speaker droned on for over 45 minutes. Finally the floor was opened up for discussion. Because he was such an eminent physician, Hertzler was asked if he had any comments. He unwound himself, stood up, and said, "Well, as far as I can tell, the boy had a bellyache."[7]

Gellenthien worked with most of the Las Vegas doctors and knew most of the pioneer doctors in the out-lying regions including Dr. Steele of Wagon Mound. He remembered chuckling over a penny postcard Steele once received in the mail. It read: "Dear Doctor: The medicine worked. Please don't tell no body that I was like I was." Of course, everyone at the village post office had seen the card.[8]

Although Dr. G. worked with Dr. Charles Mayo, Jr., a personal friend, as well as other highly esteemed physicians, he was never above taking lessons from an unknown country doctor as well. He wanted to learn from everyone he could. One lesson was learned from an old doctor from Mora. Dr. G. had been at a home between Rociada and Gascon for two days and one night with a woman in labor. The woman was in trouble so Dr. G. called in the old doctor.

The elderly gentleman from Mora came in chewing tobacco with the juice dripping into his long beard — quite a contrast to the impeccable grooming of the Mayo men. Dr. G. explained to the older doctor that he could not get the forceps in position. The first thing the old doctor asked for was an ironing board. Dr. G. couldn't imagine why. The family was too poor to own one, however, so the old doctor then asked Dr. G. to go out and bring in some planks that were lying in the yard. Questioning the old man's sanity, Gellenthien complied with his colleague's request. Then the old doctor put the planks under the mattress, raising the woman's posterior high enough so he could get the forceps in the right position. The baby was then delivered.

There were many times Dr. G. had to improvise. Most of the homes he visited were poor although they were warm and clean. The typical native houses, made of adobe, had dirt floors; and each door had an adobe threshold about a foot high in its center to keep the draft off the floors. Dr. G. did much of his work in these houses, using the kitchen table or the bed for surgery. He was even prepared to do an emergency appendectomy with improvised tools. Bent forks and tablespoons could be used as retractors, and ordinary sewing needles and thread could be used for sutures.

Once Dr. G. was delivering a baby in a home with no electricity. It was a long labor, and the kerosene for the lamps ran out. Dr. G. used his flashlight until its batteries were gone and he ran out of light. But he did not panic, even though he was alone. He just went out and brought his car up to the door of the house and aimed the headlights into the room. Thus, he delivered the baby by the light of his car. "That old Model T helped me through a lot of rough spots, but I never thought it would help me deliver a baby," Dr. G. said.[9]

At another home without running water, a house near Tiptonville, Dr. G. had to wash up using water carried from a nearby creek. He scrubbed up in a ten-pound coffee can. The baby came without difficulty. The placenta adhered, however, and the doctor had to remove it manually. Under those less-than-hygienic home conditions, Dr. G. feared the woman might get an infection. A few days later he stopped by to check on the mother. He found no one in the house, and his heart sank. He feared she had died. He walked around to the back of the house and found the healthy mother hanging up diapers.

Dr. G. thought of an old country doctor he knew who never sterilized his instruments. After washing them in soap and water, he wrapped them in newspaper. He claimed that the printers' ink kept them germ-free. As far as anyone knew, none of his patients died of infection.

Dr. G. got another fright when he was called to a home on Pecos Street in Las Vegas. Unknown to him, the family had moved to another address. Dr. G. went to the old home and knocked at the door. No one answered. Thinking that the sick woman might be unable to answer, Dr. G. went on in, announcing his presence.

Then he saw someone was in bed with a sheet pulled up over the head. He thought the woman had died. The body under the sheet was still. He approached the bed and put his hand beneath the sheet to feel for respiration. Suddenly a young woman bolted up and exclaimed, "Oh, Dr. G., it's you!" There was relief in her voice. She knew Dr. G., although she was not the patient who had called him. This woman's family had just moved into the house after the other family moved out. She had been resting when she heard a man at the door. She had been alarmed and pulled the sheet up over her. After acquiring the new address of his patient, Dr. G. proceeded to make his house call.

Dr. G. and his friend Dr. Earl Ewert were ready to enjoy an evening of relaxation at a barn warming given by Fred Thompson to celebrate the completion of his new addition to his ranch. The two doctors arrived at the barn dance near Wagon Mound early in the evening. But they soon had to work. A prominent Las Vegan, Frank Fitch, was dancing with his wife when he broke his leg. A local newspaper reported:

> Old-fashioned square dancing can be a dangerous recreation. Take the word of Frank Fitch, who is in a Las Vegas hospital with his left leg in a cast. Saturday night Fitch was square dancing in Wagon Mound. It was the third dance in the big cement-floored barn and the caller started on the "Black Hawk Waltz." As Fitch began to whirl his partner, the leg bone snapped. Two doctors and a nurse, also square dancing, gave him emergency treatment. [10]

There was no plaster of Paris in the Wagon Mound Clinic, so Dr. G. sent his nurse to get some regular plaster from one of the merchants in Wagon Mound. The two doctors worked on the leg, wondering why Frank was not complaining of any pain. He was lying near an open window and seemed quite comfortable for a man who had just broken his leg. Then they noticed that friends kept passing whiskey up to him through the window. The party didn't end until everyone had autographed the cast. It was well after sunrise when Dr. G. got home from the dance, having worked most of the evening.

When Frank went to his regular family doctor in Las Vegas, Dr. H.M. Mortimer, the physician was astonished to see the hard plaster. "Who put this thing on, anyhow?" he demanded. The circumstances were explained to Mortimer who had improvised many times himself, and he understood. He had once set a leg using plaster from a hospital supply that was so old it turned to sand the next day. He had improvised makeshift tools for repairing fractures by using nuts, bolts, and even a sacking needle from a local hardware store. [11]

Working in the home environment was not without its hazards. First, one had to get to the home. To avoid getting lost, Dr. G. usually asked someone to meet him on the main road and lead him to the patient's home. Navigating up and down primitive canyon trails in the dark to find a home via unpaved ranch roads, even with a guide, was a challenge.

One Saturday evening about 8:30, Dr. G. received a call from a father who was worried about his daughter. She had given birth about 3:00 that afternoon with the help of a midwife. Everything had appeared normal and the midwife had gone home. Afterwards the woman had a postpartum convulsion. Eclampsia could be extemely dangerous, and Dr. G. determined to get there as fast as he could. But the home was about 45 miles away in a remote area. Dr. G. didn't want to waste any time. He asked the man on the phone to meet him at a filling station and guide him to the house.

As Dr. G. prepared to leave, a friend who was visiting the Gellenthiens insisted on accompanying the doctor on his call. The man was a clothing salesman from Marshall Field & Company. He had fallen in love with the mountains and insisted that riding with the doctor on a warm summer evening would be a pleasant experience. He was wearing an expensive, stylish suit and was eager to go. Dr. G. didn't have time to argue, so he told the man to get in the car. They traveled over a dark, winding, narrow road through a deep canyon and up over high ridges.

When they arrived at the two-room home it was difficult to find the pathway to the house. There was no porch light. The only light in the home was a dim kerosene lamp. The eager businessman stepped ahead of the doctor toward the light of the open door. Unfamiliar with New Mexican architecture, he simultaneously hit his head on the low door stoop while stumbling over the two-foot high center step in the door's entrance. The fall propelled him forward and he slid under the kitchen table.

Dr. G. didn't stop to watch his friend brush off his once-immaculate suit. He hurried into the bedroom. But it was too late. The patient was dead. His hurried trip had resulted only in his attending the injured friend, who was more angry than hurt, thinking his suit would never be the same. Needless to say, he was not so anxious to accompany the doctor on another house call.

Once Dr. G. was traveling with a friend when the car lights went out. From Lamy to Las Vegas, Dr. G. stood on the running board of the car, holding on with one hand to the door post and holding a flashlight in the other. Driving slowly and cautiously, they made it home. More than once Dr. G. had to sit through a dust storm during the drought of the 1930s when visibility was zero. Other times he would get stuck in the mud. He remembered one time in particular. "There was one mud puddle between the Mississippi River and the Pacific Ocean, and I got stuck in it."[12]

There were personal risks involved in entering sick rooms, too. With contagious diseases running rampant, doctors had to overcome their own fears and enter sick rooms with courage. Before diphtheria was conquered, one woman in the Ocate area had eleven funerals in one week, having lost her husband and ten children to the disease.

After treating a patient with spinal meningitis, Dr. G. feared bringing it home to his family. He remembered a classmate who had died as an intern after treating such a patient. So Dr. G. went into the basement of his home when he returned from his call and immediately undressed, intending to shower and put on clean clothes. But when he tried to get in, he discovered that Alice had gone to

160

town and locked every door. He didn't want to put the contaminated clothes on again so he sat in the boiler room reading magazines in the nude till his wife returned.

One winter day at a small home between Valmora and Buena Vista, Dr. G. and his nurse were delivering a baby in a small room where a wood stove was used for heat. Dr. G. had his back to the stove and the patient was the kitchen table just a few feet away from it. The nurse administered ether. It was a difficult birth and Dr. G. wondered at what moment the open fire might cause the ether to explode. Later he asked the famous Anton Carlson of the University of Chicago under what conditions either might explode. In his Swedish accent he replied, "Oh, it does not explode. It just goes PPPPFFFF as it burns its way along the floor."

Another time when Dr. G. and his nurse were delivering a baby in a small, one-room home another hazard was discovered. The patient was on a table with the nurse standing in the corner of the small room administering the ether. But the ether drifted back toward the nurse. She passed out instead of the patient!

Dr. G. was grateful for the nurse who usually accompanied him to deliver babies because she spoke Spanish better than he. Once he went to deliver a baby and noticed that the family seemed unusually aloof. The patient was unmarried and her family was apparently ashamed of the unwanted child about to be born. It was a difficult delivery and Dr. G. feared the baby would be born dead, so when a healthy boy was delivered, he was delighted. Showing the family the child, Dr. G. exclaimed what a beautiful baby he was and how lucky that he'd been born alive.

"I'll take this beautiful baby home with me!" he joked.

The spokesman for the family replied solemnly, "If you want the baby, take him home, Doctor. He's yours."

Through his nurse's proficient Spanish, Dr. G. was able to decline gracefully.

Usually Dr. G. did not decline the gifts his patients offered. He often received garden fruits and vegetables grown by patients or jars of homemade jelly or relish. At Christmas he would be showered with cookies, candy, cakes, decorations and other seasonal gifts. One patient gave him a bottle of homemade whiskey known as "Mula Blanca" or "White Mule." He used it for horse colic and it was very good. Another patient gave him a beautiful Palomino.

A group of Navajos made him a diorama, the interior of a Navajo hogan with dolls in typical Navajo dress. It took ten workers six months to make the display which is now set behind glass in the reception room wall at the Clinic. The display, like everything the

Navajos make, has one imperfection. They believe that each thing they make must have a mistake in it, for if an artist is perfect, he has no more reason to live and will then be taken into the Great Beyond. The mistake in this diorama centers around the infant in the group. The baby is not tucked into his cradle properly; his arms have been left out in the air above his blanket.[13]

Patients share folk medicine and customs with Dr. G. A Navajo explained to him why the baby's cradle is constructed with the head board's frame extending out over the baby's forehead. If a mother had to run from enemies in the early days, she could toss the wooden cradle into the bushes, hoping the leather strap in the back would catch and hang from a branch. But if it didn't and the cradle rolled on the ground, the headboard would protect the baby. Nor would he smother in the sand, because the protrusion of the head board would hold his face up away from the dirt. His arms and legs were safely tucked in under blankets and he would be secure until his mother could return for him.[14]

In his office Dr. G. has a corner shelf devoted to jars of various herbs or *remedios*. *Los Remedios*, or remedies, include a variety of native plants and herbs which the older generation has passed down to the younger one. *Osha* (Ligusticum Porteri) is a widely used herbal medicine in New Mexico and there are many others. Dr. G. believes most of these herbs do no harm and some do help.

In his years of practice, Dr. G. only found one home remedy that was actually dangerous. A woman was treated for postpartum hemorrhage by squatting over a basin, a steaming hot herbal bath. The "medicated" steam was supposed to stop the bleeding. In reality, however, the heat from the steam merely stimulated more blood flow. Furthermore, there was no way such external medication could affect internal bleeding.[15]

Sharing their knowledge as well as their problems was an important way Dr. G.'s patients related to him. When he made a house call, he'd end up seeing several people besides the sick person he'd been called to see. Sometimes a home became a clinic. Once when Dr. G. went to deliver a baby, he found several people waiting to see him after he'd finished the job. One man from the village was brought in with two toes missing. He was a trapper and had tangled with a coyote. The doctor dressed the mangled foot and prescribed for the unexpected patient.

As of this writing, Dr. G. is still a busy country doctor, the oldest practicing physician in the state of New Mexico. On December 7, 1983 he got a call about 4:00 a.m. A woman in Watrous was having a baby. Her regular obstetrician was in Las Vegas, but she knew she'd never make it there in time. Dr. G. quickly dressed, grabbed his obstetrical bag and drove the four miles to her home. It was not long before he had delivered a baby girl. There were no complications. As soon as he was sure she was able, Dr. G. told the woman to go on into the hospital in Las Vegas. The ambulance came out from Las Vegas and took her and the newborn to the hospital.

Dr. G. went home, shaved, ate breakfast, and went to the clinic to meet his first morning patients. He thought nothing unusual about it. "It's all in a day's work. I've been delivering babies for 60 years. A doctor has to be prepared." He makes house calls to the most remote places in Mora and San Miguel Counties, including places like Wagon Mound, Watrous, Pecos, and Las Vegas as well as isolated ranch homes.

Sunday morning, January 17, 1982, Dr. G. was having breakfast when he received a phone call from a long-time patient in Wagon Mound. She said she had twisted her ankle and was in pain. Suddenly she broke off. The doctor feared she had passed out. He went over to his office and added a few items to his medical bag. Then, in spite of a head cold and the chill of the winter air, he went out to start his car. His 1966 Chevrolet started immediately. Dr. G. drove a Model A when he first came to New Mexico, and he always drove small cars.

"My people are poor. For me to drive up in a big flashy new car would be an insult," he said. And he always drove a car as long as it would hold up.

The 69-year-old patient lived 22 miles away. When Dr. G. arrived at her home, he was greeted by a barking dog. He spoke to the animal and entered, announcing his presence. He was relieved to see the woman, referred to here as Beth, lying conscious on her bed. One side of Beth's bed was against the wall. On the other side three bird cages were lined up together, each containing two parakeets. At the foot of the bed was a piano. A little dog yapped from its bed at the far end of the room. In spite of Beths's efforts to quiet her dog, it yapped incessantly throughout the doctor's visit. Dr. G. was unperturbed.

At medical school Dr. G. had been taught never to sit on a patient's bed so as to avoid picking up bedbugs. But there was no where else to sit so Dr. G. sat at the end of the bed, grateful that bed bugs are no longer the menace they once were, and examined Beth's foot. In spite of the dog's yapping he was able to learn that Beth had fallen during the night. The reason she had hung up so abruptly was that her dentures had come loose and she "couldn't talk any more."

She had not doubted that the doctor would come. She already had a check made out for $15.00.

Dr. G. put a light cast on the ankle and gave her instructions. He left some pills for the pain. She had a walker and would be able to get up and about when necessary. She also had her telephone within reach and a neighbor had promised to check on her every day. After leaving instructions for her to call if necessary, Dr. G. made his departure, past the larger dog standing guard outside. It had been another of hundreds of house calls he had made in this area. Beth was poor, but he had treated her as if she had been a member of a royal household, and had done so for the past 30 years.

"She lives in a prison right now," he said. "I left her house and I'm free to go. She has to just stay right there all day. She can't get up and go out. She has nowhere to go and no way to go." His voice was touched with compassion. "Her pain and infirmity have imprisoned her in her own home."[16]

Compassion is part of a good country doctor's attitude. Another is the composure and calm outward appearance that must be displayed by the person in charge of any urgent situation. As an intern, Dr. G. was conditioned to appear composed even if he felt strong emotion when others around him were on the verge of panic. The scientific approach of a doctor with a poker face may seem unfeeling to those who do not know how deep the still waters run. When Gellenthien was a medical student at the University of Illinois working nights as City Physician, he saw numerous accidents and many distraught people when he treated emergency cases at Iroquois Memorial Hospital. By the time he finished his internship, death was nothing new to him.

An old picture in a golden frame hangs in Dr. G.'s private office, "The Doctor," a famous 19th century painting by Sir Luke Fildes. It is an appropriate reminder of the sacred trust a doctor brings with him when he enters a home. The doctor in the painting sits beside a sick child, his face anxious and lined with fatigue. In the background, the parents look anxiously toward him, placing their faith in his skill. He has done all he could. Now he has nothing to offer but compassion — and his presence. Like the doctor in the Fildes painting, Dr. Gellenthien has been in this scene. He, too, has sat beside the bed of a sick and dying child and, knowing he has done all he could, offered the only thing he had left — his compassion and his very presence.

One February morning before the days of penicillin, Dr. G. was called out to a ranch near Shoemaker canyon. A ten-year-old boy had pneumonia. Dr. G. spent many long hours in that home, working with the young patient. In those days pallative treatment or supportive care was about all a doctor could offer. He could try to reduce fever. Aspirin was helpful. Application of cold clothes offered some relief. Administering baths sometimes helped. He would push fluids and see that the patient received good nutrients. Even before the discovery of vitamins the value of various foods was appreciated. Obtaining good elimination was also believed to be helpful. Enemas were administered as a course of treatment. Dr. G. did all of those things for the boy and more. But all the hours of effort failed. In the end, the boy died. He was buried in the family cemetery near his home the next day.

"I still remember the morning they buried him," Dr. G. said. "The sun was shining but there was a freezing chill in the air." [17]

Good nutrition did help some patients. Doctors at the Mayo clinic recommended the following recipe for arthritis:

3 grapefruit

3 oranges

3 lemons

Grind up in meat grinder, skins and all

3 tablespoons Epsom Salt

2 teaspoons Cream of Tarter

To this mixture add: one quart of water, boiled and cooled.

Put in refrigerator. Take one tablespoon before each meal.

Now it is known that Vitamin C is helpful; perhaps the high C content of the recipe brought about its success. It was popular for many years. [18]

In 1957 Dr. G. started the clinic at Wagon Mound at the request of the people because there was no doctor in the town of approximately 1,000 people. Dr. G. spent his spare time there, giving vaccinations, prenatal care, removing diseased tonsils, and doing whatever was called for. Dr. G. believes that a doctor should get to know his patients and their families. A family doctor should be just that, a doctor for the entire family. As a family physician for 60 years, Dr. G. is now in the fourth generation of patients. The baby he delivered in December of 1983 was the daughter of a woman he had brought into the world 22 years earlier, and it is entirely possible that he delivered her mother as well.

Many former tuberculosis patients come in for annual checkups, some traveling from distant states. One woman had not been in to see Dr. G. for several years. She was told by a young doctor in a distant city that she had lung cancer. His opinion had been based on the X-rays he had taken. She went to Dr. G., who had cared for her when she had TB forty years earlier. He took more X-rays and assured her that her lungs were healthy except for some old TB scar tissue. Apparently the younger doctor had not recognized it and had mistaken it for cancer.

Recently when a young lady met Dr. G. for the first time, she said, "I hear that you still make house calls."

"Of course," he replied. "If I didn't, who would take care of all these people who can't get out? They live on ranches long distances from town. I have to make house calls." He said that God had called him to do missionary work in the mountains of the west, and he would do his job as long as he possibly could.

Gellenthien studied comparative religion in school and realizes the importance of a person's faith. Although he was reared in a Lutheran home, Gellenthien became a member of the Episcopalian Church to which Alice belonged. Gellenthien has worked with people of all denominations and creeds. He served as doctor for the Montezuma Seminary for Roman Catholic Priests from Mexico for twenty-five years until it closed. Dr. G. had a patient who would not agree to surgery because of her religion. She had an ovarian cyst which Dr. G. had to drain at regular intervals. Finally the woman decided to have the surgery and a 35-pound cyst was removed. "But the decision had to be hers," he said.

Family members say, "When we go places with Carl, he always tells us who lived in what house, what they died of, and where they're buried." Indeed, there isn't much Dr. G. doesn't know about the past and present occupants of the houses in the Mora County area. It is a family doctor's prerogative to share a family's most intimate moments, the personal saga of birth, the ceremony of marriage, and the dramatic moment of death. Dr. G. never forgets a patient. And, like many doctors, he has come to think of them as his own personal charges. Even when they have gone on they do not seem far away. In the novel *Polly*, Dr. Maybright told his daughter:

> "You ask me not to speak of your mother, my dear; I certainly will
> mention her name to her children. She has gone away, but she is still
> one with us. Why should our dearest household word be buried? Why
> should not her influence reach you...where she now is? She is above
> — she has gone into the higher life, but she can lead you
> up...Thoughts of your mother must be your best, your noblest
> thoughts from this out." [19]

So it is natural that thoughts of patients, friends, associates, and loved ones who have gone on are often with the family doctor.

One of the most dramatic scenes in Thornton Wilder's *Our Town* is the visit of Dr. Gibbs to the cemetery. There is something about the town doctor's presence at the cemetery that grips the hearts of audiences everywhere.

Sometimes Dr. G., too, stops and visits the little mountain cemeteries and thinks of his past associations fondly. Driving along a little country road northeast of Valmora, Dr. G. pointed to the cliffs along the highway. There was the cave where one of his patients lived during the Depression. The man's wife had died, and he was out of work. He had two sons. There was nowhere to go, so he made a home out of the cave in the canyon wall. With a stove, a cot, and a chair or two, it became a comfortable home. The man worked when he could, but he would get bad asthma attacks. Then he would send his 12-year-old son for the doctor at Valmora. It was then that Gellenthein would make his house call at the cave. He had to climb half way up the steep canyon wall to reach the cavern where his patient's abode made a comfortable shelter from the elements. The man had very little, but he survived the Depression, probably better than some city folks who lived in less protected shacks. Now, driving past the cave site, Dr. G. wonders how he managed such a steep climb. When someone remarked that making a "house call" to a cave was an unusual experience for a doctor, he replied, "Country doctors have to be prepared for anything. You go where the people are. My patient lived in a cave — so I made house calls to his cave. I thought nothing unusual about it at the time."[20]

Beyond the cave Dr. G. drove until he came to a little country cemetery and stopped. He wondered if the man was buried there and what his boys were doing now. The last he had heard both were successful in their careers.

A tall man who had been standing at the far side of the cemetery wandered over and Dr. G. initiated a conversation. The man said he was visiting his father's grave. He had come to visit relatives from Albuquerque where he worked. Dr. G. said he knew the family well.

"Dr. G.!" the young man exclaimed. "You saved my grandfather's life." And then he told how his grandfather had been wasted away with TB. Cachexia left him weighing less than 100 pounds. "We used to carry him around," the man recalled, "helping him in and out of the house. He was so weak. I was afraid I'd catch TB from him. I even held my breath when I carried him. And then I developed a cough and I was scared. But it turned out to be nothing. It was all in my head." Under Dr. G.'s care the grandfather had lived a long and pleasant life after his TB was arrested. "You gave my grandfather many good years," the man said. "Well, I must be going. I just came to visit."

Gellenthien, too, just came to visit. If anyone has the right to visit the final resting place of a human being, surely it is the physician who nurtured the body and cherished the soul of the dying one. The solitude of the mountain cemetery is captured by S. Omar Barker, a New Mexican poet who expressed the deep respect and reverence for the dead that a country doctor often feels. He wrote in his poem, "Mountain Cemetery":

Pine trees grow there, God's own planting,
On a hillside gently slanting
To a little bench well hidden
From the gaze of eyes unbidden.

There the deer's step, light and quick,
Treads the green kinnikinnick
That comes leniently creeping
Where beloved dead lie sleeping.

There the bluejay's azure wing
Is a wild, familiar thing.
And green hills they loved the best
Guard good mountain-folk at rest. [21]

As a country doctor, Dr. G. has spent much time walking through the canyons and mesas of Valmora, praying for his patients, talking to The Boss about their problems, asking for guidance, petitioning Him for the patient's concerns. There was a physician at St. Luke's Hospital in Denver who inspired him when Dr. G. was an intern there, for this doctor would pray outside the patient's hospital room. "Never forget who the Great Physician is," he said.

The Great Healer did not always answer a request for healing with an affirmative response. Sometimes He allowed a sick person, even a young one, to die. One such individual was one of Valmora's special charges, Vera Martinez.

Marie Elvira Martinez, born January 19, 1940 graduated from West Las Vegas High School, attended Highlands University, and graduated from St. Vincent's Hospital School of Nursing. In 1959 she went to work for the man who had encouraged her and helped her climb the ladder of success — Dr. G. In 1963, while working at Valmora Clinic, she became ill. Acute lymphatic leukemia was diagnosed.

Dr. G. had given Vera a medical dictionary years before when he had encouraged her to attend nursing school. It was important to her that he have it back. She returned it before she died with an affectionate inscription of gratitude to Dr. G. She died on September 26, 1965 at the age of 25.

The country doctor could not always keep death away. And he wasn't always a scholar of theology or philosophy, a poet or a song writer. But he did his best to help his people in their lives and their deaths. And that set him on an equal footing with "Abou Ben

168

Adhem" in the poem about a man who told an angel, "Write me as one that loves his fellow men." [22]

NOTES

1. a pseudonym
2. Carl H. Gellenthien, interview at Valmora, October 17, 1983.
3. Paul Frank, interview at Santa Fe, New Mexico, September 20, 1981.
4. *Ibid.*
5. a pseudonym
6. Carl H. Gellenthien, interview at Valmora, October 15, 1983.
7. Carl H. Gellenthien, interview at Valmora, January 25, 1982.
8. *Ibid.*
9. *Ibid.*
10. "Swing Your Partner'—And Break a Leg," n.t., n.d., n.p., newspaper clipping in Scrapbook 2, Valmora Library, Valmora, New Mexico, p. 48.
11. H.M. Mortimer, M.D., interview in Albuquerque, New Mexico, April 12, 1981.
12. Carl H. Gellenthien, interview at Valmora, December 29, 1980.
13. Carl H. Gellenthien, personal interview, Valmora, March 18, 1982.
14. *Ibid.*
15. *Ibid.*
16. Carl H. Gellenthien, interview at Wagon Mound, New Mexico, January 17, 1982.
17. *Ibid.*
18. "Arthritis," unpublished mimeographed sheet in Scrapbook 3, Valmora Library, Valmora, New Mexico, p. 49.
19. L.T. Meade, *Polly: A New-Fashioned Girl* (Chicago: M.A. Donohue & Co., n.d.), pp. 41-42.
20. Carl H. Gellenthien, personal interview, June 10, 1982.
21. S. Omar Barker, "Mountain Cemetery," *Sunlight Through the Trees*, Las Vegas, New Mexico: Highlands University Press, 1954, p. 47.
22. James Henry Leigh Hunt, "Abou Ben Adhem," quoted in Ralph L. Woods, eds., *A Treasury of the Familiar* (N.Y.: The Macmillan Company, 1943), p. 41.

CHAPTER
X

My Doctor, The Teacher

One morning Dr. G. stopped to visit with a neighbor, an old-time cowboy who was repairing a fence along the road. News of the successful splitting of the atom had just broken.

"What do you think of them fellers splittin' the atom, Doc?"

"That's quite an accomplishment," Dr. G. replied.

"Well, Doc ain't an atom just a little bitty ol' thing?"

"That's for sure," Dr. G. replied.

"Doc, what I don't understand is how come it took so many fellers to split one little tiny thing like that?"

The cowboy was thinking of how easy it is to split a piece of wood with an ax. He'd split plenty of it to keep the wood stoves and fireplaces going the last few winters.

Dr. G. tried to explain, but the cowboy didn't think much of modern science.

"If it takes that many guys to split a teeny little thing like that they can't be very smart. I sure wouldn't hire the likes of them for hands on this spread."

His philosophy was something like another old timer in the 1930s. Dr. G. greeted him along the road one day and asked how things were going.

"Doc, the world's gittin' bummer and bummer," he replied.

Now, fifty years later, Dr. G. still remembers that expression.

The only way to keep the world from getting any "bummer" is to educate people, Dr. G. believes, and for fifty years he's been doing his part. Dr. G. has done much for education in northern New Mexico though he is not known as an educator. One reason he is a good teacher is because he has always been a good student. He was eager to learn from everyone he could.

In 1937 he worked at the Mayo Clinic in Rochester, Minnesota, learning from the most renowned physicians in the country. He worked side by side with his friend Charles "Chuck" Mayo, the son of the famous Charles Mayo who began the clinic. Dr. G. spent many pleasant hours at the Mayo home and learned a great deal from the senior Dr. Mayo as well as from Chuck. Whenever Chuck had an opportunity he would visit Dr. G. and enjoy the beautiful outdoors of the Sangre de Cristo mountains. And whenever Dr. G. was passing through Rochester he would stop by to say hello to Chuck. Once when he stopped in to visit, he found Mayo in surgery. Dr. G. stepped into the observation room where numerous other physicians were watching the famous Dr. Mayo operate. Mayo happened to glance up and saw Gellenthien behind the glass.

"Carl! When did you get into town!" Mayo exclaimed. "Come on down here!"

So Gellenthien quickly donned surgery garb and joined Mayo in surgery, leaving the surprised onlookers wondering who he was.

Though he operated with men like Dr. Mayo, Dr. G. was never above taking lessons from an obscure country doctor. A woman was having a very slow labor. Dr. G. was worried, so he called in the old doctor from Mora for assistance. The old man, who had a long, drooping mustache and smoked a corncob pipe, asked, "Did you whiff her?"

Dr. G. had no idea what he meant. But he didn't want to admit he had never learned such a technique at medical school. Not wanting to expose his ignorance, he simply said, "No, I didn't."

"Well, I'll do it," the older doctor said. He took the stem of his corncob pipe, put snuff into it, shoved it up the woman's right nostril, and blew into it. The woman sneezed and sneezed, and the baby came immediately. Thus, Dr. G. learned how to "whiff 'em." But he never did it. It worked, he admitted, but "it wasn't scientific."

Dr. G. continued to learn many techniques from men as distinguished as the Mayos or as unknown as the old Mora doctor. Dr. Ernest Irons, head of Rush Medical College, once gave Dr. G. some helpful advice. A patient came in with a common male complaint; he was worried about his virility. After Dr. G. had examined the man, the young doctor told the patient that he was fine and needed no treatment. He explained that there was nothing physiologically wrong and that no medication was needed. Dr. Irons advised Dr. Gellenthien not to send a patient away empty-handed. "He wants medicine. Give him some." The psychological effect of having received something from the doctor can often effect a cure or at least benefit the patient emotionally. Even if he offers only a vitamin capsule, the doctor can greatly encourage the patient. Ultimately, the individual may improve.

With a self-limiting ailment like the common cold, the patient will recover no matter how it is or is not treated. But medication may alleviate the symptoms and the patient often feels better and is better because of the psychological effect derived when medication is prescribed. Many doctors themselves take no medication for a cold. Dr. G. is one of them. "It doesn't do any good," he said, "because I know that nothing I take will help. I just have to wait it out."[1] Perhaps the disadvantage of being a doctor is that the psychological advantage of prescribed medicine is missing.

The advice Dr. G. recived from Dr. Irons has proven to be sound over the years. A 93-year-old man called Dr. G. for "some more of those wonderful pills you gave me." He said they had restored his virility and taken years off his age. They were nothing but hormone pills, yet the man believed in them so strongly that they helped.

"Are they really that good?" someone questioned.

"If they were, I'd take them myself," Dr. G. replied.

Dr. Irons was one of the best doctors of his time and taught the young students like Gellenthien invaluable lessons. His life ended tragically in Chicago, when he was walking home one afternoon, passed under a bridge, and was brutally attacked by a gang who robbed him and then stomped on him until his back was broken. They murdered one of the greatest minds of his time for one dollar and twenty-five cents.

Throughout the years Dr. G. learned from doctors of every walk of life — even the witch doctors in Haiti and the medicine men from the Indian reservations in the west. At an annual American Medical Association convention a proposal was under consideration a few years ago to resolve that members should have nothing to do with any doctor who was not a bona fide M.D. Dr. G. stood up and said that if the proposal passed he would have to stop associating with a good many of his practitioner friends — the medicine men on the Indian reservations. He didn't like that idea at all. The motion was not passed.

"The human mind is capable of tremendous power," he said, speaking of his experience in Haiti where he was sent by the AMA following the devastation of Hurricane Hazel. As Vice-President of the AMA, he was sent as a representative to four islands: Jamaica, Puerto Rico, Haiti and the Dominican Republic. There he attended meetings of the medical societies and was able to oversee the emergency care given to the disaster victims. He witnessed some of the voodoo ceremonies in Haiti and spoke with the witch doctors. They have tremendous power, he said, and most of it comes from suggestion, hypnotic power over the mind. Medical science has discovered that when someone dies as a result of a "curse" from a witch, he has actually been "scared to death." The victim dies of cardiac arrest at the time suggested. Actually, he simply "wills" himself to die, giving in to the suggestion.

Gellenthien never ceased to be amazed at the power of the mind. He once had a case of pseudocyesis, false pregnancy. The pseudo-pregnancy occurred in a young, single girl. One weekend before Christmas she discovered herself penniless. Being "broke" before Christmas was so unpleasant that when a man offered her $25.00 to spend the night with him, she did. The next morning she was sure that she was pregnant. Later she went to a midwife. She looked pregnant and had all the signs of pregnancy: morning sickness, enlarging breasts, nipples darkening, belly swelling, and cessation of menstruation. She said that she felt the baby kicking, too. But after 11 months, the midwife sent the girl to Dr. G. He could not hear the fetal heartbeat or detect any movement. He took X-rays and couldn't see a fetal skeleton. (Usually it can be seen at 18 weeks.) Gellenthien told the girl that he could only conclude that she wasn't pregnant. She was relieved. She began to squelch the town gossip with the news that she wasn't pregnant. She lost 30 pounds within a few days. Apparently, it was all water. Her guilty conscience had convinced her she was pregnant until Dr. G. persuaded her that she was not.

Dr. G. learned a new technique for controlling nose bleeds from a colleague in Florida at an AMA meeting. Usually when packing is necessary, a problem occurs when the plug is pulled out. The clot comes with it, and the nose starts hemorrhaging again. The colleague's advice was to enclose the pack in a rubber condom before inserting it. Then, when it is pulled out, the clot won't tear loose and bleeding won't re-occur. The next time a patient came in with a severe nose bleed, Dr. G. decided to try it. The method worked better than anything he had ever tried before.

"What's that?" the man asked, after the condom was removed.

When Dr. G. told him, the patient exclaimed, "You mean I've been sitting around here with a damned rubber up my nose?"

After Dr. G. explained, the patient was satisfied. Now the doctor carries the condoms in his bag labeled "nasal tamponades."

Besides his colleagues, Dr. G. has had many other good teachers. Will Rogers gave him advice on how to talk on the radio. Gellenthien was going to give a talk on climate and tuberculosis at the WGN Radio Station in Chicago. Rogers, a member of the Los Rancheros Visitadores to which Dr. Brown belonged, came to Valmora to visit his Rancheros friend. Dr. G. had been practicing his speech, timing it to the exact 15 minutes allotted. Everyone in the house was sick of the speech, so Gellenthien was banished to the bathroom for his rehearsals. When he came out to take a break, he saw Dr. Brown and Will Rogers standing in front of the big stone fireplace, visiting.

"I hear you're gonna make a speech, young fellow," Rogers drawled.

"Yes, that's right," Gellenthien replied.

"I 'spose you're practicin' so you ken give a good talk to the untold thousands in your radio audience?"

"Yes," Gellenthien replied.

"Want some advice young man? Forget about the multitudes out there in radio land."

"What?"

"Just talk to Doc Brown and me," he said softly. "Just like we're doin' now."

So when Dr. G. went in the radio studio made famous by the Amos and Andy show, he kept Rogers' advice in mind. He'd try to talk as if he were simply conversing with friends in his own home.

The studio was a very small room with peg board walls and ceiling, a bare table, two chairs, a radio on the wall, a speaker and a microphone. The announcer seated him, gave the signal to begin after announcing him, and quietly left the room. As Dr. G. spoke, his words seemed to be falling right back in his lap. Was anyone hearing him at all? His voice was reflected back at him so loudly he couldn't believe it was leaving the room. His Rancheros friends were always playing jokes on each other; perhaps they had set him up for a practical joke. He continued to talk, however, following Rogers' advice of speaking intimately into the microphone in a friendly, matter-of-fact manner. Then phone calls started coming with questions and comments. Dr. G. knew his voice had gone out over the air after all.

He has since given dozens of radio talks, TV presentations, and lectures. He always maintained the conversational manner audiences like so well. When he spoke to the United Nations in New York as Chairman of the Board of the National Tuberculosis Association, he was as poised and confident as he was when speaking to the Rotary Club at home. It was Will Rogers who inspired that confidence.

Two other successful speakers also inspired Gellenthien. One was The Most Reverend Fulton J. Sheen who had a weekly TV program, "Life is Worth Living." The other was evangelist Billy Graham whose speeches have been heard in person by more people than any other person in the world. Both men had charisma that made them dynamic speakers, but Dr. G. felt that Sheen was a better speaker when facing small groups and Graham was more appealing before large audiences.

Gellenthein was also inspired by other great speakers and evangelists such as Billy Sunday whose revivals he attended and Aimee Semple McPherson, the famous evangelist who founded the Angeles Temple in Los Angeles and inspired the Foresquare Gospel Church. Gellenthien attended one of her meetings and went forward when the invitation was given.

Dr. G. once matched wits in a verbal battle with Eleanor Roosevelt over socialized medicine and Communism. Mrs. Roosevelt tried to deny that socialized medicine was communistic. Gellenthein replied, "When you see something walking down the path that looks like a duck, quacks like a duck, waddles like a duck and associates with other ducks, you have to conclude that it *is* a duck!"

The doctor argued and discussed politics with local hometown folks as enthusiastically as he did with his friends in high places. He was friend of both Ernie Thwaites who owned and operated KFUN Radio Station in Las Vegas and Walter Vivian, Chief Editor of the *Las Vegas Daily Optic*. Dr. G. was Vivian's personal physician. The two men, Thwaites and Vivian, were vigorous rivals, each trying to scoop the other on local news. It was good healthy, friendly competition that kept the citizens informed of local news. The editorials of both men were stimulating and informative. Sometimes the two agreed on the issues. Other times they were staunch opponents. Both had a great deal of influence on the town.

One controversy raged after World War II when Camp Luna, where soldiers had been stationed, closed down. A proposed military base was presented. The merchants were in favor of it, as they felt it would bring in more business to Las Vegas. But others felt that a permanent base of 20,000 soldiers in a town that supported only 10,000 citizens, was unreasonable. Thwaites argued against it. Citizens presented a petition opposing it, and the base did not materialize.

Another friend of the Las Vegas area and of Dr. Gellenthien was Lloyd Bible whose flying service was of vital importance to community life in and around Las Vegas. Bible flew Dr. G. and his patients all around the country. One winter a severe snowstorm left many ranchers stranded. Bible and Gellenthien flew over their homes dropping food and medicines to them.

During the Eisenhower administration, someone had the idea of saving energy by shutting off airport lights until needed for a landing. Sometimes a pilot would radio that he was coming in, but the lights failed to come on. The night crew working at a small local airport was not always as efficient as the air controller staff in a large, metropolitan area. Thus, if no one was on duty, Bible would sometimes have to land his plane in the dark. He kept a supply of flares on hand and would throw a couple of them down in order to see the landing strip. On one occasion, Dr. G. and Alice were flying into Las Vegas when Bible's request for lights on the landing strip received no response. Bible landed in the dark. Alice decided she didn't want to fly again. Even in later years when the airport lights were again left on at night, Alice seldom accompanied her husband on his flights.

But flying never bothered Dr. G. Even the roughest flights failed to upset him. He could get seasick "just looking at a boat." But air flight never made him sick. Perhaps one reason was because he grew up with the airplane. As a youth he flew the very first planes with the single propeller, the biplane with the open cockpit. He and a friend started a flying business in 1919, taking people over the city for a small price. Dressed in high-topped boots and wearing goggles, they enjoyed "barnstorming." They had to guard the plane when it was at rest because cows in the field would chew up the wings, being attracted to the fabric which was polished with banana oil. Gellenthien's partner crashed and hung up in some power lines one day. The youth was not hurt, but that was the end of their flying business. The plane was not salvageable.

As Dr. G. began to fly more and more frequently on business, Bible taught him how to fly his plane in case of emergency. Dr. G. never had to fly the plane but was grateful for the lessons.

Having been a good student under so many able tutors, Dr. G. was an excellent teacher. He fought against ignorance as much as he fought against diseases.

Father Robert Beach of Wagon Mound said, "Knowledge is power, and to know is to prevent." He and Dr. G. believed that the youth of the area needed a program of sex education. The two friends decided to coordinate an effort to teach the community youth. Father Beach told Dr. G., "You teach them about their bodies. I'll teach them about sin, religion and morals. You don't know anything about that."[2] Although the two friends joked with one another, their ideas initiated one of the best programs in learning ever offered in the community. In a follow-up study of about 200 girls in the area, not one was found to have become pregnant before marriage, not one had contracted a venereal disease, and there had been no divorces as of that time.[3]

Dr. G.'s battle against ignorance was not always easy. One woman came to Dr. G. for a simple medical problem and he discovered that she was wearing diapers. When she had given birth a

176

few years earlier, she had not been cared for properly. The delivery had resulted in a torn rectum and it had not been repaired afterwards. The woman was surprised when Dr. G. told her that simple surgery would correct the problem. She had supposed that all women were that way after having a baby.

One young patient told Dr. G. she didn't know how she had become pregnant. She had been riding her horse near a home when someone threw some dishwater out the door, startling her horse. The girl was thrown off into some rocks. She supposed the trauma of the fall had caused her pregnancy.

A man from Rociada had an emergency appendectomy. Dr. G. preserved the appendix in a jar of alcohol and gave it to him afterwards. The patient told his friends he had swallowed a fishing worm years before and was glad the doctor had removed it. He would then show the "worm" in the bottle as proof.

One young woman came in to find out if she was pregnant. In those days a frog test was the most reliable pregnancy test. An isolated female frog was injected with the woman's blood or urine. If the frog laid eggs after that, the woman was pregnant. Dr. G. told the woman he couldn't determine whether she was pregnant and suggested the use of the frog test to find out. The woman said she would have to discuss it with her husband and went out to confer with him. After a few minutes she returned and said, "Oh, Doctor, I just don't think I could stand having that frog in there."

Each time a patient displayed a lack of knowledge, Dr. G. patiently explained the facts.

Dr. G. wrote out a prescription for a patient and was surprised to discover later that the patient wore the paper around his neck. He reported back later that it had worked. He felt much better. But now he needed Dr. G. to write out another one. He had lost the first one.

And there was a patient who did not understand the role of X-ray in diagnosis. He thought it was for treatment. He came back a few months after his first X-ray requesting another "treatment" because that X-ray had made him feel so much better.

Once Dr. G. sent a nurse out to see a pregnant woman in a small village. She was to try to ascertain information from the woman for Dr. G.'s records. The nurse questioned the unmarried woman and asked if she would reveal the name of the child's father. The village woman replied that she did not know. The nurse found this answer unacceptable and continued to question her.

"Don't you know who the father is? Surely you know his name?"

"No, I never got his name," the patient declared.

"Well, then, what does he look like?" the nurse persisted.

"I don't know," the woman replied. "It was hard to see his face. He just came by the house one night, and it was too dark to see."

"Well, can't you describe him at all?" the nurse asked. "What color was his hair?"

"I don't know. He didn't take off his hat."

At that point the nurse gave up.

Patients like these became Dr. G.'s students at every opportunity. In his office he has a small library containing books with pictures and illustrations which he uses as teaching aids. Dr. G. relies heavily on visual aids, not only because some of his patients can't read, but because "a picture is worth a thousand words." He has plastic models with moveable parts. He also has a human skeleton in the X-ray reading room that serves as an excellent visual aid.

To be a good student, teacher, or doctor, one must first be a good observer. In the old days doctors relied on all their senses. They knew the smell of measles or diphtheria. Once at a party, Dr. G. told a close friend, "That man over there has cancer." The friend asked Dr. G. how he knew. "I can *smell* it," he replied. Not long afterwards the man did succumb to cancer.

Another time a grandmother was sitting in Dr. G.'s office holding a grandchild in her arms. As Dr. G. conversed with the woman, he noticed the baby's face. One side of it was smooth, having no creases. Dr. G. asked if the baby's face had always been like that. She replied that it had not. The child was coming down with polio. Dr. G. initiated immediate treatment with success. The child grew up with no residual deformities or paralysis.

"Today doctors are too dependent on their machines and don't spend enough time with the patient," Dr. G. said. "The problem is that between the doctor and the patient are the machines, the paperwork, and many individuals: X-ray technicians, aides, paramedics and the entire hospital staff. The patient may become just another number."[4]

Dr. G. knows what it is like to be a patient. Besides his illness from tuberculosis, he spent a few days in the hospital in Waukegan as a youth after he and some of the other YMCA boys came down with gastro-intestinal trouble. Additionally, Gellenthien has had surgery four times. Early in his career at Valmora he had an attack of appendicitis. The Las Vegas surgeon, Dr. Franklin H. Crail, was out of town, so the surgeon from Raton removed his appendix at the Las Vegas Hospital. At that time the hospital was located in the old YMCA building which at the present writing is a clothing store.

Later, after prolonged coughing from his TB, Dr. G. had to have a hemorrhoidectomy and rectal repair as the violent coughing had literally torn him apart internally. This was done at the Mayo Clinic. As he was about to be anesthetized, Dr. G. heard the surgeon comment to a group of student onlookers: "See how people neglect themselves? This man's a doctor and he's got repair work that should have been taken care of a long time ago!"

Dr. G.'s most recent surgery was the removal of his gall bladder following an attack caused by gallstones. Again the work was done at the Las Vegas Hospital. This time as he was going under the anesthesia Dr. G. heard one of the surgeons comment that surgery at Dr. G.'s age was difficult but "he's a tough old bastard!" Several years later a patient called Dr. G. wanting to know if the surgeons in Las Vegas were any good. "Well, they took out my gall bladder and I'm doing all right," he replied. The patient said that recommendation was good enough for him.

Dr. G.'s most severe ordeal occurred when he had an enlarged prostate and nearly died from complications after surgery. He was in intensive care at the Mayo Clinic for weeks. He had to have numerous blood transfusions. And then, to make matters worse, he developed hepatitis as a result of one of the transfusions. His family was told that he would probably die. But Gellenthien recuperated and was finally able to leave the Clinic. He wanted to thank the surgeon who had performed his operation. But that was impossible. The man had dropped dead of a heart attack the day after the surgery.

With all his hospital experiences as a patient, Dr. G. can appreciate what his patients go through. Bishop Sheen said that he always recommeded that nurses and doctors have two things: an incision and a sense of humor. The incision is "in order that they may have a sense of pain; the sense of humor in order that they may bring joy to their faces."[5] Dr. G. has had both in sufficient quantities.

A patient who was admitted to Valmora in the early days was quite agitated after Dr. G. came into his hospital room and gave him the results of the initial tests, explaining the extent of his illness. The patient was of Italian descent, a member of a wealthy Chicago family. He couldn't accept the fact that he had tuberculosis and would have to remain at the sanatorium until his disease was arrested.

"Why me — a good, upstanding Italian citizen? A good Catholic? Why me?"

Dr. G. explained, "Anyone can get tuberculosis. It happens to the best families, the most upstanding citizens."

"It's easy for you to talk," the man said. "You're the doctor."

"And I, too, have tuberculosis," Dr. G. replied. "The only difference between you and me is that mine is apparently cured. And as soon as you follow the prescribed regimen here at Valmora, you undoubtedly will be also." Before long the patient returned home in good health.

Dr. G. believes that a good doctor will listen to the patient and take a thorough history. It is the history that "draws the picture" of the patient's needs. Dr. G. advises student doctors:

> Listen to the patient. He's telling you the diagnosis. Eighty-five percent of the time if you take a thorough history and do a physical examination, you will be able to make a correct diagnosis. A doctor should do tests to confirm what he thinks he knows. But nowadays too many do the reverse — they do the tests first and then decide on the diagnosis. The tests should simply confirm what you already know — or else prove you're wrong, and then you must start all over again. [6]

Observing patients has been an important part of Dr. G.'s career. He had a two-way mirror installed in his office so he could view patients in the waiting room. The two-way mirror was decided upon after a woman in the waiting room collapsed. The nurse saw her on the floor and called Dr. G. who was in his private office with another patient. The woman in the waiting room had gone into labor. Dr. G. and the nurse wheeled her into the operating room and delivered her baby. Dr. G. decided he should have some way of knowing what was going on in the waiting room. The window also gave him a chance to observe children in their natural, uninhibited behavior.

"You can tell a lot by the way they walk or sit when they don't know they're being watched," he said.

It also helped him identify malingerers. Some people will fake an injury in order to get a doctor to certify that they are disabled and they can then collect government money. They often put on a good act, limping around and groaning. But when they don't realize they are being watched, they show no signs of impairment.

One patient came in for the first time and said, "Doctor, do you disable your patients?"

"Not if I can help it!" he replied.

In an unusual switch, however, Dr. G. recently got a note from a social worker "putting words in my mouth." [7] She had written out a statement for him to sign, stating that the patient was malingering and did not need financial help because he was not disabled. Dr. G. had not seen the patient for a while, so he made a house call the next day. He found that the patient was still in need of help with a disabling condition, and he refused to sign the social worker's statement.

Dr. G. drives approximately 176 miles each Friday to attend medical seminars at St. Vincent Hospital in Santa Fe. He sometimes sees patients at the same time. Recently when he went on rounds with some residents, one of Dr. G's patients hugged him in gratitude. Afterwards, Dr. G. remarked that if his patients could express their gratitude in money, he'd be rich. But his patients have always been poor. One of the residents turned to him and said solemnly, "You *are* rich, Doctor."

Dr. G. is highly motivated to keep learning and seldom misses the weekly seminar. It not only gives him an opportunity to keep up with new developments in medicine but also presents the intellectual stimulation he needs.

Sometimes Dr. G.'s experiences as a tuberculosis specialist enlightens the younger generation of doctors who are not familiar with the disease. One patient was suspected of having a tumor of the lung until Dr. G. pointed out that the spot on the X-ray was simply a "coin" or lesion from the old TB the patient had had years ago. When the fight against the tubercle bacilli begins in the lungs, the body builds tubercles around the site. This develops into scar tissue which hardens, and calcium deposits then collect. These show, of course, on the X-ray.

Dr. G. has a little bottle in his office containing fragments of such calcium deposits, called calcified lesions, that he coughed up at various times during his own illness. Usually when these were coughed up, they were accompanied by pain, blood and fear. Sometimes severe hemorrhaging resulted. In the old days the expression "to throw a ruby" meant to cough up blood. Dr. G. threw many rubies, as did his fellow patients. His own X-rays show many of the old lesions. Comparison of his 1924 and his 1968 X-rays reveals the body's miraculous healing ability. The first X-ray is riddled with destructive cavities. The last one shows healthy, though scarred, lung tissue.

Before research found smoking to be a hazard to the health, Dr. G. always had a cigar in his hand. Dr. G. admitted he did not especially like cigars. But he thought that holding a cigar proved he "wasn't a weakling." No consumptive would dare smoke, so carrying a cigar "proved" he was healthy and robust. Thus, the cigar became Dr. G.'s "trademark."

"Actually, it was a childish thing to do," Dr. G. admits. "When I grew up, I quit. I was 65 years old at the time."[8]

Sometimes fate has a way of surprising everyone. A neighbor was standing up on a roof when he happened to touch an electrical wire. The live wire stopped his heart instantly. He fell from the roof, but when he hit the ground, the impact started his heart again. The current burned through his chest and lungs, but he regained consciousness. Dr. G. drove him to the hospital. On the way he asked Dr.

G. if he might have one of his cigars. After surviving such an ordeal, Dr. G. thought he should have one. The man smoked the cigar all the way to the hospital and made a full recovery.

Gellenthien took pride in teaching his own two children as much as he could, giving them practical lessons in country and city living. He took them on many trips and exposed them to as many varied experiences as possible. Sometimes the lessons were painful. When Bill insisted on climbing a tree, his father warned him that he would fall. The branches were not strong enough to hold the boy's weight; it was only a small tree. But Bill insisted that he could climb it. Dr. G. allowed his son to go ahead so that the boy could learn for himself. The fragile branch gave way, and Bill did fall. But he also learned an important lesson in physics, a lesson about weight and balance and gravity. Dr. G. knew his son would not be hurt, for the distance was short and the grass beneath the tree was soft. But Bill remembered the lesson.

Another painful lesson occurred on Christmas Eve when the children were teenagers. One of Dr. G.'s nurses had committed suicide. Her family had driven into Las Vegas to make the funeral arrangements and were on their way back to the village near Valmora when a tire blew out. The State Police called Dr. G. about 8:00 in the evening. The Gellenthiens were just ready to begin their traditional Christmas Eve celebration. Dr. G. decided to let the teenagers come along with him to the accident site so they could see for themselves the results of highway mishaps.

Editha had never known her father could drive so fast. "He didn't drive — he flew," she said.[9] It was one of those rare emergencies where seconds could make the difference between life and death if someone were bleeding to death on the highway.

A few minutes after seeing the mangled bodies on the highway, Editha remembered she had been talking with these very people that morning when they had stopped by to see the doctor after receiving news of the suicide. Editha had met them in the yard and had gone into her father's office to get him. Now those very people were sprawled on the ground; some were moaning. Two were dead, two were dying, and two were in critical condition but survived because they received prompt medical care. The impression of that accident stayed with Editha. It taught her to be careful on the highway. But it also taught her the tragedy of suicide. The nurse not only destroyed her own life and brought grief to her relatives; she indirectly caused the deaths of those who cared about her most, for if she had not died they would not have been out on the highway that Christmas Eve.

Dr. G. tried to protect his children while at the same time exposing them to experiences that would help them grow. They were protected from patients with contagious diseases and were not allowed in the hospital where they might get TB. In fact, they were so well protected in Valmora's isolated environment that they never contracted the usual childhood diseases. Editha went through them with her own children as an adult. But she and Bill were carefully nurtured. Their physical growth was monitored by their caring father who checked them periodically to detect signs of TB or other illnesses. And their mental growth was nourished by the best tutors and teachers available.

In addition to teaching his children whenever possible and instructing his patients when the opportunties arose, Dr. G. spent time teaching student doctors and nurses who worked with him throughout the years. When a young man like Dr. Lyman came to Valmora to complete a residency requirement, Dr. G. taught him as much as he could. In later years he taught other young doctors such as his protégé, Robert Smith. Much of Dr. G.'s time was spent helping TB patients teach themselves new skills in an effort to adjust to a new lifestyle.

Dr. G. was a patient teacher. But there was a point where his forebearance ended — when a person's life was at stake. When a responsible adult failed to consider the patient's welfare and put a life in jeopardy because of carelessness, incompetence, apathy, or selfish inconsideration, Dr. G. drew the line. Such was the case when a nurse did what was called "the sink test."

Dr. G. had a patient in serious condition with a failing kidney. He had to make a crucial decision as to whether it should be removed. The results of the urinalysis would be the decisive factor. Dr. G. found his nurse in the laboratory and told her that the results of this test were critical because a decision about surgery would then be determined. The nurse was in a hurry to go off duty, however, and she poured the specimen down the sink. Then she quickly falsified the report, writing in normal readings. When Dr. G. saw the report, he recognized it as false. He fired the nurse on the spot. She left Valmora the same day, never to return, banished because she had intentionally gambled with a patient's life. Such actions were strictly forbidden. When the urinalysis was repeated, surgery was indicated. The kidney was removed and the patient recovered.

The Hippocratic Oath stresses the importance of teaching those who wish to learn. Many young doctors and nurses found a mentor in Dr. G. and many grateful patients found him an able tutor. His own family depended on him as a caring guide. Dr. G. has upheld that Oath for over 57 years: "... to consider dear to me as my parents him who taught me this art...to look upon his children as my own brothers, to teach them this art if they so desire."[10]

NOTES

1. Carl H. Gellenthien, personal interview, Valmora, January 17, 1982.
2. *Ibid.*
3. *Ibid.*
4. Carl H. Gellenthien, personal interview, December 29, 1980.
5. Fulton J. Sheen, *op. cit.,* pp. 26-27.
6. Carl H. Gellenthien, personal interview, Valmora, September 5, 1981.
7. *Ibid.*
8. Carl H. Gellenthien, interview at Valmora, October 15, 1983.
9. Editha Bartley, interview at Gascon Ranch, June 10, 1982.
10. "the Oath of Hippocrates," *Hippocrates: Ancient Medicine and Other Treatises,* n.p., n.d., p. 1.

CHAPTER
XI

Saints, Sinners, and Consumption

Young Dr. Gellenthien climbed the stairs to make his usual morning rounds at Valmora Hospital. He wanted to see the new arrival from Chicago. He liked to meet newcomers as soon as they got settled.

When he opened the door of the room the man in bed moved like a startled cat. His hand shot under the pillow and he drew out a gun in a flash.

Dr. G. froze to the spot in the doorway.

"I'm the doctor," he said evenly.

The man relaxed and put the automatic back under his pillow.

"Sorry, Doc. Habit. I get jumpy in a new place."

The patient was Nick Rindoni.[1] He was Al Capone's first lieutenant. When he broke down with tuberculosis he was sent to Valmora for the cure because of its good reputation and high cure rate. He, as well as Capone's niece and aunt, came to Valmora to "chase the cure." All three recovered. Dr. G. wondered what would have happened to him if one of them had died.

After Rindoni recovered his health, Gellenthien was given an elaborate dinner by the Capone gang. He was entertained at the Congress Hotel. Everything was on the house. There was only one problem.

Capone had been known to say, "When a guy don't fall for a broad, he's through." If any of his boys failed to respond with less than expected enthusiasm for the girls, the fellow would be booted out.[2] Gellenthien was expected to accept Capone's hospitality in taking the girls from the house for his personal entertainment. He knew he would lose the good graces of his host who so generously provided them if he did not comply. He feared offending his hot-tempered friends. But he feared venereal disease even more and wanted no part of their form of entertainment.

As soon as Gellenthien got to his room and began to unpack, a pretty girl came to the door. She had been sent to accommodate his every wish. It was then that Dr. G. solved his dilemma.

Gellenthien invited the girl in and asked her how much she usually made for her visits.

"Ten dollars, Doc, but this is strictly on the house. Capone's orders."

Gellenthein proceeded to explain that he was in love with his wife and could not be untrue to her. He persuaded the girl to go away and simply pretend they'd had a good time together. He paid her ten dollars to go and leave him alone.

"Doc, you're crazy, but if you love your wife that much you must have a marriage made in heaven," she said, took the money and left.

Gellenthien heard her bragging in the hall about the good time she'd had, telling the guards that the Doc was O.K.

Gellenthien sighed with relief. His plan had worked. He shuddered when he thought of a woman he'd seen once waiting for the "L". Syphilis had eaten away at her face, eroding a once lovely countenance. An ugly, gaping orifice had replaced her nose.

While he was taking a bath, Dr. G. was startled to see another pretty girl come into the room. He quickly dressed and told her the same thing he'd told the first girl, gave her ten dollars, and asked her to leave. Again, he was relieved to hear the girl telling the guards what a great time she'd had. The vision of Capone's wrath was bone-chilling. But so far the plan had worked.

Then, after dinner, an even more gorgeous girl was sent to his room. Again, the doctor gave her ten dollars to leave. Late that night when Dr. G. was sound asleep, someone again knocked at his door. It was another beautiful girl. And he was out another ten dollars.

Altogether he lost forty or fifty dollars just to get the girls to leave him alone. He was the talk of the gang because the girls bragged vociferously. Gellenthien later tried to tell some of his buddies about the incident, but none of them would believe him. They didn't understand his fear of venereal disease and his desire to remain faithful to Alice. Gellenthein's quick thinking and persuasive manner kept the girls happy, the gangsters congenial and himself in their good graces.

"The boys may not believe it, but that's how I got along with Al Capone and his gang," Gellenthein declared.

Indeed, they were grateful to him for the good care given their people at Valmora. When Nick Rindoni left Valmora he gave Dr. G. his 38 automatic which he'd kept under his pillow for the duration of his stay. He was grateful to Dr. G. for his recovered health and it was the best token of gratitude he could offer.

The gangsters respected Dr. G. because of his medical expertise and because the doctor never judged his patients. His interest in them was simply that of a physician concerned about sick people, about his patient. They were grateful to him for taking in their sick, regardless of their reputations. He treated everyone the same no matter who they were or what they had done.

Throughout his career, Dr. G. got to know many celebrities including Jean Harlow, Carol Lombard, and Greta Garbo. He traveled all over New Mexico with Greer Garson in the American Cancer Society's drive. And he and Marlene Dietrich won the prize for the best waltzing couple on the floor one night at the Pennsylvania Hotel in New York.

Gellenthien was introduced to Arthur Schnabel, the famous pianist and composer. During World War II when his native Austria was under siege, he came to Gascon Ranch. He was given a summer haven there to relax and compose. In his haste to flee the Nazis, he had buried some of his manuscripts in his garden at home to keep them from being destroyed. After the war he went back and dug them up. They were still intact. Once Dr. G. was driving Schnabel and several of his musician friends — including Paul Hindemith and Victor Babin — to the ranch. It was raining hard and Dr. G. was worried about the unpaved road. But his friends were chatting "shop talk" and paid no attention to the mud and water in the road. Finally the water got so high it came up over the running board and into the car. There were several inches of water on the floor. Dr. G. was disconcerted, but the musicians were so busy talking they never noticed. "They were sitting in water and didn't know it," Dr. G. recalled. [3]

Gellenthien also knew Wernher von Braun, the German-born American rocket engineer. He had invented the rocket in Germany and then fled to America after he saw Hitler's insanity. He became an American citizen and contributed much to scientific knowledge.

Gellenthien described him as an austere man with the attitude, "Ich bin er Herr" — I am the master.

As Gellenthien came to know people in all walks of life, he learned how true it is that disease is no respecter of persons. It struck the most promient and respected as well as the pariahs of society.

One of the greatest acts of Christian charity Dr. G. ever witnessed was brought about through the kindness of a group of prostitutes in Chicago. One Sunday when Dr. G. was making his routine examinations at the clinic, a young girl burst into tears. It was discovered that she had been forced into prostitution out of desperation. She had left her Iowa farm for the glitter of city living only to find out that she had to hit the streets to survive. The other women in the clinic didn't realize her plight until she began to cry and her story came out. The women gave her a change of clothing and enough money for a bus ticket back to her hometown. One of them said, "If we ever see your face in this city again, we'll tan your hide."

Dr. G. never tried to reform anyone. He believed in accepting people just as they were. One time he did help a nurse overcome her addiction to morphine, however.

The tremendous power of the mind, already illustrated in the false pregnancy case mentioned earlier, was again demonstrated in the case of this addict referred to herein as Catherine. When Dr. G. discovered that Catherine was an addict, he did not want to fire her or turn her over to the authorities. He wanted to help her. He decided to try a bold experiment, perhaps the most astounding one he ever conducted.

The morphine came in small white tablets which were easily accessible to Catherine in the office. She would take one and dissolve it in a teaspoon of water, heating it over a flame. Then she would fill a syringe with the liquid and inject herself. The nurse did not suspect that anyone knew she was addicted.

Dr. G. replaced the tablets with identical tablets which were actually harmelss sugar pills. Catherine continued to dissolve the tablets and inject herself. Dr. G. watched her every move and knew she had no other source of morphine. Yet she continued to experience the effects of the "morphine" which she was getting from the office, the drug she believed she had to have.

About two years later, Dr. G. decided to tell her that she was no longer an addict. She couldn't be. She had been off of morphine and taking the harmless placebos for two years. At last Dr. G. took Catherine aside and told her what was really in the bottle she had been using.

"You've had absolutely no morphine for two years," he told her. He expected her to be overjoyed at the news that she was no longer an addict. "You're not an addict any more. You've been taking placebos — sugar pills."

To Dr. G.'s surprise, Catherine proceeded to go through withdrawal symptoms. The physical withdrawal came, not when the injections of morphine actually ceased, but only when Catherine's mind registered the news that she had no morphine to take and had not had any for two years. The physical withdrawal was just as real as that experienced by any addict deprived of morphine. She went through a miserable period of time before she was finally free mentally as well as physically.

Afterwards she was grateful to Dr. G. for helping to free her. She married an orthopedic surgeon and moved to a city where she continued to work as a successful nurse. If Dr. G. had not intervened, her addiction might have destroyed her. If he had fired her or turned her in, she would not have been able to continue her career. Dr. G. was glad he had undertaken the experiment. But he never ceased to be amazed. He was never able to explain why she reacted as she did except to underscore the tremendous power of the mind.

There were no family or marriage counselors in the early days, so people turned to the family doctor for advice. Much of Dr. G.'s counseling involved helping people deal with guilt feelings. Sudden Infant Death Syndrome was one of the most difficult problems to deal with. One woman near Valmora thought she had rolled on her baby and smothered him as he slept next to her. Another woman thought the plastic cover on the crib had choked her baby. These women were overwhelmed with guilt and grief, blaming themselves. It took time and patience to help them realize the truth. Often people needed counseling after amputations for they sometimes felt mutilated, inadequate, and helpless.

In addition to his practice at Valmora, Dr. G. was kept busy serving on the staffs of the Colfax Memorial Hospital at Springer, St. Anthony's Hospital in Las Vegas, and the Las Vegas Hospital. He also served at the Wagon Mound Clinic. Dr. G. traveled all over the state as a consultant, as well. He made frequent trips to the State Tuberculosis Sanatorium in Socorro, to the sanatorium at Fort Stanton, located 4 miles southeast of Capitan, to the sanatorium at Fort Bayard, 10 miles east of Silver City, and to Bruns Army Hospital located in Santa Fe. Additionally, he was attending physician for the Montezuma Seminary, located 6 miles northwest of Las Vegas, from 1945 to 1975. It was established after the Catholic Church's seminaries were closed down by the Mexican Government. When the government changed its policy in the 1970s, the young men could again train for the priesthood in their own country, and the Seminary subsequently closed.

Gellenthien encouraged the young priests to complete their education. Some of them had tuberculosis and he treated them there. None were sent home.

"There were so many of them — the young men I knew who became priests, and each of them invited me to come to visit his church in Mexico. I promised each that if I ever went to Mexico, I would. Now, how can I visit Mexico? If I go, I'll have to spend all my time in church!" he joked. [4]

Dr. G. cared for many men of the cloth, both Protestant and Catholic. Father Edward Bryne, Chaplain at St. Vincent Hospital for many years, stated that TB is now the least of his worries. He and his brother, also a priest, both "took the cure" under Dr. G.'s guidance years ago. Men such as Harold Walters, the Methodist minister from Bloomington, Illinois, remained life-long friends after leaving Valmora.

John Ransdell, a Southern Baptist minister, was a patient whose fascinating story has been written up in *Promises Kept* by Bonnie Ball O'Brien. In February of 1944, Ransdell and his wife Marguerite moved from Kentucky to New Mexico after he had been bedridden with TB for 4 years. When he arrived in Las Vegas, Ransdell was too weak to stand or to walk. The day after he arrived, he phoned Dr. Gellenthien, stating that he would take a taxi out to the hospital. Gellenthien laughed; the hospital was over twenty miles from Las Vegas. He ordered Ransdell to stay where he was. The doctor would come and see him. He brought his pneumothorax machine along and administered the treatment where air was forced into the patient's side via a tube, causing the ailing lung to rest. [5]

Gellenthien was an expert at performing the difficult technique. He had, in fact, invented the particular pneumothorax machine being used at that time. Dr. G. had administered the treatment to hundreds of patients and he never lost one. Some of the most renowned chest physicians of the time could not say as much. It was a dangerous procedure because the needle had to be inserted into an exact spot, not too close to the surface or else the procedure would be useless, and not too deep, or serious damage, even death, would result. If air got into a blood vessel, the patient could die within seconds as an air embolism traveled to the heart. Only once did Dr. G. nearly lose a patient that way. When an air embolism got into the patient's blood stream, Dr. G. knew it immediately because he kept his patients talking during the procedure. The man suddenly stopped responding and Dr. G. knew he had to act fast. He quickly turned the man upside down and the embolism did not travel to his heart; it was harmlessly dissipated before it could do any damage.

The Ransdells were grateful that God had led them to a physician of such eminence as Gellenthien, one of the foremost chest physicians in the nation. They were impressed when they learned that he had dedicated his life to medical missions as a young man, and by the fact that he knew the trauma they faced because he himself had experienced tuberculosis. [6]

One day Mrs. Ransdell returned home to find her husband's room empty. She was alarmed until she saw a familiar car pull up.

Dr. G. helped Ransdell out of his car and explained that he felt it was about time John had a ride, and he himself wanted the privilege of providing it.[7] For five years treatment was continued. While recovering, Ransdell had been converted and felt the call to preach the Gospel of Christ. After his recovery, he was licensed and ordained by the First Baptist Church of Las Vegas where he was pastor for nine years before moving to Albuquerque and serving as pastor at Fruit Avenue Baptist Church for 14 years. Affectionately called "Brother Johnny" by his congregation, Ransdell is presently pastor emeritus at Fruit Avenue.[8]

Dr. G.'s associations with ministers and priests have enriched his life and made his job of counseling patients much easier. Dr. G. had known God's call to service was real, but he had not known that the place was to be New Mexico. When death stalked him, he turned defeat into victory. If he could not go to India, he would serve where he was. His mission was to provide a place for the invalid who needed a hideaway to recover his health, whether he be a priest from Ireland or a gangster from Chicago. Dr. G. believed that in serving men he served God, as Jesus said, "Inasmuch as ye have done it unto one of the least of these my brethren, ye have done it unto me."[9]

When the Great Physician healed Carl Gellenthien in 1924, He required no payment but the same generosity He had given. The fee He exacted was in-kind service. When Dr. G. met each patient with kindness, Dr. G. performed his own mission of healing — payment enough for the mercy he had received. Many times he was paid off by his patients in trade, receiving pinto beans, fruit, or vegetables, whatever the patient had to offer. Many times he was never paid in a monetary sense. But payment took many forms, even the simple satisfaction that a life had been saved.

Returning from a trip to California from his Los Rancheros Visitadores trek one spring, Dr. G. was sitting in the airport at Las Vegas, Nevada when he saw a little boy run into a plate glass window, slashing his arm. The main artery was severed. Dr. G. went to the boy's aid and stayed until an ambulance arrived. His quick action kept the boy from bleeding to death. There was no fee. The reward of knowing a boy's life had been saved was priceless.

NOTES

1. a pseudonym
2. Edward Baumann and John O'Brien, "Capone's Old Hotel Now Just a Tomb?" *Chicago Tribune,* June 18, 1981, sec. 1, pp. 20-21.
3. Carl H. Gellenthien, interview at Valmora, July 5, 1982.
4. *Ibid.*
5. Bonnie Ball O'Brien, *Promises Kept* (Nashville, Tennessee: Broadman Press, 1978), p. 159.
6. *Ibid.*
7. *Ibid.*
8. "Ransdell Announces Retirement," *Baptist New Mexican,* June 12, 1976, p. 1.
9. Matthew 25:40, *The Holy Bible, op. cit.,* p. 848.

Dr. G. playing his accordion at a picnic in March, 1942.

Gascon Ranch cabins.

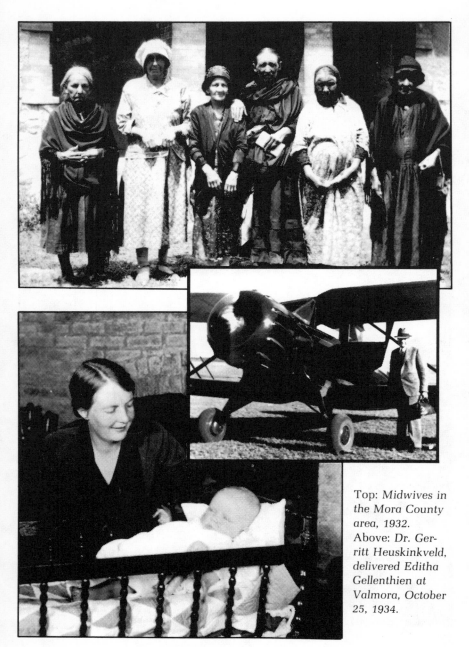

Top: *Midwives in the Mora County area, 1932.*
Above: Dr. Gerritt Heuskinkveld, *delivered Editha Gellenthien at Valmora, October 25, 1934.*

Alice Gellenthien with Editha, March 20, 1935.

Alice Gellenthien, Billy, Dr. Gellenthien, Editha, about 1939.

Above: Bill, Editha and their mother, Alice Gellenthein, about 1941. Left: Editha and Bill with their pets, December, 1949.

Above: *Steam engine at Watrous
station, 1930s.*
Right: *Valmora Station*

The bridge at Valmora where Editha Hassell Brown was killed.

Top: *The impact of the collision threw Brakeman Kincaid out on the roadbed through the glass vestibule of this pullman.*
Center: *This photo was taken at dawn, September 5, 1956 at Robinson Siding. Miss Marjorie Shea, Valmora's secretary, and Dr. Gellenthien; right.*
Bottom: *Dr. Gellenthien speaking with the roadmaster.*

Left: John Boles (left) movie actor and light opera star with Carl Gellenthien, 1948. Below: Dr. Gellenthien, Pres. New Mexico Division, American Cancer Society; Greer Garson and Alva A. Simpson, late 1950s.

Dr. G. (left) with Rancheros Visitadores friends including Ronald Reagan (right).

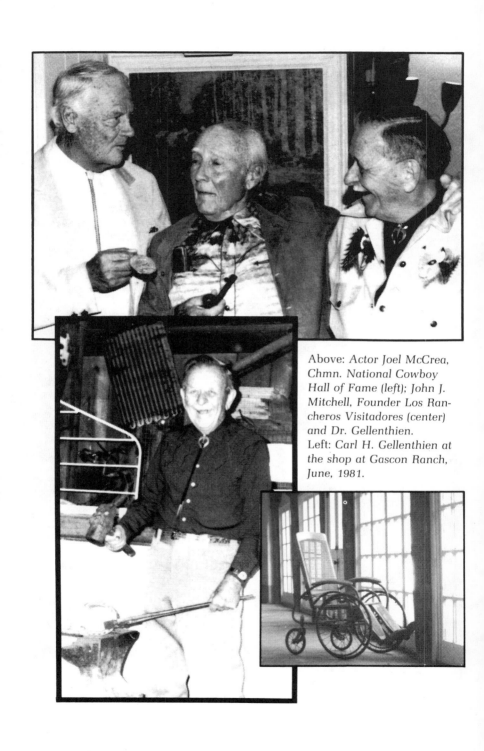

Above: *Actor Joel McCrea, Chmn. National Cowboy Hall of Fame (left); John J. Mitchell, Founder Los Rancheros Visitadores (center) and Dr. Gellenthien.*
Left: *Carl H. Gellenthien at the shop at Gascon Ranch, June, 1981.*

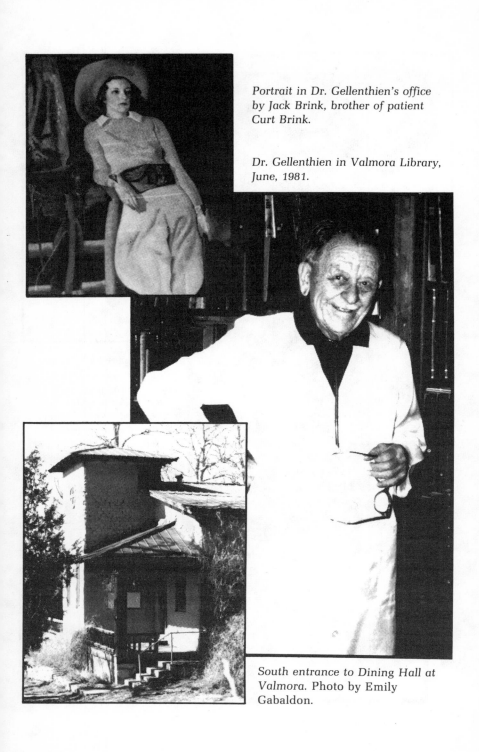

Portrait in Dr. Gellenthien's office by Jack Brink, brother of patient Curt Brink.

Dr. Gellenthien in Valmora Library, June, 1981.

South entrance to Dining Hall at Valmora. Photo by Emily Gabaldon.

CHAPTER XII

The Wreck at Robinson Siding

At 3:00 a.m. on Wednesday, September 5, 1956, Santa Fe Railroad's speeding streamliner, "the Chief," was headed west. The Number 19, en route from Chicago to Los Angeles was doing its usual speed, 60 to 70 miles an hour. Inside were 45 Pullman passengers, 227 adult coach passengers and 40 children, most of them sleeping peacefully to the rhythmical click-clicking of the wheels and the even rocking motion of the train.

In the pitch black darkness the Number 8 eastbound mail train sat at the Robinson siding 3 miles south of Springer waiting for the number 19 to pass, ready to pull out for its journey to Chicago. There was a small crew on the mail train. A carload of Navajo Indians were being taken to work. The clerks would sort the mail and have it ready by the time they arrived at their destination. Engineer L.J. Rush of Raton looked at his watch, the diamond ring he wore on his left hand glittering in the artificial light. Rush knew it was only minutes before he would pull out — as soon as the Number 19 passed — and he was ready to go. He looked forward to another routine day.

At 3:02 a.m., a night club operator from Springer locked up his club and drove out for some fresh air, taking the highway along the railroad track. It was his habit to drive around a few minutes after closing up so he could unwind before going home to bed. He planned on a good sleep after his long hours at the club.

At 3:08 a.m. Charles Kincaid, a brakeman on the Chief and resident of Albuquerque, was standing in the vestibule of one of the pullmans of Number 19. He opened the upper half of the vestibule window to see if train Number 8, the mail train, had any signals for Number 19 as they passed.

Passenger Jack London of Beverly Hills, California was awake in Car CC3. Nearly everyone else was sound asleep, but London was restless. He didn't know why.

Chief J.P. Reinhold, Santa Fe Railroad Vice President in charge of public relations was aboard the business car with his family. They slept soundly.

Sleeping soundly, too, at Valmora, about 30 miles south of Springer where the Chief was racing through the darkness, was Dr. Erle S. Ross, Medical Director of the Brotherhood of Railroad Trainmen. He had arrived from Cleveland, Ohio the night before to vacation in the lovely Valmora Valley and visit the Gellenthiens. It was good to get away from it all for a while. He had determined to forget all about work and just relax the next few days in the company of his good friends, Carl and Alice. The fresh mountain air had already begun its salubrious effects. Erle had retired to his cabin early, planning to sleep as late as he liked in the morning. Right now, at 3:09 a.m., he was sleeping like a baby.

At his own home Carl Gellenthien, too, was in deep slumber. He lay in the big bed beside Alice. Both were lost in deep dreams.

At 3:10 a.m. the fireman from Number 8 saw the Santa Fe Chief bearing down the tracks toward him. After fourteen years of experience the fireman knew his job routine perfectly. What happened next has never been explained except in the two words "human error." Seconds before Number 19 hit the switchpoint he reached out and threw the hand switch, sending Number 19 hurtling off the main line and onto the siding, smack into the front of the waiting Number 8. The fatal movement of his hand could not be retracted. The result was one of the biggest catastrophes in the history of the Santa Fe: The Robinson Switch Point disaster.

At Robinson siding there was an earsplitting crash as metal and steel met like two gignatic monsters at war, twisting, grinding, ripping at each other, metal slashing and disembowling metal.

The Springer night club owner saw the head-on collision, gasped, and sped to the nearest phone.

At the main railroad office in Amarillo, Texas, trouble was seen on the lighted map. Moments later Mr. Cecil Hope, Chief Dispatcher in Las Vegas, knew there had been a wreck. He got on the phone.

At about 3:20 a.m. the telephone by Dr. Gellenthien's bedside rang. Mr. Hope from the Las Vegas depot said there had been a wreck three miles south of Springer and medical help was urgently needed — fast.

Dr. G. tumbled out of bed and scrambled into his clothes. Alice knew the familiar sounds — the shirt jerked off its hanger, the shuffling of shoes, the scramble for car keys, and the familiar snap of the brown leather bag.

"What is it Carl?" she asked sleepily.

"Train wreck near Springer," he told her. "I'll get Erle to go with me." And he was out the door.

He pounded on the cabin door once, then finding it unlocked, pushed it open and entered the darkness where his colleague lay sleeping.

"Get up, Erle. There's been a train wreck. A bad one. We've got to go!"

Erle thought his friend was kidding. Carl was always playing jokes on his friends. It would be a perfect joke to play on the head doctor of the railroad union — wake him up in the middle of the night on the first day of his vacation and tell him there had been a head-on collision just up the track.

"Go on, Carl, save your jokes for tomorrow. Let me sleep," he muttered.

"This is no joke, Erle. It's true. There's been a wreck and people may be dying. Come on."

The urgent tone of Carl's voice convinced him. He got up and somehow tumbled into his clothes.

Meanwhile, Dr. G. woke his secretary, Marge Shea, and told her to get Ellen Dominguez, Valmora's nurse, and get emergency medical supplies together as quickly as possible. He and Erle wouldn't wait. They left immediately. Erle Ross had never had such a fast ride.

At 3:35 a.m. Carl and Erle were headed north on the highway toward Springer. It was the kind of emergency decribed by Editha later as "the type when my father didn't drive the car; he flew it." This was one of those occasions when Dr. G. drove like the proverbial bat out of hell, knowing that minutes counted when someone was bleeding.

On the way the two doctors discussed how they would organize their activities, dividing the work between them. Location of the victims and triage would be the first problem. The dispatcher had notified State Police and would get medical personnel and ambulances as quickly as possible to the scene. But both Springer and Las Vegas, the two towns closest to the wreck on either side, were small and limited in their medical facilities. They hoped there would be enough help.

Approximately 4:10 a.m. the doctors arrived at the scene and knew there wasn't enough help. All was quiet, an ominous sign of death. Dr. Gellenthien and Dr. Ross were the first physicians on the scene. The giant wreckage, twisted grotesquely and groaning the final death throes of its fatal impact, lay sprawled on the flat grazing land under the first rays of dawn.

Dr. G.'s handwritten notes give an interesting account of his initial observations and actions:

Head on Collision

West bound Chief Train #19 - traveling usual speed, (60-70 miles per hour - Engine speedometer tape supposedly destroyed) on Main Line Track

East bound mail train #8, ready to head out on mainline track Robinson Switch Point - 3 miles south of Springer, New Mexico

Time: 4:10 a.m. Wednesday morning, September 5, 1956.[1]

Head end of Number 8 - Mail train

Motors running and lights on. Dr. Ross and I raced through looking for injured or dead....We did not know how to shut off motors (the Diesel engines) but there was no fire.[2]

Dr. G.'s notes indicate that he attended many people with minor injuries in the passenger car and a few with more serious injuries. The passengers were trapped inside the twisted wreckage until a porter grabbed a sledge hammer and broke open a window. Rescue workers broke the window glasses so that doctors could make their way inside the cars to administer first aid. No passengers were killed, but most of the Chief's crew were either killed or injured.

Dr. G. expected the worst when he started out that morning. But he did not expect the carnage that met his eyes as be began looking for the injured; he had never seen anything like it. It took some time before he and Ross realized they had been walking across the body of a brakeman in the Chief's baggage car as they went through looking for the injured. No one was supposed to be aboard it, and they weren't looking for any one in there. But the brakeman was "deadheading" in the baggage car — traveling without official railroad permission — to get to his next destination. It was done quite frequently. This time it didn't pay. A flying trunk took his head off.

Dr. G. found his friend, W.L. "Walt" Schriever, Conductor of the Chief, wedged between Pullman cars. Schriever had been standing in the entrance way of the passenger sleeping cars when the collision occurred. For a split second Dr. G. hoped his friend could be helped. He could see that he was bleeding profusely. But when the doctor saw the mutilated body crushed between the cars, embedded between the vice-like steel walls, he realized Schriever was dead. His notes read:

We can see the mutilated body of Conductor Walt Schriever jammed right side of this Chief Pullman Car vestibule. (reference to photo.) He obviously is dead, but is still bleeding. It took several hours to get Walt

204

out. Undertaker was unable to embalm. [3]

The job of finding and matching the parts of human bodies took hours, but Dr. G.'s immediate concern, of course, was to aid the survivors. He and Ross were soon joined by Marge Shea and Ellen Dominguez with medical supplies. Soon other medical assistance arrived from Springer, Raton, Trinidad, and Las Vegas.

Brakeman Charles Kincaid was found lying on the roadbed in shock. The sounds around him were dimmed by the surging forces mobilizing in his body and brain in the battle to survive. He was not seriously injured but he was stunned. Dimly he was aware of the doctor from Valmora, his friend Dr. G., kneeling beside him, examining him. And then there was the stretcher, the ambulance, the motion and noise. Later he remembered he had been standing at the vestibule window and opened the upper half to see if Number 8 had any signals.

"I never did see the train. I don't remember much until I got to the hospital," he said.

Dr. Gellenthien noted:

Impact threw Brakeman Kincaid out on roadbed
not seriously injured through this glass vestibule door
(reference to photo). [4]

At about 4:30 a.m. the phone rang and woke Walter Vivian, editor. It was a police officer telling him of the wreck. He called his photographer and hurried out to the site. He was the first reporter on the scene. Others would follow, from Santa Fe, Albuquerque, Chicago, even New York. Vivian wrote in his daily colum for the *Las Vegas Daily Optic*, "Along the Banks of the Gallinas":

Phone rings in the early morning, thanks to a cooperative police officer, and we learn of a train wreck...Scramble and away we go with Gordon Terrill and his trusty camera in tow...North into the budding sky...Highway nearly empty as the miles roll along...Then suddenly an ambulance, another — seven of them returning to Las Vegas...There it is to the right and State Patrolman Benny Trujillo briefs us on the tragedy...We learn with a shock that Walt Shriver, whom we've known for years, was one of the dead...Tangled wreckage. Steel bent like wire. Smashed and battered...The grim search for bodies amid the twisted debris that only a few hours before were live and shining diesels..."We haven't got to that yet," said a doctor pointing to a section of the wreckage. "But we think there are four more in there." (In there behind luggage and debris.)...The curious gather in increasing droves...We head back pondering the tragedies we have seen and add another... [5]

A photo taken of the early morning scene, probably by Vivian or

Terrill, shows Valmora's nurse, Ellen, standing in the center staring at the wreckage, and the secretary, Marge, taking a step toward Dr. G. beside the train. Dr. G. has just reached out his hand to help her move forward into the mangled wreckage. A group of men stand in the background.

"We were busy as a cat on a hot tin roof," Gellenthien stated afterwards. But sometime in between his trips in and out of cars looking for bodies, Walter Vivian caught him and said, "Doc, I got a lot of good pictures of you, but I can't use them."

"Why not?" Gellenthien asked.

"Because your pants are unzipped," Vivian pointed out. Indeed, the doctor had dressed so rapidly that he had not zipped up his pants, so the fly was open.

The greatest casualties were in the dormitory car where the crew of the Chief slept. Gellenthien's notes read:

> Dormitory car with 20 men utterly demolished. Wreckage on ground and on top of Pullman car about all that remained. Difficult task of finding and matching parts of dead men. [6]

The crew in the Number 8 was lucky. The engineer, L.J. Rush of Raton, did not survive, but the other mail train occupants escaped death. In his notes, Dr. G. wrote:

> 2nd day — Still looking for left hand of Train 8 engineer L.J. Rush — Raton. Found it on top this engine (Reference to photograph.) He always wore a diamond ring. [7]

When the hand was finally found, the ring gave it unmistakable identification.

Passengers in the Number 19, too, made written notes or gave verbal accounts of their experiences. One of them wrote: "I had been unable to sleep. The first I knew, there seemed to be a sharp braking and then a rending crash. Screaming broke out in my car, so I started yelling at people to take it easy." [8]

Seven of the cars of the 13-car Chief remained on the track. Ted Teprick of Ponca City, Oklahoma en route to Riverside, California said seats in his car were turned about 10 degrees from the impact. But he said he had no immediate realization that there had been a severe crash. [9]

"When help arrived and threw lights on the scene, it seemed like bodies were lying all over," said Mrs. Lillian Marks of Chicago who had been asleep at the time of the wreck. She may have been referring to the bodies of the Chief's waiters trapped in the dormitory car two cars ahead. "Everyone seemed calm. There was no panic," she said. "One man kept yelling, 'Help, help, here I am.'" [10]

One passenger from Ohio gave the following account:

We were on a sleeper on the Chief going to Albuquerque. I was in a roomette with Everett Ruddell of Springfield, Ohio. Our car was about four back from the engine.

I was asleep and woke up when we began bouncing around. It didn't hurt anybody in our car but we sure had a rough ride for a while.

There was quite a lot of noise. The train's undergear rumbled and the rails and ties were breaking and it got pretty loud for a minute. Then everything went quiet.

No one screamed in our car. They were all asleep and awoke like I did, wondering what was happening.

We piled out of our beds and got into the aisle. The car was tilted but hadn't turned over. Then we found that the doors were locked tight.

But a porter and a couple of passengers grabbed a sledge hammer and broke open a window and we got out that way.

We all talked back and forth while waiting to get out. Someone mentioned the possibility of fire so no one lighted any cigarettes.

When we got out there was wreckage all around us. Some of the cars ahead of us were really smashed up and there were a number of them overturned.

All the dead seemed to be in the front one or two cars on our train. There were a number of injured standing and sitting there.

It was still dark. We waited at the scene until after dawn and a bus brought us into town. [11]

Public affairs vice president J.P. Reinhold and his family were not injured. He stood and looked at the twisted, mangled and telescoped cars, stunned.

Associated Press Staff Writer John B. Curtis wrote, "It was as though some giant hand had picked up the silvery gleaming cars of the streamliner and crushed them together like a fantastic accordion." [12]

Another reporter wrote, "The force which sent the railroad passenger cars tumbling like a child's blocks early this morning south of Springer ripped up the rail..." [13]

In a story entitled, "Worst for Veteran Newsman: Nightmarish Scene Near Springer As Crews Start Cleanup," the *Optic's* Walter Vivian wrote a description of what he saw:

This spot three miles south of Springer is a nightmarish scene of tangled wreckage and shattered bodies where at least 20 trainmen were killed and 11 passengers injured when the Santa Fe Chief plowed through an open switch.

I have seen some bad wrecks, but this is really the worst.

There were four diesel units on each train and then they were smashed together — practically fused together. One was riding on top of the other in piggy-back style.

Officials believe there were four bodies trapped in the sleeping car of the Chief's diesel. They were the crew and no doubt didn't know what hit them.

Police were having a problem in keeping the crowd back. [14]

Gellenthien noted that the police were very efficient. Springer National Guardsmen were pressed into service to guard the mail train. Traffic along U.S. 85 jammed up temporarily as awestruck passersby slowed down to get a glimpse of the wreck. State Police Chief Joe Roach arrived around 8:00 a.m. to take command of the police forces. Later in the morning nearly 500 onlookers crowded around, gawking from behind the shoulders of State Police troopers and Colfax County peace officers. Dr. G. was acquainted with most of the officers, as he was with the railroad workers. He knew Officer Don Hammond whose father, a minister, had started a church in Wagon Mound.

Dr. G. wrote:

N.M. State police who helped at R.R. wreck officer Don Hammond arrived at 5 a.m. stayed with me and helped me personally for over 48 hours until I was finished with my work. Officer Dick Lewis, Springer - Officer Benny Trujillo, Raton - Captain C.A. White, Springer - also helped. Chief of Police Roach - Santa Fe arrived after breakfast. The 1st morning nothing much for him to do. Dr. G. [15]

Walter Vivian's story continued:

The area is scattered with wreckage, both human and mechanical.

Identification of many of the fatalities is difficult because the bodies are so mangled.

The State Police and members of the Springer National Guard are policing the area. When I arrived at the scene shortly before 7 o'clock this morning there were about 25 persons there with Capt. White of the State Police and Benny Trujillo and Don Hammond of the State Police were directing traffic.

When I left there were at least 700 morbid and curious spectators flocked to the scene. [16]

Before long help began to arrive. Doctors from Raton, Trinidad and Springer rushed to the scene to give aid and ambulances from Las Vegas, Springer, Raton, and Trinidad soon arrived. Buses were supplied from Springer to carry the uninjured and injured alike to Springer facilities. All passengers were given check-ups. The dead were hurried away to mortuaries in Raton and Trinidad, Colorado. [17]

Walter Vivian concluded his story:

Santa Fe crewmen were laying track around the wreckage to avoid a delay. I would imagine they would have the track cleared by tomorrow.

I was impressed by the grim faced National Guardsmen patrolling the area. Some of them were kids and looked pretty sick faced. [18]

One of the seriously injured was James Wolter, age 24, a dishwasher hired for the summer crew. This was to be his last trip before returning to Northwestern University School of Law in Chicago. He was serving aboard the streamliner, working in the dining car when the impact sent him flying, crushed under the wreckage.

A report of injuries treated by Dr. G. included the following:

Passengers - last car No. 19:

Mrs. D. - Bruise, right leg - Bandaid applied.

Mr. D. - cut, left shin. Dressing applied.

Mrs. N. - Cut, left shin - dressing applied.

Miss W. - Headache, 1 dz. ASA; Sprained left ankle.

Mrs. R. - Lying across both seats. Rolled off; Diplopia, both eyes, right clearing. 1 dz. ASA.

Mrs. M. - Bruise and swelling, right elbow. Bandage applied. [19]

Dr. G. noted one crew member treated from Number 8's baggage car:

C.B. - slid length of car. Bruised right elbow and right knee. [20]

Investigations into the wreck were launched by the FBI at Albuquerque, the State Corporation Commission and the railroad itself. T.J. Anderson, Assistant General Manager of the Santa Fe, arrived by mid-morning and said that apparently somebody threw a switch by mistake; there was no probability of sabotage. [21]

The Robinson Siding wreck was one of the worst disasters in the history of American rail experience. The fireman who threw the switch in a moment of confusion had no explanation for the error.

"I don't know," he could only say when asked how the switch error came about. "It was a great shock...they were my friends." He was given sedatives and had to remain in bed all the next day under the care of a physician. [22]

An inquest was conducted by Peace Justice Harry Smith and District Attorney Arthur Noble. C.C. Boatright of the State Corporation Commission said, "human error, period" was the cause of the train wreck. [23]

The fireman had been Dr. G.'s patient for some time and was treated for Nervosa Anorexia or nervous indigestion. Dr. G. wondered if the man had been taking his medication properly or if it might have affected his judgement in some way. But that question was ruled out.

Naturally the fireman lost his job. He was unable to find another. No one wanted to hire him. Dr. G. tried to help him get a job with U.S. Steel Corporation in South America but they wouldn't have him. He ended up doing part-time work as a musician in his home town.

After the investigations were completed, bulldozers were brought in to bury the wreckage. There was much paper work to be done, too. On September 11, 1956, Dr. G. wrote the following letter to Mr. Cecil Hope, Chief Dispatcher, AT & SFRR in Las Vegas:

Dear Mr. Hope:

When you telephoned me in the early morning hours of Wednesday, September 5, advising that there had been a head-on collision of No. 19 and No. 8 at Robinson, we loaded the car with splints, bandages, tourniquets and opiates, expecting the usual mutilated, hysterical, bleeding casualties.

Dr. Erle S. Ross, Medical Director of the Brotherhood of Railroad Trainmen at Cleveland, Ohio had just come in the evening before on his vacation. Dr. Ross, our Valmora nurse Ellen Dominguez, R.N., my secretary Marjorie Shea, and I left immediately for the wreck scene. While driving up, we worked out plans for assigning a doctor to each car, if possible, to limit our first aid efforts to shock and hemorrhage treatment and to get the cases into the local hospital as promptly as possible, but when we arrived at the wreck, there was an ominous silence with a few men walking around dazed, some moaning from the Dormitory Car (which soon ceased) and everyone we found was dead.

It wasn't long until the State Police, Railroad men and National Guard had the remains out and taken to the central morgue in Raton. I don't know the porter's name, but the porter in the first Pullman deserves recognition for his outstanding rescue work. He broke out a window with a sledge hammer, made sure there were no fragments of glass to cut, put a ladder out the window and was taking his passengers out of the car when we arrived.

Fortunately the passenger cars did not overturn and there was no bedlam or panic. With State Patrolman Don Hammond, we went through the cars and dressed the wounds which were all superficial. Most of the injured were in the last car of the train. Mrs.—— of Los Angeles conceivably could have some cerebral injury. We advised each passenger to check with the Railroad people in Los Angeles when they arrived. One Indian on No. 8 had been pushed up against the glass of the car door and broken it, but we could find no Indians injured.

The Springer Hospital had only one Registered Nurse and I left our Valmora nurse, Miss Dominguez, to help them at the hospital all day Wednesday.

It was the worst accident in my professional life and I am sorry there was no more that we could have done medically. We at Valmora deeply appreciate your confidence in us in calling us for our help. [24]

Enclosed was a list of the injured treated by Dr. Gellenthien.

Dr. G. received a letter from the Office of Division Superintendent, dated September 17, 1956, thanking him for his assistance in the disastrous accident of September 5th. Appreciation was extended to Dr. G. and Dr. Ross for their prompt action to relieve the injured at the scene of the accident.

Superintendent W.H. Jones also wrote Dr. G. that they would be glad to accept his bill in connection with this case, as he certainly must have incurred some out-of-pocket expenses, and for his professional services. In response, Dr. G. replied in a hand-written note for his secretary Marge Shea, dated September 17, 1956:

Advise Mr. Jones that we at Valmora Sanatorium are unanimous in our decision that it is unthinkable to put the dollar sign on such a dreadful tragedy. The injured and the 22 railroad employees killed are our friends and neighbors. For years Walt Schriever, Conductor of the Chief, a graduate of Valmora, has been collecting newspapers and magazines on his train and throwing them off at Valmora for our patients. Other employees likewise and in other ways, contributed to our patients' welfare.

There is not —

There will not be —

Nor can there ever be — a bill or charge for our medical services.

Our only regret is that we could not have done more. But the wreck was so deadly.

There is no need to write Superintendent Jones this. Telephone him or tell him when you see him and ask him for pictures for our files.

Dr. G. [25]

Certainly Dr. G. could take consolation in the fact that he and the other doctors from surrounding communities did indeed "relieve the injured at the scene of the accident." Records show that many cuts were bandaged. Shock was treated. A man with a back injury was given a shot to relieve his pain. The more critically injured were carefully treated and transported to hospitals.

One of those was the young law student and dishwasher, James Wolter, on his last journey before leaving his summer railroad job to return to school. After initial emergency treatment he was taken to the Springer Hospital. Sadly, Dr. G. learned that he died days later. Upon hearing of his death, Dr. G. wrote to his parents, Mr. and Mrs. Fred W. Wolter of Rockford, Illinois:

We at Valmora, are grieved to learn that James has lost his valiant fight for life.

Dr. Erle Ross, medical director of the Brotherhood of Railway Trainmen, Cleveland, Ohio, my medical secretary since 1934 Miss Marjorie Shea born and raised in Chicago, our Valmora nurse Miss Ellen Dominguez, a graduate of the Sherman Hospital Nurses Training School in Elgin, Illinois, stayed at James' bedside the first critical twelve hours, gave him blood transfusions, etc., and rewrote and sent his confused telegram to you.

These three and Don Hammond, our New Mexico State patrolman helped me at the wreck. Dr. Blakely (Henry Blakely) and Dr. Gunter (Joe Gunter) of Springer you know. I write you this background so that you may take comfort in the knowledge that James' first critical hours were in the hands of well trained, skilled, and conscientious medical personnel and that everything humanly possible was done.

We all join in extending to you our deepest sympathy and condolences. [26]

Dr. G. had never faced such a devastating disaster of such widespread wreckage and loss as the wreck at Robinson Switch Point. He and Dr. Ross had arrived at the scene first and handled the triage well. They had remained on the job for over 48 hours. And Dr. G. took the time to follow up with compassionate letters afterwards. He would accept no fee. His kindness extended, also, to the man who had caused the wreck, for his life was ruined. Yet everyone is capable of mistakes, errors which occur in a thoughtless moment. His error was deadly. But, Dr. G. said, who can cast the first stone?

In all, 23 people died. Years passed. Memories dimmed. But the wreck at Robinson Siding left a vivid imprint on Dr. G.'s memory. "I never saw anything like it, before or since," he said. "And I hope I never again see an accident as tragic as the wreck at Robinson Siding." [27]

NOTES

1. Carl H. Gellenthien, handwritten notes composed following the accident at Springer Siding, September 5, 1956, in Scrapbook 6, Valmora Library, p. 17.
2. *Ibid.,* p. 25.
3. *Ibid.,* p. 39.
4. *Ibid.,* p. 33.
5. Walter T. Vivian, "Along the Banks of the Gallinas," *Las Vegas Daily Optic,* September 5, 1956, n.p., in Scrapbook 6, Valmora Library, p. 53.
6. Carl H. Gellenthien, handwritten notes composed following the accident at Springer Siding, *op. cit.,* p. 26.
7. *Ibid.,* p. 35.
8. John B. Curtis, "'Giant Hand' Crushes Train Like Accordion," n.p., n.d., clipping in Scrapbook 6, Valmora Library, Valmora, New Mexico, p. 50.
9. *Ibid.*
10. *Ibid.*
11. Herbert Hudson, "Rough for While," n.p., n.d., clipping in Scrapbook 6, Valmora Library, p. 41.
12. Curtis, *op. cit.*
13. Newspaper clipping, caption for photography, in Scrapbook 6, Valmora Library, p. 32.
14. Walter Vivian, "Worst for Veteran Newsman," *Las Vegas Daily Optic,* September 5, 1956, p. 1, in Scrapbook 6, Valmora Library, p. 43.
15. Carl H. Gellenthien, handwritten notes written after the Springer Siding accident, *op. cit.,* p. 46.
16. Walter Vivian, "Worst for Veteran Newsman," *op. cit.*
17. Neil Addington, "Crews Hunt More Bodies in Wreckage," *Santa Fe New Mexican,* September 5, 1956, n.p., clipping in Scrapbook 6, Valmora, New Mexico, p. 53.
18. Walter Vivian, "Worst for Veteran Newsman," *op. cit.*
19. Carl H. Gellenthien, typed notes written up after accident at Springer Siding, in Scrapbook 6, Valmora Library, p. 62.
20. *Ibid.*
21. William B. Dickinson, "Santa Fe's Chief Rams Mail Train," n.t., n.d., n.p., newspaper clipping in Scrapbook 6, Valmora Library, p. 52.
22. "Santa Fe Fireman Shocked," *Albuquerque Journal,* n.d., n.p., newspaper clipping from Scrapbook 6, Valmora Library, p. 53.

23. "Human Error Cited in Train Accident Claiming 20 Lives," newspaper clipping in Scrapbook 6, Valmora Library, p. 47.

24. Carl H. Gellenthien, letter to Cecil Hope, September 11, 1956, in Scrapbook 6, Valmora Library, Valmora, New Mexico, pp. 16-17.

25. Carl H. Gellenthien, handwritten note to Marge Shea, secretary, Valmora, September 17, 1956, in Scrapbook 6, Valmora Library, p. 19.

26. Carl H. Gellenthien, letter to Mr. and Mrs. Fred W. Wolter, October 22, 1956, in Scrapbook 6, Valmora Library, Valmora, New Mexico, p. 20.

27. Carl H. Gellenthien, interview at Valmora, June 25, 1983.

CHAPTER XIII

Saga of a Railroad Surgeon

The Grand Canyon Limited pulled out of Dodge City, Kansas one evening, taking Dr. G. and about 200 other passengers on its routine journey west. Dr. G. sat by the window and watched the barren terrain as light snowflakes fell and dusted everything in white. They passed through farms and saw the solid farm houses in the distance, smoke rising from the chimneys in defiance of the bitter cold. After a while there were no more houses visible. The snow blotted everything out, and only the blinding white flakes could be seen caressing the windows in frigid, feathering patterns. It made one dizzy to look too long, and there was nothing more to see. Darkness was descending. The wind grew stronger.

Dr. G. sat back in his seat and tried to read. He dozed. Then he awoke with an uneasy feeling. Something was amiss. The train had stopped. It was engulfed in swirling snow, trapped in heavy drifts, a captive prisoner of the strong arms of a bitter enemy, a raging Kansas blizzard.

Dr. G. recalled the stop at Dodge City earlier that evening. He had gone into the Harvey House to call home. He wanted to tell Alice not to be worried if his return was delayed. Weather conditions did not look good. Mr. Duffy, an "alumni" of Valmora, was the dispatcher. He became a dispatcher after leaving Valmora because the job would not tax his bad lungs. Dr. G. had visited with his old friend and asked him to try to get a line. But the lines were down. Duffy thought he could go via Denver where one line was still in operation, but even it failed. Dr. G. visited with Duffy until the Dispatcher told him it was time to get back on the train.

"All aboard for Garden City!"

But now the train had stopped and they were not even near Garden City.

The snow fall of early evening had turned into a heavy blizzard that night. Snow drifts began to stack up. At last the train could no longer push through the heavy drifts and was trapped.

At first the passengers were only slightly alarmed. They were in the middle of a Kansas prairie between Dodge City and Garden City but they anticipated only a slight delay. The problem was that there was no communication. The Garden City folks thought that the Grand Canyon had stayed in Dodge City because of the bad weather. The Dodge City people assumed that the train had reached Garden City. Thus, there were no concerns and the Grand Canyon sat on the prairie unaided.

As the hours stretched on the train ran out of coal. There was no more comfortable steam heat. The interior of the train began to cool as it became a frigid ice box. The passengers put on layers of clothing and wrapped up in blankets. Those in the Pullman got into bed and covered up. They began to worry.

Then the food and water ran out. Morning came and went. Anxiety was not confined to the passengers as the afternoon dragged on. The crew felt helpless. As darkness of the second night set in, the passengers and crew felt a growing desperation. As the train sat in the darkness of the second night, the wind howling at the windows, the interior was like a refrigerator.

Dr. G. carried an emergency medical bag with him on every trip. Now he began to worry about the passengers. Babies were crying. They needed nourishment and warmth. People with border-line health problems could succumb under the stress of these conditions. He was able to offer some assistance to a few. He had insulin for diabetics. He could help with minor complaints. But if the train wasn't rescued soon, people would be in real trouble.

That second night was the coldest, most miserable night Dr. G. ever spent. He tried to think of a way to warm up his compartment. He even tried stuffing newspaper in the toilet and lighting it, hoping to build a safe little fire, but all he created was a smoke house. It was a good idea but it didn't work.

Nearly 40 hours elapsed before the stranded train was discovered. Two small planes flew over on the second day and noticed the frozen giant on the track. They contacted Dodge City. An engine and a wrecking crew came out with plows to clear the track. The rescue crew had to break up the train because it was frozen to the track. They made up a new train and got the passengers back to Dodge City. There the train was heated up, re-supplied with coal, food, and water. There were no fatalities. But the Grand Canyon was luckier than the Rock Island Express caught in that same storm. Its route was from Chicago to Kansas City and then down to Amarillo, Texas and Tucumcari, New Mexico. The storm hit it with the same crippling force that stopped the Grand Canyon. Before reaching Tucumcari it, too, was stranded on the plains. The passengers did not fare as well as those on he Grand Canyon. Some died of exposure or hypothermia. A newspaper crew then went out on another train to get the story and it, too, ran into trouble. The passengers on that train ended up burning the car seats for warmth before they were rescued.

The saga of the American railroad is replete with the stories of unsung heros, and the railroad surgeon has a definite place among them. Rail travel was hazardous in the early days. Injuries were commonplace. "Railroad spine," a concussion of the nerve center, "railroad brain," a mental shock caused by the jolting of cars, and eye injuries from flying cinders were common. Engineers were often scalded by the steam from the boilers. Sometimes limbs or fingers were crushed by the crude coupling devices and had to be amputated. Frequent derailments and collisions resulted in shock and bodily injury.

Cleanliness and hygiene left much to be desired in the early days. Food poisoning was a danger. Water was frequently taken from a common cup or dipper. Typhoid spread quickly. In the day coaches the floor would be littered with peanut hulls, tobacco juice, and trash. Consumptives would expectorate on the floor. When the division point was reached the brakeman would taken his broom and brush all the filth into a stifling dust which the passengers had to breathe — dust laden with deadly tubercule bacilli. [1]

Sometimes passengers required special attention. Babies have been delivered by railroad surgeons among other duties. "When a physician traveled aboard a train, he could count on giving emergency medical attention to somebody before his journey was over." [2]

Although conditions had improved by 1929 there was still a definite need for the railroad surgeon and Dr. Gellenthien was appointed Local Surgeon at Valmora in November of that year.

A section hand was trying a pry a rock loose earlier that year above the tracks between Wagon Mound and Valmora when a loose rock slipped and hit him, fracturing his femer. He then went to a doctor in the area to have the thigh bone set. But it was still bothering him later so he went to Dr. G. After X-rays were taken, it was evident that the young man's leg had been improperly set, and he would remain crippled unless the leg was broken again and reset.

The claim agent feared a lawsuit. The railroad offered the youth a choice. They would pay to have his leg re-broken and reset properly or they would give him $1,000 cash outright. He took the $1,000, bought a new car, and by the end of the year was broke — and crippled. It was because of the need for a competent doctor in the Valmora area that Dr. G. was appointed for the job. He held the position of railroad surgeon for the Atchison, Topeka and Santa Fe Railway Company until March of 1979 when the service was discontinued. As local railroad surgeon for the AT & SFRR Hospital Association, Dr. G. received railroad passes and traveled thousands of miles a year.

The claim agents continued to keep busy making settlements. Someone's haystack would catch fire from a spark and the railroad would have to compensate for fire loss. Or someone's cow was hit by the train and the company would have to pay for it. But at least the company was assured of a good doctor in the area to care for the sick and injured.

In caring for railroad employees and passengers, Dr. G. treated dozens of people each year. His "Discharge from Treatment" records for the Santa Fe Hospital Association show a variety of conditions, including hypertension, influenza, pulmonary tuberculosis, pneumonia, pleurisy, puncture wounds, foreign bodies in the eye, and various injuries such as crushed index fingers. Routine company physical examinations were also done.[3]

On June 26, 1936, an employee was injured near the Shoemaker Bridge. A description from the "Official Superior's Report of Injury" stated:

> Operating Stump Puller and chain broke and struck patient on chest on June 26, 1936 - contusion and scar of sternum and right costo chondro conjunction - Bony frame work of chest is normal - X-ray negative - Chest strapped with adhesive, heat applied and anodynes given.[4]

When he was brought in to see Dr. G., the patient was spitting blood. Two office calls and X-rays were required. Twenty-nine dollars and fifty cents was the total charge.[5]

Passengers as well as employees had to be cared for. Pullman Conductor J.L. Stoudt sent a woman to Dr. G. with this note:

> Claire, Mich. enroute Pasadena to Chicago - Roomette 2 car 208 - Stooping over when basin fell and cut scalp at top of head approximately 8 p.m.. 4/12/62 J.L. Stoudt, Pull. Cond.[6]

Dr. G.'s handwritten note described his findings and treatment:

> Sagittal sutural
> Parietal bones midway between Lambdoid and Coronal sutures
> Abrasion and small superficial laceration requiring no suturing, along the sagittal suture between parietal bones and midway between Lambdoid and Coronal sutures.
> Wound cleaned with soap and H_2O

Tr. Merthiolate and band aid dressing applied. [7]

When a passenger en route from city to city became injured or ill it could be quite disconcerting for his fellow travelers in close proximity. Dealing with an emergency required discretion and tact. On his way to Chicago for the annual scientific meeting of the American Railway Surgeon's Assocation, Dr. Gellenthien, occupying Bedroom J, Car 208, was summoned one morning by the Pullman Conductor. The man spoke in subdued tones, asking the doctor if he would come and look at one of the passengers. The following is Dr. G.'s written account:

Pullman Conductor C.H. Beaver asked me to see a very sick lady in Bedroom Suite E & F, private Tour Car No. 51. Found an elderly lady lying in berth, dressed in nightgown as if asleep. Head was slumped to the right, lower jaw hung agape. There were no vital signs; no heart sounds, no pulse, no respiration. Pupils of both eyes dilated, rigid, no reflex. Typical whiteness of skin and slight cynaosis of mucous membranes of mouth and lips. Skin felt cold. I pronounced her dead at 10:45 A.M. of an apparent heart attack. There was no evidence of struggle or violence. At 10:45 A.M., No. 20 was traveling between Trinidad and La Junta, Colorado at Hoehnes, Colorado.

Mrs. ——'s sister and traveling companion, occupying the same bedroom suite, stated that she and her sister had taken a walk on the Williams, Arizona platform the night before and Miss —— had complained of some shortness of breath. They returned to their bedroom suite and her sister had slept well all night, but thought she would have her breakfast in bed. She ate a light breakfast and promptly vomited all of it. She did not complain of any chest, epigastric, neck or arm pains; did not seem cynaotic and stated that she would take a nap and would be all right. She died quietly while asleep. . . . I would guess that Mrs. —— waited about one-half hour before calling the Tour Director, Mr. Fred Sperie. [8]

After this description of the woman's illness, Dr. G. added a personal comment:

It was pleasant for me to see how efficiently, quietly and unobtrusively both conductors worked. The adaptation of the short wave radio to railroad use is certainly wonderful. When we pulled into La Junta, the ambulance and proper personnel were waiting. Very few people realized that anything unusual was happening and I doubt if the train lost very much, if any, time. The surviving sister was most appreciative of the kindness and sympathetic care in which everything was done. [9]

Having the railroad track right at his own front door at Valmora made life easier for Dr. G. He had access to quick transportation, communication, and supplies. Patients could come and go conveniently. But sometimes having the track so near presented problems, too, such as when Dr. G.'s deranged neighbor sat on the track intent on committing suicide and Dr. G. had to stop the train.

One day Dr. G. got a call telling him there was a man lying sprawled across the railroad track and a train was speeding closer to the Valmora site each minute. Dr. G. got into his car and hurried to the location. Sure enough, there was a body lying on the tracks. He could hear the train barreling down the tracks. It was too late to stop the train. Dr. G. scrambled over to the unconscious man. He recognized him as a local trapper who lived in a cabin nearby. Dr. G. tugged and pulled the heavy body off the tracks, not a moment too soon, for just as he had the body clear the train went by.

Apparently the unconscious man had fallen and convulsed as he walked along the track. The ground showed signs of the body's struggle during the seizure. Dr. G. checked the man's vital signs. He was dying. By the time he was taken to the hospital he was dead.

Dr. G. did most of his own autopsies at Valmora in those days. Now he wanted to determine the cause of death and proceeded to perform the autopsy. To verify his findings, he sent tissues, including the stomach, to the lab in Albuquerque. The findings showed strychnine in the stomach. The question was, how did such a deadly poison get there? Was the man murdered?

An investigation concluded that the trapper had accidentally poisoned himself. He had a habit of keeping his rat poison, containing strychnine, in a can on a shelf in the kitchen. He kept his baking powder in a can of the same size and shape. The day of his death he had made biscuits, using what he thought was baking powder. He inadvertantly reached for the wrong can, put in a teaspoon of the "powder," and baked his biscuits as usual. Only one to two grams of strychnine by mouth can be fatal. The man ate his biscuits and then went out to check his traps, walking along the tracks. Within 15 minutes he was overcome by a violent seizure, fell to the ground, struggled convulsively and finally lay still, sprawled where Dr. G. found him.

"I thought I was rescuing the man from death, but my efforts were futile. He was already a dead man. Nothing I could have done would have saved him," Dr. G. said later, realizing he had risked his own life to rescue a man who could not be saved.

On a similar occasion, however, Dr. G. did save a man's life. A work train was backing up from Shoemaker to Watrous when a freight train ran through the automatic box signal. The two met on the bridge at Valmora. The caboose of the work train smashed into the freight train, demolishing it. The crew saw it coming and they all jumped clear of the train except for one young man, a student who had not worked for the railroad long. He was thrown from the top of the freight train, landing alongside of the engine, and lay on the ground unconscious.

At Valmora patients and staff heard the loud crash of the collision. Dr. G. got into his car, taking his nurse Georgie with him. They hurried down to the site. The engine was upright, but it was sitting precariously on the track, tilted sideways. The doctor knew it might fall at any moment, crushing the young man under it. He and Georgie, oblivious to their own danger, made their way through the tilted engine, hoping their weight would not cause it to fall. They then got to the young man and dragged him out of danger, put him on a stretcher, and carried him up to the hospital. He was "banged up" pretty badly and was in shock. Dr. G.'s quick action may have saved his life.

For fifty years Dr. G. served as railroad surgeon. He traveled thousands of miles. Train travel was one of his most enjoyable experiences. From the eastern cities through America's breadbasket and into the tunneled hills and high ridges of the Rocky Mountains he could watch his country unfold in a colorful panorama. Many of his speeches and lectures were prepared during this travel.

Dr. G. learned a great deal from his railroad friends, the crew of the Santa Fe — their habits, their lingo, their values. He learned to put his money in his sock, then tuck it into the pillowcase before going to sleep. No one could steal it, and when he reached for his shoes the next morning, he'd remember it.

As the train's rhythmic rocking lulled him to sleep, Dr. G. would think of the vast country he was traveling through and how much its freedom meant to him. The train seemed to be the pulse of the continent as it passed through its heartland. It was a time when the country depended on its railroad system, when the train was the vital artery system of the country and the cargo its lifeblood. The railroad has adapted itself to new times. The railroad surgeon's role has slipped into the proud pages of history. Men like Carl Gellenthien helped write those pages.

NOTES

1. Richard Dunlop, *Doctors of the American Frontier* (N.Y.: Ballantine Books, a Division of Random House, Inc., 1965), p. 160.
2. *Ibid.*, p. 161.
3. Carl H. Gellenthein, "Discharge from Treatment," Form 1784 Standard, Santa Fe Hospital Association Record Book, in Scrapbook 6, Valmora Library, Valmora, New Mexico, p. 62.
4. Carl H. Gellenthien, "Official Superior's Report of Injury" form, September 10, 1936, n.p., in Scrapbook 6, Valmora Library, Valmora, New Mexico, p. 65.
5. *Ibid.*
6. J.L. Stoudt, handwritten note in Scrapbook 6, Valmora Library, Valmora, New Mexico, p. 64.
7. Carl H. Gellenthien, handwritten note reporting injury, in Scrapbook 6, Valmora Library, Valmora, New Mexico, p. 64.
8. Carl H. Gellenthien, Report sent to Dr. O.L. Hanson, ST & SF Hospital Association, Topeka, Kansas, Dr. John R. Winston, Medical Director, AT & SFRR, Chicago, Illinois, Mr. C.B. Kurtz, Superintendent, Colorado Division, ST & SFRR, La Junta, Colorado, April 29, 1967, in Scrapbook 6, Valmora Library, p. 66.
9. *Ibid.*

CHAPTER
XIV
From Hovels to Haciendas

President Dwight D. Eisenhower leaned back in his chair and smiled his famous, broad smile as he and Carl Gellenthien completed their talk. Gellenthien, representing the AMA's stand against socialized medicine, visited the White House several times. He was impressed with the way Eisenhower tried to put people at ease in his presence, appearing relaxed and comfortable. He was so casual, in fact, "he did everything but put his feet up on the desk," Gellenthien observed.[1]

Dr. G. was briefed by Sherman Adams of the White House staff about talking to the President prior to his visit. He was told not to initiate a topic. "You don't bring up a subject; let the President bring it up. And don't quote the President to anyone afterwards," he was advised.

As the conversation concluded, Dr. G. said he had a memento for Eisenhower, a small token of his appreciation. It was a little iron horseshoe, about the size of a quarter, perfectly formed. Dr. G. explained that an elderly blacksmith in Wagon Mound, Ed Howe, had made it. His father, James Howe, also a blacksmith, had salvaged the metal after the mail robbery in 1850 near Wagon Mound. From the broken wagon, the metal had been collected and melted down. Dozens of the little shoes had been made.

Eisenhower was familiar with the history of Fort Union and New Mexico Territory in the early days. He wanted to know more about the mail robbery. Gellenthien told him the story briefly.

The mail carriers were traveling from Fort Leavenworth to deliver the mail to Santa Fe when they were attacked at Wagon Mound. All eleven men were killed with arrows. The tongue of the wagon was broken as the terrified mules ran in circles. Three mules and two horses were killed with balls from muzzleloaders. The mail bags were ransacked and some envelopes were torn open. It was thought that a combined force of at least two tribes, including Jicarilla Apaches and Utes, carried out the massacre. What was left of the mail train was discovered about 15 days later. Identification of bodies was hindered because of the extent of decay and the fact that some had been almost entirely devoured by wolves. It was evident that two members of the party had been scalped, and all were stripped. The story is told in *Leading Facts of New Mexican History* by Ralph Emerson Twitchell and in correspondence from James S. Calhoun, Indian Agent at Santa Fe to Orlando Brown, Commander of Indian Affairs in Washington D.C. and similar correspondence at Valmora Library.[2]

Eisenhower was fascinated. He rubbed the little horseshoe in the palm of his hand, realizing that the metal was 100 years old. "It came from a U.S. mail caravan taking letters to New Mexico Territory. I'll keep it with me for good luck." And he put it in his pocket. Dr. G. later sent two of the little horseshoes to Mrs. Eisenhower and she had earrings made out of them.

The next time Dr. G. visited Eisenhower and the interview concluded, Eisenhower reached in his pocket and drew out the little horseshoe. "I've got mine, Doc. Have you got yours?" Eisenhower's only complaint was that the little pointed edges kept wearing a hole in his pocket.

When Eisenhower suffered a heart attack in 1955 and was hospitalized in Denver, Gellenthien was summoned as a medical consultant. He, with numerous other physicians, examined Eisenhower and provided the best treatment available.

Dr. G. has an autographed photo of Eisenhower hanging on the wall of his home.

Dr. G.'s medical career took him from the poorest one-room hovels with dirt floors to the richest haciendas. He saw the extremes of human conditions, both poverty and luxury. He was comfortable in homes without electricity or running water, and he even enjoyed visiting his patient who lived in a cave. He was just as much at home in the elegant haciendas of the prosperous ranchers, in the well-furnished mansions of business tycoons in Chicago or Los Angeles, and even in the princely suite of the President of the United States.

Whether Dr. G. had to travel miles through mud, snow, or sand storms to reach a humble little farmhouse or whether he was flown first class to consult in a case involving one of the richest, most powerful men in the world, Dr. G. always tried his best to bring cheer and comfort along with the benefits of medicine with him.

Besides Eisenhower, many other influential and powerful men

were his patients. They were individuals such as W.A. "Pat" Patterson, President of United Airlines, John J. Mitchell, a founder and President of Los Rancheros Visitadores, and his wife Lolita Armour, and M.D. Anderson, a cotton merchant from Galveston who founded the M.D. Anderson Cancer Hospital in Houston in 1941. Clarence Darrow, the famous attorney, was also once a patient of Dr. G. after the lawyer had an allergic reaction to seafood. He looked "like one big hive." Dr. G. was impressed by his charming personality. Dr. G. also treated Irving S. Cobb, the famous writer and humorist. He was a heavy man. "Treating him for a bellyache was like treating a giraffe with a sore throat," Gellenthien said.

One of Dr. G.'s patients was Sir Anthony Eden, Prime Minister of England. Earl Ewert, head of the Department of Urology at Lahey Clinic in Boston, asked Dr. G. to come to Boston as a consultant. Eden needed surgery. The question was whether he would be able to survive the amount of surgery needed. Dr. G. examined Eden and expressed his opinion that Eden could withstand the surgery. Eden subsequently had the surgery and made a successful recovery. Dr. G. never sent a bill.

"I thought maybe the Queen would send me her garter but she never did," he said.

Dr. G.'s biggest fee was $5,000. Dr. Frederick Tice of the University of Illinois asked Dr. G. to investigate the Woodman of the World Tuberculosis Hospital in Colorado Springs after the successful chemotherapy treatment was discovered and sanatoria were no longer needed. He was asked to make recommendations. Dr. G. took along his friend, Dr. Fred Zapffe, Executive Secretary of the American and Canadian Medical Colleges, who happened to be visiting at the time. Dr. G. recommended that the hospital be closed as it was no longer necessary. It became the site of the present day Air Force Academy.

Dr. G. casually mentioned to a friend that he didn't know what to charge for his services. He was told, "Bill them for $5,000." Dr. G. protested that the amount of $5,000 was too much. He hadn't done that much work. "They're paying you for your expertise," his friend replied, "for what you know, not for what you do. Besides, if they object, you can always come down."

They did not object. They thought it was fair and sent a check for $5,000 by return mail.

Dr. Tice, who had recommended that Dr. Gellenthien be given the job, was the same professor who objected in 1927 that Dr. G. was too young to be medical director of Valmora. Gellenthien was indignant and wrote an angry letter to Tice. Before he mailed it, he told Dr.

Brown what he had done. Dr. Brown knew about Tice's reservations in appointing Gellenthien to the position.

"Give me that letter," Brown told his son-in-law. "You don't need to send it. I'll take care of this matter."

The letter was never mailed, but there were no more objections from Dr. Tice. When Dr. Brown said he'd take care of something, he did. He persuaded Tice that Gellenthien was the right man for the job, despite his young age of 27. In time Tice realized the right decision had been made. He sent many patients to Valmora to be placed under the care of Dr. G.

Dr. G. attracted some of the world's most outstanding personalities because of his reputation as a tuberculosis specialist. He had studied under some of the best minds of his day including Dr. Joseph De Lee of the University of Chicago, his obstetrics professor; Dr. Samuel Slaymaker of Rush Medical School, an outstanding cardiologist called "Daddy" Slaymaker by his students; Frederick Tice of the University of Illinois, an expert in internal medicine; Dr. Ernest Irons, Dean of Rush Medical School; Dr. Frank Billings of Rush Medical School, an internist and specialist in gastro-intestinal disorders; and L.G. Davis, the father of Nancy Davis (Mrs. Ronald Reagan). Dr. Davis, a specialist in neurosurgery and professor at Northwestern University, was called "Lord God Davis" by the students. Such men worked together to teach the medical students, exchanging lectures at the universities and converging at Cook County Hospital for surgery and clinics. Each would contribute questions for the exams which the students had to pass.

Dr. G. needed every bit of his background and expertise when he came up against "the curse" of King Tut. A team of archeologists under Charles A. Brested of the University of Chicago's Oriental Institute, went to Egypt to excavate the newly discovered tomb of King Tutankhamen. The team worked for months under Brested's direction, living on location. As a result of their work they were stricken with what some believed to be the curse of King Tut's tomb. Every one of them who had been working on the site was stricken with tuberculosis. They were sent to Valmora.

All the archeologists arrived at Valmora hairless. Another "curse" they had brought back with them was body lice. They had to shave off all body hair to get rid of the lice. But TB was not so easily shaken. They had to remain at Valmora for some time. Working in the poor living conditions on the field and being exposed to the natives who had TB was what brought the disease to the American workers, Dr. G. said. They all recovered at Valmora — 100 percent of them. All went on with successful careers afterwards. Those who had insisted that the team was "cursed" had to admit that at Valmora the curse was broken.

In gratitude the group left a set of lantern slides showing the tomb before it had been touched, before anything had been removed or disturbed.

"Curses" were not confined to the tombs of Egyptian mummies. There were plenty of them to be found among the living in Haiti. Dr. G. was sent to Haiti when he was vice president of the AMA during the rescue operations after Hurricane Hazel. People were dying of starvation and lack of medical care as a result of the disaster. The U.S. Navy Caribbean task force with its aircraft carrier sent medical supplies and personnel in by helicopter, parachute and other means soon after the hurricane hit. The American Red Cross and various U.S. Government agencies gave over two million dollars' worth of material and supplies to the country. Dr. G. was one of the people sent in to supervise the rescue work there. While he was there he was invited to visit some of the native communities and sit in on some of their meetings. He got to know some of the local witch doctors. He found out that people who were "cursed" by voodoo spells were actually in danger of their lives. The victim would believe he was going to die and would then die of fright — cardiac arrest. The doctors would try to break the evil spells and convince the victim that the curse was broken. Then he would not die. The hypnotic force of suggestion among the superstitious is very powerful and very real, Dr. G. learned.

But witchcraft and superstition were to be found back home, too. Sometimes patients would come to Valmora Clinic with complaints such as the evil eye. A *bruja* or witch had placed a spell on the patient and powerful medicine was needed to overcome it. Dr. G. took such complaints seriously, for even if they were the product of the mind's fear and superstition, the effects were very real. Usually Dr. G. would refer such a patient to the local expert in such matters, a *curandero* or "good witch doctor" who knew how to remove evil spells.

Dr. G. was respected because he didn't laugh at people whose beliefs were different from his. He honored each individual's inherent right to his own religious and political convictions. Patients who brought Dr. G. samples of home remedies were pleased when he inquired about how they should be used and put them on a display shelf, labeled appropriately for future reference. Dr. G. associated with presidents and vice presidents in the fight against socialized medicine; and even when his views opposed those of others, he respected their rights.

Once Dr. G. had to catch a flight from Cleveland to Washington

D.C. and bad weather was settling in. He had attended a meeting with the Brotherhood of Railroad Workers and met with their medical director, Dr. Erle Ross, to discuss business. Valmora was where they sent their employees who had TB. After giving a progress report, Dr. G. hurried to catch the plane for Washington D.C. to meet with John L. Lewis, head of the United Mine Workers Union, and his Union Board.

Dr. G. liked Lewis, though he didn't always agree with him. Lewis was a "bull-dog mean, tough," Dr. G. said, but the self-educated man had "something of a poet's heart; he was always quoting Shakespeare."[3] Lewis wanted to build a chain of ten hospitals in Appalachia where the mine workers needed them, but Dr. G. advised him against it, saying that it would break the unions financially. But the Union went ahead and built the hospitals — and suffered the financial consequences.

On this particular day there was only one seat left on the plane, and Dr. G. was given the place next to a distinguished looking gentleman. The flight was very rough. Everyone was getting sick except Dr. G. and the man sitting beside him. They struck up a conversation while they listened to the ice hitting the fuselage. In those days, to keep the wings from icing up, a flexible rubber tubing was put on the leader edge of the wing. The pulsating motor pushed air through it and expanded it to break off the ice. Then the ice flew back and hit the fuselage. It sounded just like a machine gun. The two men talked for a few minutes, and Dr. G. mentioned his sentiments about socialized medicine.

Suddenly the gentleman next to him declared, "Why you sound like a Goddamned Republican!" Then the gentleman introduced himself. He was the Vice-President of the United States — Alben William Barkley. Dr. G. continued expressing opposing viewpoints about President Truman's policies. He and Barkley engaged in a friendly debate. They enjoyed one another's company throughout the turbulent journey, discussing everything from politics to the weather.

When it was time to get off, Barkley stood up pompously, stretched deliberately, and turned to face the people in the back of the plane. Then he turned to get his hat but couldn't find it. When Dr. G. got up they discovered that he had been sitting on the Vice-President's hat the whole time. Barkley, his hat no worse for wear, asked Dr. G. where he was staying. Then he offered to have his chauffeur drop him off at his hotel. Dr. G. rode in the Vice-President's limousine and was escorted to his hotel where the two parted as friends even if their politics did not agree.

One time on his way into the White House to see Eisenhower, Dr. G. was approached by a man who asked to take his picture. With visions of his photo in front of the White House on the front page of the newspapers, Dr. G. agreed, only to discover that it was a tourist trap. The photographer wanted two dollars for the photo. Dr. G. brought it home as a souvenir and a reminder for future visits to Washington, D.C.

A close friend who was a member of Rancheros Visitadores, Pat Patterson, President of United Airlines, told Dr. G. how he was invited to have dinner with President Franklin D. Roosevelt. Patterson was lobbying against Roosevelt's plan to take away the air mail service from the airlines and give it to the Army. One day his phone rang and a woman indentified herself as the President's secretary. She said that the President wished to invite Mr. Patterson for dinner at the White House that evening. Thinking it was all a gag from one of his Rancheros buddies, Patterson said, "Sure, sure," and hung up. The woman called again. "President and Mrs. Roosevelt want to have dinner with you at the White House tonight. Will you be there?" she asked. Finally Patterson was convinced that the call was authentic and went to a tailor and bought some appropriate dinner clothes. Then he got a cab and went to the White House where the butler ushered him into the Lincoln Room which was decorated in red. The President came down in an elevator and they had dinner. Then he entertained Patterson with an old movie, "The Last of the Mohicans," which Patterson had already seen. Afterwards the President said it was a wonderful evening and told him good night.

"The next morning he took the air mail contract away!" Patterson told Gellenthien. Roosevelt was simply sizing up his opponent. The Army's operation of the mail service was so unsuccessful, however, that before long it was given back to the air lines.

Many of Dr. G.'s influential friends came to visit him both at Valmora and to spend time at Gascon ranch. Dr. Irons had a strawberry patch that he carefully cultivated in the summer time. People from a big city like Chicago, who saw nothing but concrete, glass, and steel all day, had a particular longing to get out into the country and grow something in the rich earth. Dr. Irons was no exception. Dr. Slaymaker like to ride horseback but a special saddle had to be made for him to accommodate his large size.

The wealthy patients who came to Valmora were not given special privileges over the poor, for illness and death were the great equalizers and everyone was treated with the best medical treatment available. Once the wealthy M.D. Anderson came to see Dr. G. about his health. He was brought by a chauffeur in a big limousine to

Valmora Clinic. He went into the waiting room to wait. As he waited he visited with a native who lived near Tiptonville referred to here as Juan. Juan was called in next and was seen by Dr. G. for a bad leg condition. When Juan returned to the waiting room to get his jacket and leave, Mr. Anderson asked if he had a ride. He told Anderson that he did not own a car and intended to walk home, about 6 miles. Anderson's turn was next and he asked Dr. G. if he could defer his time. He wanted to leave for a while but he would return. Dr. G. told him that would be fine; he would see him when he got back. Then Anderson offered Juan a ride. When they arrived at the two room adobe house, Juan invited Anderson in for coffee. Then Anderson returned to the Clinic and saw Dr. G.

The next time Juan came to the Clinic, he told Dr. G. that the nice man who was in the waiting room with him last time was a real gentleman. He took him home in his nice car and came in for coffee.

"He looked around and told me and my wife what a nice house we had," Juan said. "And he said he liked the way he had everything fixed up. And then you know what that nice man did? He took out a hundred dollar bill and he gave it to me and said, 'You go buy some more of these nice things.'" Juan had no idea that he had been visited by one of the richest men in the nation, and he didn't care. He was just a nice man.

Death was the great equalizer, visiting rich and poor alike. Disease was no respector of persons. The doctor counted princes and presidents as well as common laborers and blue collar workers among his patients and friends. He talked with labor leaders like Walter Reuther and John L. Lewis. He spoke with religious leaders like Bishop Fulton J. Sheen and Rev. Billy Graham. He worked with bankers, farmers, ranchers, and railroaders. Comedians, movie stars, songwriters, artists, and novelists were among his friends. And so the doctor visited the homes of both rich and poor and made himself welcome in the hovel or in the hacienda. In the end, the hearts of the occupants were grateful.

NOTES

1. Carl H. Gellenthien, personal interview, Valmora, August 16, 1983.
2. Letters from James S. Calhoun to Orlando Brown, May 20, May 23, 1850, in Scrapbook 3, Valmora Library, Valmora, New Mexico, p. 51.
3. Carl H. Gellenthien, personal interview, Valmora, June 12, 1982.

CHAPTER
XV
Standing the Heat

"I'm not going to Cuba and that's final," the doctor said.

A group of Cubans had followed Dr. G. to his New York hotel room and pushed their way through the door. "We want you to reconsider, Dr. Gellenthien," the spokesman declared. "You must go to Cuba and give your lectures. We insist."

Dr. G.'s patience was wearing thin. His uninvited guests were proving more troublesome than he had expected.

"Cuba's Castro has turned out to be pro-Communist. As long as we thought he was an ally of this country, nothing was changed. But now that there's no doubt about his sympathies, it would be wrong for me to go and lecture there. I won't betray my country and the AMA by parleying with the enemy," Dr. G. declared.

The Cubans continued to argue, their voices growing more hostile.

"If you don't leave now, I'm going to call the F.B.I.," Gellenthien said. "You've harrassed me long enough. I've cancelled my lectures. There's no more to discuss."

Gellenthien knew he was at their mercy. If they chose to pull a gun on him, he would be helpless. Indeed, they began to threaten him. True to his word, Gellenthien picked up the phone.

"Give me the F.B.I.," he said into the phone.

Thirty seconds later, like the fast action of a melodramamtic movie, the F.B.I. men came charging into the room. They arrested the Cubans and handcuffed them after searching for weapons and finding none.

"How did you get here so fast?" Gellenthien asked, flabbergasted.

"We've been following you around for weeks, Doctor," one of the agents explained. "The telephone operator is one of our agents and besides, we were standing right outside your door. We suspected these guys would start some trouble."

"Why follow *me* around?" Dr. G. asked.

"Because Castro would love to get you to Cuba — and keep you there, that's why. We've been monitoring your telephone conversations for quite some time, keeping a tail on you for fear you might be abducted and taken to Cuba against your will."

"Well, some of the doctors are going to continue giving their lectures in Cuba, but it's against my convictions. But how did you know I'd turn them down?" Gellenthien aksed.

One of the agents replied, "Because Dr. Gellenthien, we know you."

They explained that they knew Dr. G. to be a loyal American and that he would not give into Communist threats, even if his very life were threatened.

Two physicians who did agree to go to Cuba were subsequently ousted from the AMA. The Cubans who gave Gallenthien a difficult time were put on a plane and sent back to Cuba.

United States' and Cuban relations were strained. Fidel Castro had shown his true colors and the U.S. was reacting coldly. Gellenthien, who was Vice-President of the AMA in 1953-54, did not realize how powerful his position was in the eyes of those who hoped to take advantage of his authority and use his power for their own purposes. Dr. G. had been in the AMA House of Delegates from 1938 to 1955 and was an Ex Officio member for life. He was on the Past Vice-President Council and various AMA committees. He was a life member of the American College of Physicians and a founding member of the World Medical Association. He belonged to the Royal Society of Health and the United States-Mexico Border Public Health Association. He was a founder and life member of the American College of Chest Physicians and served on its Board of Regents. He was a member of the American Academy of Tuberculosis Physicians and was President from 1954 to 1955. He was a Fellow of the American Association of Railway Surgeons in 1950-51, on the National Board of Directors of the American Cancer Society from 1950 to 1956, and was a member of the Aero-Space Medical Association. He was a life member of the National Tuberculosis Association and was on its Board of Directors from 1947 to 1953. He was on the Board of Directors, United Public Health League and was a life member of the Washington Institute of Medicine. Additionally, he was powerful in his influence as the Scientific Editor of the *Rocky Mountain Medical Journal*, the official journal for state medical societies of Montana, Utah, Wyoming, Nevada, Colorado and New

Mexico, from 1944 to 1956. Moreover, the Cubans knew of Dr. G.'s reputation as a practicing physician. It is no wonder the Cubans wanted such an authority to give medical lectures in their country. Indeed, Dr. G. had lectured in Cuba prior to Castro's take over.

> The Cuban Medical Society had invited Dr. Gellenthien to participate in the Third International Congress for Diseases of the Heart and Lungs held at the Curie Institute of the Cuban Medical School in Havana.
>
> The Gellentheins next went to Cameguey, in the lower central part of Cuba, to inspect the new Children's Hospital built on the ground of the old Leper Hospital.
>
> They next stopped at Montego Bay, Jamaica, where they were met and taken by auto down through the center and length of Jamaica to Kingston. Here the Jamaica Branch of the British Medical Association was holding its annual congress. They had previously invited Dr. Gellenthien to participate as their guest.
>
> The last stop of Dr. Gellenthien's medical speaking tour was in Port au Prince, Haiti. Haitian Medical Society was scheduled to meet three days... [1]

Gellenthien's reputation had, therefore, been widely known among the Cubans and because of his earlier speaking tours, his return visit was greatly desired. But Gellenthien was well known, too, for his outspoken stand against socialized medicine and against Communism. He had been Chairman of the New Mexico Physicians Committee to Combat Socialized Medicine and Communism from 1944 to 1949. Yet because of his scientific expertise and background, Gellenthien was asked to lecture in Russia. His work with developments in aviation medicine and research in aero-space was of great interest to them. The State Department advised Dr. G. not to go to Russia because "they'd never let you out again."

It was because of Dr. G.'s background and influence as a "king maker" that Castro's Cubans wished him to return to Cuba to lecture. But no amount of pressure would make him work with Communists.

President Truman's statement, "If you can't stand the heat, get out of the kitchen" made Dr. G. realize that if you want to be where the action is and accomplish your goals, you've got to be able to take some discomfort. He realized early in life that all of life is a struggle, a fight, in order to reach one's goals. Those who fail, who do not survive the battles, go under. "You have to be a fighter to survive," Dr. G. observed. "And you have to stand up for what you believe is right."

Gellenthien had survived because he had learned to "stand the heat." As a youth he struggled through school. He fought the battle to regain his health before he could finish medical school. Financing his education required many long hours of work. As a medical student, he went to school all day and worked from six p.m. to six a.m. for the City of Chicago as night surgeon. Existing on only a few hours of sleep between times, it is no wonder that his health broke down. But even after his recovery at Valmora he had a struggle to get through his internship. It was always one battle or another.

As a doctor, Gellenthien fought for the lives of his patients. The fight wasn't always against disease. The fight was sometimes a quest for a patient's mental well-being, as when he persuaded someone not to commit suicide. Sometimes the fight was against outside forces pitted against a patient. Sometimes the battle carried Dr. G. into the courtroom or the judge's chambers.

A court battle in 1969 took Dr. G. to Colorado to testify regarding the life of an infant who had been battered by his mother. In 1983 Dr. G. was called to Mora to testify for a woman whose husband had beaten her.

Gellenthien's dogged determination to win his battles for his patients' lives was displayed more than once. Even as the priest was administering the last rites to a TB patient *in extremis*, Dr. G. was working to pull him through.

But many of Gellenthien's battle scars were received outside the sick room. One of those fights was against socialzed medicine and the threat of Communism. The battle against socialized medicine was a long one. The first conflict over the federal role in medical care was from 1948 to 1952 when the AMA opposed Truman and the Wagner-Murray-Dignell proposal for national health insurance. Organized labor backed Truman. The AMA sponsored a multi-million-dollar advertising campaign, the "National Education Campaign" launched under the direction of California's Clem Whitaker and his wife Leone Baxter, who ran a successful public relations firm.

"It was to be a holy war. In those days, AMA and its allies considered themselves in the front line of a battle between freedom and 'socialism.'"[2] The AMA recommended "Voluntary Health Insurance," stating that it was the American Way. Physicians expanded membership in Blue Cross-Blue Shield during 1945 -1950 from 19 million to 39 million.[3]

Britain had nationalized its medical system. Whitaker argued against bringing "socialized medicine from sick England to healthy America."[4]

The Wagner-Murray-Dingell bill was first proposed in 1943, and for most of the 1940s the AMA was led by Morris Fishbein, M.D., who was editor of the *Journal of the American Medical Association,* and Olin West, M.D., the secretary-general manager. Fishbein, a friend of Dr. G., encouraged his colleagues in the fight. He was so well-known throughout the medical world and by the public in general that he was given the title, "Mr. AMA."

The years from 1943 to 1952 were years of intense crusading against the socialism of the Wagner-Murray-Dingell NHI bills. Whitaker and Baxter shrewdly zeroed in on the public's reluctance to politicize medicine. In his memoirs, Harry Truman wrote that his most bitter defeat was to the AMA.[5]

But the movement did not die with the end of the Truman administration. The Kennedy Administration backed the King-Anderson bill to have Social Security take over hospital care for the aged. Leonard Larson, President of the AMA, spoke out against it on national television, but he could not compete with John F. Kennedy's popularity. Kennedy had organized labor behind him. On July 17, 1962 the bill came to a vote on the Senate floor. AMA representative David Baldwin recalled:

> I don't suppose I'll see anything like it again. Every single senator was there, including Dennis Chavez, who was near death and had to be brought in a wheelchair. Vice President Lyndon B. Johnson presided. The nose count AMA had was so close we couldn't call it.[6]

The AMA won, 52 to 48, but in 1965 Congress passed Medicare over AMA's violent objections by a 3 to 1 margin.[7]

Dr. G. opposed Senator Chavez on the issue of socialized medicine throughout the years. When Chavez was at Lovelace Clinic, losing the battle against his illness, he met Gellenthien in the hall. The Democratic Senator said he was glad to see his old adversary. "We always fought a clean fight," he said. "Usually I beat you — but sometimes you beat me." It was the last time Gellenthien saw his old opponent. They parted as friends. Chavez died while still in office, November 18, 1962.

In his speech "Socialized Medicine is the Keystone in the Arch of Communism," Dr. Gellenthien stated that trouble began in the 1930's when so-called social reform coming from a small section of the Democratic Party called the New Deal was introduced. When the AMA began its attempts to influence proposed legislation in Congress, President Roosevelt ordered the U.S. Attorney General to indict and prosecute the AMA as a monopoly and trust. This was done and a "packed" and "rigged" New Deal Supreme Court of the U.S. pronounced the medical profession guilty, forcing abandonment of organized resistance on the part of the medical profession. He stated that the year 1939 marked a milestone in the history of American medicine, for in that year the first bold attempt of the group of collectivist thinkers was manifested through open action. They planned through the enslavement of medicine to impose a bureaucratic political control over the lives of citizens. American medicine was indicted and physicians were charged with being members of a trade union. Dr. G. stated that the case was not tried in the courts; it was tried in the newspapers. "All of the resources and facilities of the government's hundred million dollar propaganda machine were devoted to besmirching American doctors and the private practice system."[8]

The National Physicians Committee for the Extension of Medical Services was organized as a trust on November 18, 1939 and incorporated as a non-profit corporation. American medicine wanted an agency that could speak for the professions in awakening the American public to a recognition of its priceless heritage and the basic part that free medicine plays in maintaining individual initiative and our American concept that the individual is all important in any form of free government. Pamphlets, radio and news commentaries plus speeches explained the basic issues and the inherent danger in the regimentation of health care services. The N.P.C. released editorials telling of the progress, aims, and achievements of American medicine under the private practice system.

Gellenthien, as a member of the AMA House of Delegates and as President of the New Mexico Physicians Committee, traveled all over. He gave testimony to the U.S. Senate regarding the Wagner-Murray-Dingell Bill and they called him back for a supplementary statement and more information. Gellenthien strongly believed in the cause as indicated by statements from his speeches: "As a result of the WMD Bill, we gradually realized that the medical profession had been singled out deliberately for the first attack and that here existed a master plan for Communizing the United States."[9] Gellenthien cited evidence to support his opinion:

> The campaign for Socialized Medicine in the United States stems directly from Kremlin Communism. Louis F. Bundez, former editor of the Communist Daily Worker in New York, and one-time Communist Central Committee member for the U.S., relates in his recent memoirs that Dimitri Manuilsky, Secretary of the Communist International, first urged compulsory social insurance as a segment of the world revolution program in 1930.[10]

Dr. Gellenthien said that Lenin, in his Communist Manifesto, stated, "Socialized medicine is the keystone in the Arch of Communism." Gellenthien stated that the Communists felt that when they move into a new country, they could wield a tremendous influence if they could socialize medicine.[11]

Socialized medicine was defeated by one vote in Hawaii after the N.P.C. sent informative material and some staff members over to fight against the proposed program.

In his statement to the U.S. Senate Committee on Education and Labor, April 17, 1946, Dr. G. gave some background on New Mexico and Mora County. New Mexico's 122,303 square miles was sparsely populated, with roughly 3.5 people per square mile. The State's area is approximately twice the combined area of all the New England states, divided into 31 counties, the smallest being Bernalillo which is about the size of Rhode Island, Dr. G. said. The largest county is Socorro, which has about the same area as Massachusetts. Mora County had a population of 10,387 at that time. The size of the average family was 4.5. The area of Mora County is 1,942 square miles. There were no towns over 1,332 population in Mora County. Only two towns, Mora and Wagon Mound, had electricity and few of the natives enjoyed running water or indoor toilets. The average income per family was $2,200, up from $1,500 the previous year. Dr. G. stated that the cost of medical care to New Mexicans was being taken care of by the voluntary medical service plan of the New Mexico Physicians Service. He pointed out that the charity cases were always taken care of while those who could afford to pay did so.[12]

He said that the most critical need of New Mexicans was for good all-weather, ranch-to-market roads.

> A glance at a map of New Mexico shows several large counties sparsely populated, that have no doctor. They have never had a doctor or hospital, and no doctor could afford to practice in these counties. If, instead of looking at a political map, one looks at a topographical map, one immediately sees the county is bisected by a mountain range or canyon, thus making it impossible to get from one part of the country to another. In Rio Arriba County, the towns of Tierra Amarilla and Gobernador are 45 miles apart but one has to drive 345 miles to get from one town to the other. Sickness does not recognize political and artificial boundaries.[13]

Dr. G. pointed out that there were only two doctors of medicine in Mora County at that time, one 73 year old who was physically incapacitated, and himself. There were no general hospitals in the county. He concluded his statement to the Committee with the following:

> So, in summarizing, I express the sentiments of my fellow New Mexicans when I say, "We emphatically do not want more government interference with our daily lives; we want less. We do not want more taxes; we want less. We definitely do not want the provisions of

Senate Bill 1606 and its political regulation of our lives. We feel that if you must do something, then give us larger appropriations for the betterment of our public health and general welfare; give us good, all-weather, ranch-to-market roads and help us build small dams to insure ample water for irrigation so that we can raise bigger and better crops... We do not wish to be regimented, socialized, communized, or regulated by Federal Government business.

We New Mexicans detest and resent emphatically the interference of well-intentioned but uninformed social workers, the professional "do-gooders," and other parasites on Government payrolls. We do not enjoy driving down our highways and seeing car after car pass us with tax exempt license plates from a multitude of Federal bureaus.

In the west we rid our cattle of parasites by dipping the herd in nicotine. The non-producers on the range we eliminate by shipping to market.

If Congress feels that it must do something for the people of New Mexico, then HELP US TO HELP OURSELVES, BUT DON'T TRY TO MAKE US WARDS OF THE GOVERNMENT. [14]

In his "supplementary statement" of July 19, 1946, Dr. G. stated that medical care is intimate, personal, and varied according to the character and personality of every patient and that as such it can never lend itself to impersonal mass-production methods. He stated that every patient presents a distinct problem, varied by many complex factors of heritage, environment, training, personality and self-discipline. "To ignore, submerge or neglect these vital factors of personality in the relationship of physician and patient would destroy at one stroke the very foundations of America's supremacy in medicine today." [15]

He again stressed the need for improvement in roads. This would increase rural incomes sufficiently to raise living, housing and sanitary conditions to the proper health level, he said. "It will make medical facilities available almost everywhere, since distances are a matter of time rather than miles." [16] He concluded by stating that Communist medicine is not for free America. He stated that America leads the world in the quality and availability of medical care for all the people, not because bureaucrats and trade unions swarm our hospitals daily with their forms, inspections, and certifications, but because American medicine has always been guided and stimulated by the sacred inspirations of liberty, freedom and enterprise. [17]

We must not — we dare not — risk the loss of those inspirations and ideals for a capricious experiment in state medicine.

Sitting by the side of the desert trail under the clear skies of New Mexico, we find time to reflect on the progress and opportunities of

mankind and medicine under our American way of life. With clearly
thinking heads we differentiate between the advantages gained by
progress through individual initiative rather than political largesse. In
New Mexico we simply want the kind of help that will assist us to
solve our own problems in our own way. [18]

Gellenthien's role as spokesman for New Mexico was appropriate as he had been a member of the New Mexico Medical Society since 1927, served as its President from 1944 to 1946 and served on its Executive Council from 1947 to 1956. He was a founder of the New Mexico Physicians Service in 1944, New Mexico Medical Society's Prepaid Medical Care Plan and served on its Board of Trustees from 1944 to 1956. He also belonged to the New Mexico State Tuberculosis Association and was its President from 1942 to 1946 and served on its Board of Directors and Executive Committee from 1936 to 1954. He belonged to the New Mexico Public Health Association and was Chairman of the New Mexico Physicians Committee to Combat Socialized Medicine and Communism from 1936 to 1954. He was also a member of the New Mexico State Hospital Association and served as President. He was a New Mexico Division Chairman and served on the Board of Trustees of the American Cancer Society. He belonged to the Rocky Mountain Medical Conference and was Chairman from 1950 to 1952. He was the New Mexico Representative from 1949 to 1952. He was a Life Member of the East Mora County Health Association of Wagon Mound and served as President of San Miguel-Mora County Medical Society from 1934 to 1935. He belonged to national organizations such as the American Geriatrics Society, American Heart Association, American Public Health Association, Society for Nuclear Medicine, Southwestern Medical Association and United Public Health League where he served on its Board of Directors. He was also a life member of the Washington Institute of Medicine. Certainly he was well qualified to speak as a medical representative from New Mexico.

Dr. G. visited the White House no less than ten times in his battle against socialized medicine. Wilbur Cohen, Secretary of Health, Education and Welfare in President Roosevelt's cabinet told Dr. G., "We will put the program down tile by tile. When the mosaic is completed we will have socialized medicine." [19]

The best way Dr. G. knew to fight socialized medicine was to offer an attractive alternative. That was why he became one of the founders of the New Mexico Physicians' Service. It would offer affordable health care without selling out to socialistic or Communistic forms of regulation.

A good description of Dr. G.'s role in New Mexico's fight against socialized medicine by offering an alternative is found in a letter written on January 2, 1982 by Lou Lagrave, Executive Director of the Physician's Service who worked closely with Dr. G.

In the middle thirties...a Committee for the Study of the Costs of Medical Care was authorized in Washington...The bottom line, after several years of intensive work, was that the quality of medical care practiced in the country was tops, but that its cost, or its availability to patients at a price they could afford, was a matter of serious concern. The implication was obvious. If patients could not obtain the medical care they needed because of its cost, a government which under FDR had tried the most amazing social and economic programs, was the logical instrument to find a solution. The economic despair of the period practically assured acceptance of some form of socialized medicine. None knew this better than physicians in the industrialized states...in 1939 two states, Michigan and California, started to offer, to their low-income patients, pre-paid surgical and in-hospital medical care on a service basis. Service is the critical word. Participating physicians would provide their service, be compensated by the pre-paid plan, according to an accepted schedule, without additional cost to the patient for that covered service.

The practice had always been that to whatever health insurance the patient had, the physician would tack-on enough to make his fee, or a fatter fee.

Very shortly after Michigan and California doctors started these service plans...Hitler...invaded Poland. Our best physicians were gobbled up for the Armed Services. Everyone in the industrial states went to work including Rosie the Riveter, and who cared about the cost of anything, including medical care?

For the next few years over worked physicians met no resistance whatsoever to their ever-rising fees. Medically-sponsored service plans were available, but were sabotaged regularly by physicians when management, or labor, called on their own physicians for a recommendation.

Unfortunately, all good things come to an end and so did our World War II economy. Eager physicians were coming back to private practice, but you need patients, preferably paying patients, to practice. Although New Mexico had prospered little from the war, it had no scarcity of physicians coming...

Carl G. was president of the New Mexico Medical Society on two successive years, 1944-45 and 1945-46. This period was the ending of the war, with its relocation and adjustment problems for his colleagues. His frequent attendance to national and regional meetings exposed him to the rumblings against the cost of medical care...Carl

*was in personal contact with very prominent national business
leaders, many of whom were directors or sponsors of Valmora
Sanitorium. He got the message (about the need for a low cost health
care plan) everywhere. The demand for some sort of socialized
medicine was growing in the industrial states. If it got going it would
sweep the country, with bureaucrats dictating the quality of medical
care to the detriment of tax payers, and most important, the patient.* [20]

Lagrave described Dr. G.'s efforts in setting up an affordable
medical care program for low-income New Mexicans. He visited the
California Medical Association to investigate its service medical program and he visited all over New Mexico, all at his own expense. He
selected the first Board of Trustees for the proposed New Mexico
Physicians Service, along with John Conway as its president. Conway, a surgeon in Clovis, along with Gellenthien "were targets of bitter attacks from many in the New Mexico medical profession
who...thought it was their God-given right to soak the patient and
his responsible relatives." [21]

The New Mexico Physicians' Service started with a capitaliza-
tion of nine hundred dollars. Each Trustee donated a hundred and
physicians around the state were asked for donations. The premium
for New Mexico Physicians' Service was $1.55 per month, per fami-
ly, making affordable medical care available to low income families.
The Service was finally phased out after numerous changes and considerable opposition to it took place.

*The struggle that creating, sustaining, and fighting for the survival
of a system entailed for all connected with it was mellowed by the
fabulous hospitality of Dr. G. and that unequalled great lady, Alice, in
their annual entertaining of the Board of Trustees and their families
at the beautiful Gascon Ranch. Alice would do wonders on that huge
wood stove and Carl would wake the guests playing "Home on the
Range" on his accordion. (No matter what one asked for, it always
came out "Home on the Range.")...They finally crushed us — but of
all the medical plans started, New Mexico was one of the toughest to
beat.* [22]

Not all the battles were in the legislative halls of Congress or in
the small rooms of council or committee assemblies. Some were at
home where the political web had ensnared innocent people in its
trap. The New Mexico State Hospital — called the Insane Asylum —
was always a political battlefield in those days.

Dr. G. did not intend to get involved in such battles, but
somehow he seemed to fall into them. And when he saw an injustice
being done, he soon found himself in the heat of the battle, trying to
protect the innocent or to oust the wrong-doers. He went into the bat-

tle with the same attitude he had discovered when he saw a man struggling in the river, drowning.

"There were other people standing there watching, people who could swim. But no one jumped in to rescue him. So I had to. What else could I do?" And he did.

On January 15, 1943, Governor John Dempsey appointed Dr. Gellenthien and Pablo Lopez of Las Vegas to the board of the state insane asylum. Conditions at the Hospital in the early days were primitive by today's standards. As Dr. G. began to become familiar with the day to day functioning of the hospital, the work of the personnel, and the treatment of the patients, he felt that something had to be done. No one else was offering to jump in and help, so it was up to him.

A commonly used technique that was supposed to somehow shock patients out of their insanity was called the Scotch Douche. Patients were put into a room where they were suddenly doused with ice water. Then they were immediately squirted with hot water.

Arsenic was used in treatment for syphilis before penicillin. An experiment was done at the Insane Asylum to try another cure. Patients who had syphilis at the Asylum were exposed to the malaria mosquito under controlled conditons. When the victims got the fever, which was high enough to kill the syphilis germ, they were given quinine to cure the malaria. Later the fever cabinet was invented. After that patients were put into the cabinet to produce fever instead of being given malaria. The cabinet enclosed the entire body except the head. Cold packs were put on their heads so they could survive the high fever. They had to stand in the fever cabinet until the temperature was high enough to kill the syphilis organism.

As a past Vice-President and Ex-Officio member of the AMA's House of Delegates, Gellenthien became a part of the policing of the AMA in keeping unqualified or unethical doctors out of the country. One time Dr. G. discovered that the Superintendent of the New Mexico State Hospital was not a physician at all, nor was his wife the nurse she claimed be. The couple were actually ex-convicts from the state prison at Joliet, Illinois. They were masquerading as doctor and nurse. The man was in charge of the entire hospital and had been given the position on his false credentials. After Gellenthien's investigation uncovered the facts, the man and his wife were sent back to Joliet.

There was also a doctor at the Insane Asylum who proclaimed to be a good surgeon. He performed operations which involved scrambling the front lobes of the brain, supposedly to cure dementia praecox (precocious dementia). He was paid a handsome fee for each operation, so he advocated the operation frequently. Then he split the fee with the individuals who helped him set them up.

"They were a bunch of crooked politicians," Gellenthien said.

Gellenthien also found that hospital staff members were pilfering just about everything, including the livestock. The hospital had its own dairy and small farm. Employees were getting away with pigs, chickens, and even cows. Of course the tax payer was absorbing the cost. What enraged Dr. G. the most was when he discovered hospital employees pimping. They were exploiting the female patients by setting them up for sex with any man who wanted to pay the pimp. Dr. G. had all the dishonest employees he could find fired.

About two years later, however, there was another political upheaval and three members of the Board of Directors of the New Mexico Insane Asylum were removed "for *incompentency*," among them Dr. Gellenthien. Dr. Gellenthien, whose name was misspelled in the Governor's declaration, noticed that the word "incompetency" was also misspelled. He bought a ten-cent dictionary and sent it to the Governor for Christmas. They became good friends after that.

There was considerable political controversy over the Governor's decision but Gellenthien was glad to be out of it.

Gellenthien couldn't stay entirely away from the political arena, however. There was a movement to run Dr. G. for Governor of New Mexico. Before the campaign got underway, however, he backed out of the race. For one thing, it was the Roosevelt era and he felt he didn't have a chance to win. The investment of energy, time, and money would take away from his medical work, and he didn't feel it was worth it. His job was to serve his patients, he believed, not to become Governor.

"Besides, I'd only get a couple of votes," he said. "Alice and I are probably the only Republicans in Mora County."

Dr. G.'s honesty was tested when a patient was asked to resign from her position at a local company. She came in bringing insurance forms which Dr. G. was supposed to sign, showing that the woman was no longer able to work. The woman wanted her job and was able to work. The company was supposedly doing her a favor by sending her to get a medical statement that she was no longer "able" to work. They assumed the doctor would cooperate. Gellenthien was irate to learn that he was supposed to lie, saying the woman was sick when she wasn't. Dr. G. filled out the form with the truth. Under "Diagnosis" he wrote "None." Under "Why she left work" he put, "Should not have left; not sick."

The next day the vice-president of the company was in Dr. G.'s office. Gellenthien said he'd write an editorial as editor of the *Rocky*

Mountain Medical Journal, disclosing the dishonest practice of the company for trying to make a doctor party to a lie. He reminded the gentleman that he was also a member of the AMA House of Delegates. The company backed down, and the woman kept her job.

Another time a representative of a large drug company, referred to here as Tony Spencer, came to visit with Dr. G. in his office. He had been coming to Valmora for years to check the pharmaceutical supplies and take new orders. On this particular day he was downcast, saying it would be his last trip as the company was letting him go. The company was merging with another company, and he was being dropped. Dr. G. wrote a diplomatic letter to the company, telling them now much he regretted the news that Mr. Spencer would no longer be the company representative to Valmora and that without him, Valmora Sanatorium would no longer be purchasing supplies from the company. A letter came back stating that a decision had been made not to fire Mr. Spencer after all. Valmora was one of their largest accounts, and they did not want to lose it. Thus, Mr. Spencer's job was saved.

"Sometimes a man is trapped and can't help himself, but a third party can step in and fight for him," Dr. G. explained.[23]

Dr. G. helped Ralph Marshall, Executive Secretary of the New Mexico Medical Society, in the early days. In 1949 the House of Delegates of the New Mexico Medical Society created the job of Executive Secretary at $4,000 a year. Marshall applied for the job and offered to have his bride Elaine help at $1.00 an hour. The young couple went to work and did an excellent job. But Marshall was on a yearly contract and had no job security, always wondering if his contract would be renewed the next year. Dr. G. told him he'd see what he could do.

At the meeting that year the delegates were all gathered around the evening before the business was to be conducted. Most of them had indulged in alcoholic beverages and were feeling cheerful. Dr. G. suggested to the delegates that Ralph deserved a five year contract, at $10,000 a year. They all agreed and said they'd draw up a new contract, a five year one, in the morning. Dr. G. told them he'd already had it done, so they wouldn't have to bother. They all signed the contract that night. The next morning some of them had second thoughts about it.

"What if we decide we don't want Ralph? This five year contract isn't so good."

"Well, if you don't want Ralph any more, all you have to do is pay him off for the total amount — $50,000 — and hire someone else," Dr. G. explained.

The delegates were happy with the job Marshall was doing and he continued to hold the position where he is still working as Executive Director as of this writing.

Dr. G. helped to keep the Veterans Administration Hospital open at Fort Bayard. President Johnson's Administration had decided to close eleven veterans hospitals. The President asked VA Administration officer William J. Driver to personally visit each of the hospitals and make another review. Johnson said some of the testimony he had received about the hospital at Fort Bayard had raised doubts in his mind as to "whether we are 100 percent right in ordering the closings." Some of that testimony came from Dr. G. The House Veterans Committee approved the bill giving it veto control of such closings unless the administration came up with a compromise. The President said, "I will be reviewing it and I may ask some other people to help me with that task."[24] Johnson had been reading the testimony and statements of Congressmen from the hospital areas and said "Some doubt in my own mind has resulted from reading their statements."[25] Dr. G. was asked by Congressman Thomas G. Morris to serve on the medical evaluation team to investigate Fort Bayard in 1965.

On February 10, 1964, Dr. G. wrote a report to the Congressman saying, "After a diligent attempt to ascertain a true state of affairs at Fort Bayard Hospital, I am convinced that the present attempt to close this hospital is ill-advised, and not based on facts or horse sense, and is an extravagant waste of money."[26]

In spite of his prominent position in American medicine, there was a time when Dr. G. was refused admittance to a hospital to care for an injured man in the emergency room. Dr. G. was bringing a new station wagon from Denver, a gift, back to New Mexico, when he saw a one-car accident on the road ahead. He stopped to render aid. The driver of the car was bleeding profusely where his arm had been nearly severed and was just hanging by a piece of skin. Using a belt as a tourniquet, Dr. G. removed the arm with his pocket knife and tossed it into the back of the new station wagon. Then he got the man into his vehicle and rushed him to the small hospital in the nearest Colorado town.

At the hospital the nurse refused Gellenthien entrance, although he explained that he was physician and a man's life depended on his getting immediate treatment.

"There was a one-car accident on the highway. I stopped to help," he explained. "This man needs medical attention fast or he'll die."

The nurse remained adamant.

Gellenthien's patience ran out. He literally broke through the door and wheeled the man into the operating room himself. Then he ordered the astonished nurse to assist in sewing up the arm. Just as he was finishing up the surgery, one of the local doctors showed up, so Dr. G. turned the case over to him and made his departure, leaving the severed arm at the hospital.

He drove on to the port of entry. Since he had no license for the new vehicle, the officer asked Dr. G. to get out and then carefully inspected it to make sure it wasn't stolen. When he saw blood stains on the back seat, he asked, "What's that all over the back seat?"

"Blood," the doctor replied.

"What kind of blood?" the officer asked suspiciously.

"Human blood," Dr. G. stated.

The officer got very excited. Dr. G. explained what had happened and suggested that he call the State Police to verify the story. He agreed.

Impatient to be on his way, Dr. G. got behind the wheel again, determined to be off. It was then that he found himself face to face with the officer's gun. Dr. G. decided to wait until the fellow made his call and cleared him. He did — and he was.

Nothing made Dr. G. more angry than incompetence and waste in public health care. When he learned of a health officer who was going to close down a school cafeteria because venereal disease had been discovered in the community, he wrote the following letter to a citizen who had expressed concern over the matter:

> Many years ago my fellow doctors recognized the need and value of preventive medicine...These old time doctors, like my father-in-law, Dr. W.T. Brown at Valmora, started the State and County Public Health Department in New Mexico to carry out the public or preventive health programs of the New Mexico Medical Society.
>
> Somewhere in the 1930's, by the time I was active in state medical affairs, I thought that one could improve the so-called Public or Preventive Health program by setting up Health Districts similar to the District Judges.
>
> We did this; for a while it worked fine...Then due to the war, lack of proper planning, or maybe politics at the State level, the State Health Department had 'kinda' fallen apart...I am sorry that the State Health Department is in such poor shape.
>
> Today...I came in contact with a gonorrhea snooper or venereal disease contact finder who now has the exalted title of "district sanitaritan"...I am sorry and I apologize to you that the New Mexico State Medical Society's program of prevention of disease has been so prostituted by the hiring of an egotitstic, overbearing, dumb, and inef-

ficient representative for the State Health Department as Mr. ——.

I shall do everything in my power to see that the State Health Department stops its German Gestapo practices of sneering, threatening, brow beating, and causing you to waste money on unnecessary changes in your stores, businesses and school cafeterias. Your many unpleasant experiences that you have told to me are incredible and I am staggered to realize that this could happen in the United States...money has been wasted by unnecessary travel and expense...They have offered me those all-expense first class hotel trips but I have never accepted one from the State Public Health Department. Just the opposite; I have raised hell about them and thought that bribery like that should be stopped.

I can only say that I am sorry for the unnecessary unpleasantness, mental anguish, distress, and foolish spending of money that these tyranical bureaucrats like Mr. —— have forced upon you.

As an officer of the American Medical Association, I promise you Mr. —— will leave New Mexico and in his place let us all try to find someone who will help and guide us in our common goal — HEALTH FOR ALL. [27]

The unethical officer was replaced soon thereafter and he left the state.

In his lifetime Dr. G. has fought many battles, some of them in an attempt to win victory over disease. He witnessed the conquering of the bacterial world with antibiotics. This he cites as the greatest accomplishment he observed in his lifetime. Some of the goals, he personally attained through much perseverance. The battles were many, but Dr. G. was a winner. He agreed with Winston Churchill who said:

Never give in, never give in, never, never, never, never — in nothing great or small, large or petty — never give in except to convictions of honor and good sense. [28]

NOTES

1. "Gellenthiens In West Indies Trip," n.t., n.p., n.d., newspaper clipping in Scrapbook 3, Valmora Library, p. 1.
2. "AMA's Washington Office — Its Legend and Its Legacy," *American Medical News*, June 18, 1982, p. 9.
3. *Ibid.*
4. *Ibid.*
5. *Ibid.*
6. *Ibid.*, p. 9.
7. *Ibid.*
8. C.H. Gellenthien, "Socialized Medicine is the Keystone in the Arch of Communism," manuscript of speech, Scrapbook 4, Valmora Library, p. 81.
9. *Ibid.*
10. *Ibid.*
11. *Ibid.*
12. Carl H. Gellenthien, "Statement of Carl H. Gellenthien, M.D., President of the New Mexico Medical Society, Presented to the U.S. Senate Committee on Education and Labor," reprint from *Rocky Mountain Medical Journal*, September, 1946, p. 1, in Scrapbook 3, Valmora Library, Valmora, New Mexico, p. 35.
13. *Ibid.*, p. 2.
14. *Ibid.*
15. *Ibid.*
16. *Ibid.*
17. *Ibid.*
18. *Ibid.*
19. *Ibid.*
20. Lou Lagrave, Letter to Dorothy Beimer, January 2, 1982.
21. *Ibid.*
22. *Ibid.*
23. Carl H. Gellenthien, personal interview, Valmora, June 9, 1983.
24. "LBJ Heeds Capitol Hill Criticism, Orders New Study of VA Hospitals," n.t., n.p., n.d., in Scrapbook 3, Valmora Library, Valmora, New Mexico, p. 54.
25. Willard Edwards, "Johnson Puts Off Shutdowns by VA," n.t., n.p., n.d., in Scrapbook 3, Valmora Library, p. 54

26. C.H. Gellenthien, letter to The Honorable Thomas G. Morris, February 10, 1965, in Scrapbook 3, Valmora Library, p. 55.
27. Carl H. Gellenthien, letter in Scrapbook 20, Valmora Library, p. 21.
28. Winston Churchill, quoted in *Medical Aspects of Human Sexuality*, 16 (November, 1982), n.p.

CHAPTER
XVI

The Movers and Shakers

When Carl Gellenthien was a student he developed a desire to do medical research. That desire did not develop overnight. It was budding even when he was a child. One of his earliest memories depicts the curiosity of a two-year-old child looking out the window at a streetcar passing by. Carl would push a little button near the window to see if it would make a streetcar go by. He soon found that there was no casual relationship between the window button and the streetcar outside. Apparently it had a schedule of its own beyond his control.

When Carl attended St. John's Elementary School, he was told not to question, only to believe. But sometimes blind belief seemed unreasonable to young Carl. When his aunt had a miscarriage she was convinced that God was punishing her for some reason. Later, when his brother Henry died, Carl was told that it was God's will. Yet 30 years later Henry would have been saved by a simple shot of penicillin. Thus, the question "why" remained in Carl's mind. He wanted more education. He wanted to find more answers. He believed in God, but he believed that God gave man intelligence to be used for his own benefit and progress. Carl liked the philosophy of the desert Arab, who trusting God, sees that his camel is well-tied. He believed that God helps those who help themselves. Ignorance was the great sin that kept man from helping himself. If it could be overcome, man could do greater things, and God would be glorified.

Carl realized that it is often impossible for a person born in the ghetto to break out, to become educated and develop a career, to rise above the crowd. Carl was not born in the ghetto, but it was difficult enough for him.

When he attended Tuley High School, determined to finish, he had to fight the attitudes of family friends and of relatives who said

Carl should drop out and get a job. At least he should take some short, "practical" course in business and get right into the job market. But Carl's ambitions ran in a different direction. When he said he wanted to study science and medicine, he had to overcome the scorn of some of his elders. His aunt laughed at him for wanting to become a doctor. His uncle thought if he must go to school he should become a minister for the Lutheran Church. Someone else advised him to become an accountant.

Carl finished high school in less than the usual four years because he carried an extra heavy load. He went right on to Crane Junior College to obtain his basic courses. At the same time, he worked as Secretary at the YMCA and took on any other jobs he could get. He graduated from Crane Junior College June 17, 1921. His father helped him obtain a small scholarship and he entered the University of Illinois School of Medicine.

There Carl was introduced to the microscope and the wonders beneath it. He learned to identify the various organisms and to spot the deadly ones. His professors were demanding and meticulous. In his pathology class Carl and his classmates were given difficult tasks. The professor would hold up a muscle or a nerve and ask the student to identify its proper location in the human body and to describe its function. Students had to give case histories of patients who had died, stating what diagnosis had been given by the doctor, what treatment had been given, and what the final outcome. Then the pathologist would step forward with the final diagnosis — the facts revealed by autopsy.

"It was like gambling," Dr. G. stated. "Sometimes were were wrong. Most of the time we were right. But there was no arguing with the final diagnosis."

The first cadaver Carl had to dissect came from a common tank where medical students would fish one out with a hook. The one Carl got still had stockings on. In the early days bodies available for medical science were scarce. But when word got out that "no grave was safe" from the zealous curiosity and scientific endeavor of medical students, efforts were made to obtain bodies more officially. By the time Carl was in medical school, there were plenty of bodies to study. But the methods of preserving them in a common tank of formaldehyde left much to be desired. On that first day of fishing in the tank, several students became ill. A good number dropped out after that because they couldn't take the strenuous work load.

In June of 1982 Dr. G. attended the AMA Convention in Chicago and while there visited the campus of the University of Illinois. He visited his old pathology department on the campus of the College of

Medicine. He marveled at the changes that have taken place since the early 1920s. Modern techniques have replaced the near-primitive methods of those days. Refrigeration has replaced the "tank," and the autopsy room is well-lighted and well-ventilated.

One of Dr. G.'s first research studies was on climate and health, especially the effects of altitude and barometric pressure on the lungs. He made a climatological data chart which illustrated these effects. The chart compared Valmora, 6200 feet in altitude, with Chicago, 550 feet in altitude. In Chicago, one pound of air occupies 13.2 cubic feet; at Valmora one pound of air occupies 16.3 cubic feet. In Chicago the oxygen was 18 to 19 percent by volume due to impurities and smoke while at Valmora the oxygen was 20.8 percent by volume at the time of this study. In Chicago water boils at 211 degrees Fahrenheit. The average barometric pressure in Chicago is 14.4 pounds per square inch or 29.4 inches of Mercury; at Valmora the average barometric pressure is 11.7 pounds per square inch or 23.7 inches of Mercury.[1] This meant that at Valmora there was less air pressure to tear the diseased lungs and they had a better chance of recovery. This study was one of Gellenthien's first original research projects and was significant in its findings. It meant that consumptives had a better chance of recovery in a climate like Valmora's. The knowledge that there was less barometric pressure at high altitudes gave hope to consumptives with lung cavities. A blood vessel running through a lung eaten away by tuberculosis was like a fragile balloon in the wind, unprotected and uncovered. The slightest pressure could cause it to burst. There was no surrounding tissue to cushion it. The vulnerable vessel was stretched from one area of the lung to another in helpless solitude. Weakened by the eroding process of the tubercle bacilli, it became as fragile as a frayed, old rubber band. If it broke, the patient could hemorrhage and die. Thus, less pressure on the lungs was highly desirable. Dr. G.'s study proved to be a pragmatic experiment. Valmora had fewer deaths than any other sanatorium of its size.[2]

This study on climate led Dr. G. to complete an original research project on the study of altitude and artificial pneumothorax. In the early days one method of treatment was to let the diseased lung heal by collapsing it and letting it rest. Early in his career Dr. G. developed the Valmora Artificial Pneumathorax Apparatus, a simple one-valve machine for use for pneumothorax pneumoporitenoeum and thoracic aspiration. There were other pneumothorax machines in use but his was unique. Apparently he had excellent results with it. None of his patients ever died from the procedure. By the time Dr. G. got around to applying for a patent on it, the machine was no longer needed.

The research problem was to determine the effect of pressure on the collapsed lung of a tuberculosis patient during air travel. He had realized the necessity for such research when a patient was flown in to Valmora and arrived *in extremis*. She had left New York with a collapsed lung (artificial pneumothorax) but the altitude of air travel had altered the air pressure in her thorax.

Dr. G. quickly inserted a hollow needle into her lung and let the air out "just like you'd let it out of an over-inflated tire." The woman recovered with no complications. It was then that Dr. G. realized that patients could not be flown safely until the changes in air pressure were considered and the proper adaptations made.

Gellenthien worked out a mathematical chart to determine how high one could go without obtaining a positive pressure at any given time after a fresh supply of air had been introduced into the pleural cavity.

There were several factors to be considered. One was the altitude at which the patient had been living at which the last supply of air was added to the pleural cavity. The time interval for replenishing air was important. The total capacity of pleural cavity in cubic centimeters when the lung is completely collapsed was important, as was the capacity of pleural cavity in cubic centimeters after absorption had taken place. He considered the fact that standard sea level pressure is 29.92 inches of mercury. Thus, he figured that one should reduce one inch for each thousand feet above sea level. He had to consider the atmospheric pressure at maximum safe altitude or the maximum altitude in feet above sea level to which one can go without difficulty, varying, of course, from day to day after pneumothorax has been given. He figured out calculations for an entire ten day period on his table. His conclusions were that in pneumothorax the air within the pleural cavity is subject to the ordinary physical laws of the expansion of gas; a knowledge of the application of these laws in individual cases may be valuable in determining the size of injection when changes of altitude are contemplated. The method presented in his study was based on the measurement of the ordinary six foot roentgenogram of the chest combined with known data of altitude, present and contemplated, and the size of the pneumothorax injection.[3]

One of the problems in transporting patients from the east to Valmora and/or beyond to the west, was that to get over the Rocky Mountains, commerical airlines (usually flying at a minimum altitude of 2,000 feet) had to rise at least 15,000 feet. Such high altitudes produced definite, sudden physiologic changes which could profoundly affect any patient with artificial pneumothorax.[4]

The first results of the research on the effects of high altitude and decreased barometric pressure upon the pneumothorax and the normal physiological functions was published in the *Journal of the American Medical Association* on March 2, 1940 under the caption, "Altitude and Artificial Pneumothorax."

> To overcome the hazards accompanying rapid changes due to sudden variances in altitude, Dr. Gellenthien worked out a formula to determine how high a person can go without occurence of positive pressure after a fresh supply of air has been injected into the plural cavity.[5]

Pneumothorax was of particular interest to the physician dealing with problems of aviation medicine because under no other conditions is such a large quantity of gas enclosed within the body cavities with no means of escape. This large quantity of gas is enclosed by tissues which are usually elastic, offering little resistance to expansion. The adjacent organs are of extreme physiological importance and their functions may be seriously impaired if they are much compressed.[6]

A news story clearly detailed the significance of Dr. G.'s findings:

> A method for calculating just how high an altitude is safe for plane travel by patients with tuberculosis of the lungs after pneumothorax (lung collapse) treatment, is presented by C.H. Gellenthien, M.D., Valmora, in The Journal of the American Medical Association for March 2.
>
> Pneumothorax treatment involves the introduction of air or nitrogen gas into the space surrounding the lung. This procedure collapses the lung and gives it partial or complete rest from the processes of breathing. Changes in altitude and the consequent changes in air pressure may upset the patients' equilibrium.
>
> The application of his method... may be valuable in determining the size of injection of air in the lung when changes of altitude are contemplated.
>
> The method takes into consideration such factors as the altitude at which the patient has been living and at which the last supply of air was added to the lung, the interval of time between injections of air, the length of time since the last injection, and the capacity of the lung when it is completely collapsed. While the safe altitude varies for each individual, Dr. Gellenthien points out that a typical patient can safely fly 2,000 feet above sea level four days after pneumothorax treatment and can fly at an altitude of nearly 4,000 feet on the tenth day.
>
> Explaining how flying may affect the pneumothorax patient, Dr. Gellenthien says that when the atmospheric pressure changes abrupt-

ly, as it does in traveling by plane, the pressure in the cavity around the collapsed lung does not adjust itself, as the lung is not functioning normally. Pressure is therefore obtained that is greater than that of the atmosphere. "As the pressure on this cavity acts directly on the heart and other organs," he states, "any increase in pressure, if allowed to go high enough, may result in serious difficulty and even death, if the heart and other organs are not able to readjust themselves properly.[7]

Undoubtedly many lives were saved due to Dr. G.'s research, for more and more patients were traveling by air, either by choice or by necessity. Their physicians were able to prepare them for this air travel due to Dr. G.'s research.

The *Las Vegas Daily Optic* reported:

Another outstanding contribution in scientific research has been made by a New Mexico physician to advance American aeronautics. This knowledge is given to the public in the current issue of The Journal of the American Medical Association which published an article by Major W.R. Lovelace of the United States Air Corps and Dr. H. Corwin Hinshaw of the Mayo Clinic reporting on and confirming the findings in research work in Aviation Medicine done at Valmora Sanatorium by Dr. C.H. Gellenthien. Dr. Gellenthien is the well known superintendent of the Valmora Sanatorium.[8]

This study on altitude led to Dr. G.'s continued interest in the effect of barometric pressure upon the gases within the human body and led to his involvement in submarine, rocket and space medicine. It eventually led to his nomination to the Aviation Hall of Fame.

Gellenthien's research in aviation medicine flourished when he worked with the Army during World War II. In 1930 Dr. G. was a First Lieutenant with the Army Medical Corps Reserve. He became Captain and then attained the rank of Major. He was with the School of Aviation Medicine, Brooks Field, Texas, in 1936. Then, during the war he worked in Burbank, California on one of the most serious aviation problems of the time. Pilots were losing consciousness when dive bombing. Several had died. What could be done to keep pilots from blacking out?

Increased efficiency of anti-aircraft batteries is compelling pilots to fly at greater increased altitudes for longer periods of time. Dive bombing, with its spectacularly rapid changes in altitude and barometric pressures causes marked changes in the aviator's body. A "blackout" or loss of consciousness, at the end of a bombing dive that lasts seconds too long, may mean the loss of the plane and its pilots in a crash. Or, he may get too low and be destroyed by the explosion of his own bomb in the target. Improved oxygen masks, forced oxygen breathing on the ground before going up in high altitude flights, throat microphones, scientific bandaging and constriction of the body for dive bombing attacks...are some of the improvements already the result of medical aviation research. [9]

It was Gellenthien's previous research on the effects of high altitude and decreased barometric pressure that contributed to solving the problem. His study was carried on in military and civilian research centers throughout the world. [10] The research team with which Dr. G. worked tried several experiments and finally came up with the idea of a pressurized suit. Dr. G. felt it was the best solution to the problem. At first the United States military rejected the idea of the pressurized suit. The Canadians, however, accepted it immediately and found it successful. Then it became universal.

Gellenthien's method for determining the effect of rapid or marked atmospheric pressure changes in confined internal gases within the thorax is included in the textbook *Human Factors in Air Transportation* by Ross A. McFarland, published in 1943 by McGraw-Hill Book Company.

From Gellenthien's article, "The Effects of Barometric Pressure Upon the Gases of the Human Body," based on his original research, many continued studies were carried on. Dr. G. was honored at various times and places, as indicated by news items such as the following:

"Doc" will also tour the Submarine Base at New London, Conn., and will be honored for his original research work in the fields of aerospace and submarine medicine. [11]

Gellenthien also worked at Alamogordo to help put a monkey into space in 1953. Space travel brought about much new research. It was his work with aviation medicine that brought Dr. G. into contact with Wernher von Braun who contributed so much to the science of astronautics, especially in the development of rockets necessary to make possible manned space flights, lunar landings, orbiting satellites, and deep space probes. [12]

Gellenthien's name ranks among those of von Braun and Frederick Brant Rentschler in the Aviation Hall of Fame. (It was Rentschler who developed and produced reliable aircraft engines and was widely known as "Mr. Horsepower.")

In his quest for knowledge, Gellentien had to sacrifice other things. "I had to keep working. I missed out on a lot of social and cultural activities," he admitted. Indeed, his sisters sometimes remarked that Carl was "illiterate" when it came to art, music, literature, poetry, history, and other such areas of the fine arts and humanities. Parties, theatre and art shows, any of the social and cultural events others usually enjoyed, were denied him because he was driven by the mandate that his patients came first and the obsession that his research must be done. When O'Shaughnessy wrote of the "world-losers and world-forsakers on whom the pale moon gleams" he may have been thinking of those great humanitarians who have given their lives to making the world a better place, who have made great discoveries and acted on profound ideas, "the movers and shakers of the world for ever, it seems."[13]

Once Dr. G. went to hear Albert Einstein speak on his theory of relativity. A German professor sitting next to Gellenthien declared, after Einstein sat down, "Rein Wie Schmutz!" — "Clear as mud!" Still, the scientific mind never stops seeking to understand.

Gellenthien also did research involving an attempt to create a beneficial micro-climate within the respiratory tract by using ionizing air for bronchial asthma. He published numerous articles based on his findings in journals such as Chest, Diseases of the Chest, Industrial Medicine and Rocky Mountain Medical Journal.

At Bruns General Hospital at Santa Fe, an Army hospital for diseases of the chest, Dr. G. did more research. During world War II he was hired as a consultant by the Army. He traveled to Santa Fe two or more times a week to see ailing soldiers.

A mysterious development occurred during the War. American soldiers were training in the desert in the San Joaquin Valley near Needles, California, preparing to fight the Nazis under General Erwin Rommel in the Sahara Desert. Many of the soldiers came down with symptoms of tuberculosis in training. They were fatigued and losing weight, coughing, spitting up blood, had fever and night sweats, and cavities in the lungs, shown by chest X-rays. But doctors were unable to confirm a diagnosis of tuberculosis. No evidence of the tubercle bacilli could be found.

Lieut. Col. George J. Kastlin was Chief of the Medical Service at Bruns. Dr. Isador Pilot, Professor of Clinical Laboratory Medicine in Chicago, was in charge as the bacteriologist. Dr. Pilot insisted that the tubercle bacilli must certainly be there. But slide after slide showed nothing under the microscope. "It's got to be there! Why can't we see it!" he stormed.[14]

Then someone noticed some "little twigs" in the sputum specimens under the microscope. It was then that the research team made a significant discovery. The soldiers did not have tuberculosis at all. They were suffering from the invasion of fungi. It was then discovered that from El Paso to Phoenix through the San Joaquin Valley and to the Pacific Ocean, the fungi thrived in desert places. Another fungus was found in Oklahoma when it spread through the school yards by bird droppings. Another was discovered in the clay in Georgia. Two of the culprits to be discovered in these early studies were the *coccidioides immitis* and the *histoplasma capsulatum*.

Before the fungi were discovered, Dr. G. would check patients with the pseudo-tuberculosis and tell them they were free of TB; he found no tubercle bacilli. If their X-rays were negative there was nothing to worry about. In the absence of tubercle bacilli, Dr. G. assumed that the patient had overcome his TB because of good resistance and was "apparently cured." No treatment was necessary. After the Bruns study, the serious problems caused by fungi were known and physicians began finding methods of treatment.

Working with a microscpe in the laboratory did not remove Dr. G. from the problems of everyday living. He was compassionate in trying to solve those, too. In January of 1939 one of the worst storms of the century left ranchers west of Sapello marooned. Highways leading to Tecolotenos, Upper and Lower Rociada, and Gascon were shrouded by snow drifts up to five feet deep. More than 100 persons were stranded.

As owner of Gascon ranch, Dr. G. issued orders to his ranch foreman, Secundino Martinez, "to kill as many beeves as necessary" and to ration food supplies, "among the families whose larders are diminishing." [15] It was reported that 14 or 15 families were in dire need of immediate help, but not all of the 121 persons in the district were suffering. It was also reported that some were critically ill — including some children. [16] Dr. G. telephoned those families and found that no one was in serious condition. He prescribed what he could via phone. Then he flew with Lloyd Bible over the homes and dropped food and medicines down to the people.

The *Las Vegas Daily Optic* chartered Bible's plane, and Stewart Hensley of the *Optic* staff flew with Bible over the mountain regions to drop sacks of food near isolated cabins. Starting out on the mercy flight, Bible was barely able to lift his plane from the snow covered airport. He flew to Gascon country, circled over the area and made "direct hits" with the foodstuffs. When he returned to Las Vegas from his bitter cold flight, he was "suffering from cold and a cut hand, incurred when his hand caught on a strut when dropping a bundle of food." [17] The *Optic* praised Bible's courage for being willing to fly over the mountain region at the risk of crashing. Dr. G. and others who helped were also praised. Local people thought Bible and his passengers were brave, but they had flown so much that it hardly occurred to them to be afraid of flying. Dr. G. had ridden in open cockpit planes and flown "by the seat of the pants" in all kinds of weather. Bible's modern plane seemed very safe by comparison, even in bad weather. Once when Bible was flying Dr. G. home from a medical meeting, the plane ran out of gas. Bible had to make a forced landing at Showlow, Arizona. Neither he nor Dr. G. were disturbed. "You have to expect those things," Dr. G. said.

Second to his love for trains is Dr. G.'s love of planes. He grew up with aviation. He was a member of the Aerospace Medical Association. He was given recognition by United Airlines as a member of their 100,000 Mile Club and by Continental Airlines for having flown the equivalent of two and a half times around the world.

Dr. G.'s research brought him into new areas of discovery. The advent of isoniazid in 1952 opened up a new era of TB control. Not only did it have bactericidal effects on tubercle bacilli, but it was especially effective in treating childhood TB due to its good tolerance by children. Dr. G. initiated research using Isonicotinic Hydrazide in the treatment and prevention of TB. The New Mexico Indian Children Tuberculosis Study was conducted from July 1, 1954 to July 1, 1959, with 5,500 Navajo Pueblo children from birth to 15 years of age given the new treatment. It was directed from Valmora and sponsored by the American College of Chest Physicians in cooperation with The University of Pennsylvania School of Medicine, Henry Phipps Institute in Philadelphia, and the U.S. Department of Health, Education, and Welfare's Public Health Service under its Bureau of Indian Affairs.

In 1957 Dr. G. reported:

...doing well is our five-year research study with over 5,000 Pueblo and Navajo Indian children and Isoniazid in the treatment and prevention of tuberculosis. We have been pleasantly surprised to find:

a) The spread of infection in children has been prevented.

b) Positive tuberculin skin test have changed back to negative.

c) The development of positive tuberculin skin tests has been prevented among extensively exposed children with active positive sputum cases in their families living in the hogans and pueblos. The research study will continue into 1960 and by then our results should be definite. [18]

From 1950 to 1954 Dr. G. also did a study on the treatment of syphilis in the Navajo Indian by three massive intramuscular injections of penicillin every four days. The results were excellent.

In 1951 Dr. G. did a study of the effects of Osonicofinie Hydrazide (INH-Nydrazid - Squibb and Co.) upon sputum count, urine, blood pressure and clinical symptoms of tuberculosis.

Although Dr. G.'s major research interest was directed at a cure for tuberculosis, his interests were diversified. Much of his research was done with a partner, Dr. Lora Shields, Professor and Head of the

Biology Department at New Mexico Highlands University. Dr. Shields, an internationally known botanist who was with the Atomic Energy Commission, did much study and work at the Yucca Flats, Nevada testing site. In 1963 when the student body at Highlands was about 1,200, Dr. Shields and Dr. G. worked on several projects. They did numerous studies including some of the original research on the so-called "Miracle Pill" for TB. They also spent a year of study on leucorrheas due to fungi and also evaluated various fungicides and antibiotics.

An herb in the southern part of Mexico led Dr. Shields and Dr. G. to another study. The natives claimed that the herbal tea made from this particular plant would cure diabetes. After three years of work, Dr. Shields and Dr. G. found that the herbal tea did lower the blood sugar in dogs and other animals. Then they turned their data over to the Sloan-Kettering Institute, where the effects of the herbal tea upon humans were determined.

Next, the two partners launched into a study regarding the clotting of blood and the blood serum fats present in members of the different New Mexican cultural groups: Spanish-American, Mexican-National, Navajo, and Anglo. The study attempted to throw light on the aging process, why heart attacks are the number one killer, and whether endocrines and bio-chemistry are a factor in causing coronary occlusion. This was the first time Dr. G. had worked with a computer. In a progress report, Dr. G. wrote:

> Our graduate bio-chemsitry student assistants get their masters degrees after one year with us, if their theses are accepted. Naturally they are all champing at the bit to get their names in print in some scientific publication. This spring, we allowed two of them to read papers at the regional meeting of the American Association for the Advancement of Science in Albuquerque. I would not allow one student to use my name because I doubted his mathematical conclusions. Just this past week the IBM 1620 computer proved me right. Dr. Shield's report is the usual required progress report for government agencies. The clinical significance of this study is my personal responsibility. To date we have examined over 1,500 individuals. The chemistry takes about three weeks per individual and the intricate mathematical computations used to take over one week per individual. There were many chances for error with the pencil but this computer is marvelous, although at times it lays eggs. [19]

He went on to state that any conclusions from the study would be withheld until all the data was analyzed and valid conclusions could be drawn.

Dr. G. encouraged young people in their scientific endeavors.

Once he attended a scientific exhibit of the AMA at Atlantic City demonstrating the growth of algae under space conditions in the lab. The algae was made into a variety of goods. An 18-year-old senior from Nashville, Tennessee had done the experiment. The algae had been made entirely from recycled waste. Dr. G. wanted no part of it, but since President Eisenhower ate one of the sweet rolls made of the algae, Dr. G. felt he had to also. Besides, it was in the interest of science. Neither suffered any ill effects.

Gellenthien's most extensive research project throughout the years was to try to find a cure for TB. He was always finding new ways of dealing with old problems. Besides his research on climate, his study of altitude and barometric pressure, and his invention of the Valmora pneumothorax machine, Gellenthien studied methods of more effective treatment. He had learned to pay attention to details, even the smallest details. For instance, he noticed that patients would usually lie on the side of the affected lung. Relieving pressure on the lung seemed to help. Thus, he learned to help patients sit and lie in the most beneficial positions. He also helped patients keep their breakfast down by having them drink two glasses of warm water before breakfast. Then the patient would vomit before breakfast instead of after breakfast. (Morning vomiting was caused by phlegm in the stomach which had been coughed up and swallowed during the night.)

Dr. G. also worked out a schedule of daily exposure for heliotherapy at Valmora. The first day a patient was exposed a few minutes, but each successive day he could be exposed longer. Following a precise schedule was extremely important for patients with pulmonary TB. Too much exposure could be harmful. The rays of the sun could cause a blood vessel in the lungs to burst and the patient could die of hemorrhage. Therefore, the chest was always covered during exposure. Patients with TB of the throat, of the bone or other types of TB could stand more direct exposure. Dr. G.'s careful calculations prevented complications and produced excellent results.

Early in his career at Valmora Dr. G. also did a study of average temperature and pulse. The results of his "Average Temperature & Pulse of 129 Cases at Valmora" gave him interesting data to work with. He found that the average temperature at 7:00 a.m. was 97.6 and pulse was 74. At 1:00 p.m. the average temperature was 98.7 and pulse 83. At 7:00 p.m. the average termperature was 98.7, pulse 83. These studies were done frequently.[20]

He also did studies on the various conditions of the TB patients. These statistics were used in progress reports. From September 15,

1927 to September 15, 1963, a total of 2,800 were treated and discharged. An analysis of the records of those 2,800 patients disclosed the following: Pulmonary tuberculosis cases: 1,732 or 61.9 percent; Non-pulmonary tuberculosis cases, 70 or 2.5 percent; and non-tuberculosis cases, 998 or 35. 6 percent. Patients from the United States totaled 2,774; from the Canal Zone, 4; and from various foreign countries, 22 or a total of 2,800 in all. This total did not include the number of patients seen in the out-patient department or clinic nor those seen in their homes. [21]

Dr. G.'s attention to detail gave him great success with his TB patients before chemotherapy was available, and even afterwards helped him in his dignostic abilities. Soon after the discovery of chemotherapy, Dr. G. had a patient who was recovering from TB in Room 2 at the hospital. She had been very ill and her recovery was slow. One day her son came to visit her and was very depressed. He told Dr. G. that doctors in the nearby town had told him that he had a tumor of the femur, the large leg bone. He was scheduled for surgery the next day to have the leg amputated. The young man was a star basketball player at the local high school. He was devastated by the thought of losing his leg. Dr. G. offered to X-ray the leg. He did, and when he examined the X-ray he saw no evidence of a tumor. He saw, instead, definite erosion of the bone. Tuberculosis was "eating away" at it. The boy had obviously contracted TB from his mother — TB of the bone. Dr. G. explained what he had found to both mother and son. The young man cancelled his surgery. Dr. G. started him on chemotherapy that day. It was totally effective. Both he and his mother completely recovered.

Country doctors were experts at improvising. Dr. G. once prescribed for a professor of music who had used his voice constantly on the job until one day he could no longer speak above a whisper. When Dr. G. examined him, he saw that his vocal cords were strained. He prescribed a drug to tighten them up, and it worked. The professor regained the normal use of his voice. The drug Dr. G. had prescribed was strychnine — in a very small dose, of course.

It was through improvising, experimenting, and observation that doctors found a cure for TB. Dr. G. and others realized that the Benzene Ring could be the key to the drug that would conquer the tubercle bacilli. They knew the waxy, protective layer of the bacilli had to be penetrated by something strong enough to break through the cover and kill the bacilli but remain harmless to the patient. Through much research work, such a drug was finally refined. Dr. G. was one of many pioneers who worked to conquer TB. Following Waksman's discovery of streptomycin in 1944, isoniazid (INH) and many other effective drugs were developed.

NOTES

1. Carl H. Gellenthien, "Climatological Data Chart," Valmora Library, Valmora, New Mexico.
2. Carl H. Gellenthien, personal interview, Valmora, June 9, 1983.
3. Carl H. Gellenthien, "Altitude and Artificial Pneumothorax," *The Journal of the American Medical Association* (March 2, 1940), pp. 727-728.
4. *Ibid.*
5. "Research Work of Gellenthien Gets National Notice: Article in Medical Journal Tells of Findings in Aviation Medicine Field," newspaper clipping from Las Vegas newspaper, n.t., April 22, 1942, in Scrapbook 2, Valmora Library, p. 6.
6. *Ibid.*
7. "Pneumothorax Patients Should Consult Doctor Before Taking Trip in Airplane," n.t., n.p., n.d., clipping in Scrapbook 1, Valmora Library, Valmora, New Mexico, p. 139.
8. "Research Work of Gellenthien Gets National Notice: Article in Medical Journal Tells of Findings in Aviation Medicine Field," *op. cit.*
9. *Ibid.*
10. *Ibid.*
11. "Optic Topics," *Las Vegas Daily Optic,* May 16, 1969, in Scrapbook 2, Valmora Library, Valmora, New Mexico, p. 65.
12. "Frank Borman, Barry Morris Goldwater, Frederick Brant Rentschler, and Wernher von Braun to be Enshrined," *National Aviation Hall of Fame,* Issue 2 (Dayton, Ohio), 1982, p. 1.
13. O'Shaughnessy, *op. cit.*
14. Carl H. Gellenthien, personal interview, Valmora, June 29, 1982.
15. "Help Provided for Needy in Snowbound Area; Crew Works on Clogged Roads," *Las Vegas Daily Optic,* Las Vegas, New Mexico, January 12, 1939, p. 1.
16. "Optic Sends Food to Isolated Area," *Las Vegas Daily Optic,* Las Vegas New Mexico, January 11, 1939, p. 1.
17. "Help Provided for Needy in Snowbound Area; Crew Works on Clogged Roads," *op. cit.*
18. Carl and Alice Gellenthien, "1957 - For Alice and Me," *op. cit.*, pp. 1-2.
19. Carl H. Gellenthien, letter to Dr. Eugene L. Walsh, Medical Director, International Harvester Company, Chicago, Illinois, November 5, 1963, pp. 1-2.

20. "Average Temperature & Pulse of 129 Cases," Scrapbook 1/, Valmora, Library, p. 50.

21. "Total Patients Treated and Discharged from September 15, 1927 to September 15, 1963," Report in Scrapbook 11, Valmora Library, p. 27.

CHAPTER XVII

Hijos y Hijas

They were the darlings of Valmora, a girl and a boy with the charm and comeliness that would have upstaged the likes of Shirley Temple and Mickey Rooney, the famed child stars of the early days. Indeed, they were the stars of Valmora, adored and cherished by their nurturing parents and their "public" — the patients and staff.

No child star could have enjoyed the spotlight any more than those two and yet remain unspoiled. Editha made her debut on October 25, 1934, and her brother Bill was born almost exactly two years later, October 18, 1936. He was named Carl William but was dubbed "Billy" or "Bill" from the beginning. The Gellenthiens' *hija* (daughter) and *hijo* (son) lacked nothing in the way of attention. Their parents protected them, their grandparents indulged them, the staff and patients "spoiled" them.

The children were kept in a kind of protective isolation for fear of getting TB from the patients, for it was well known that children are especially susceptible to the disease. They were not usually allowed in the hospital. On special occasions when they ate in the main dining room with the patients, such as for Christmas celebrations, their mother provided dishes from their home, never allowing them to eat from hospital dishes. They were regularly subjected to medical check ups and chest X-rays.

The patients would sometimes make paper airplanes for Bill. But the nurses would insist on letting the little gifts sit out in the sun for three days before he was allowed to play with them.

The father feared for his children. He felt a pang of remorse each time he had the impulse to throw his arms about them and kiss them. He knew that a kiss could mean a kiss of death, for a consumptive is never sure of being free of the deadly bacilli. So he cherished his children but would not kiss them. He gave them protection, security, and love. He taught them everything he could. Yet he chastened himself for being a poor father. Each party, each special event, each recital or school program that he had to miss because of his work, brought a bitter disappointment to him, perhaps more than to the children. They understood his unique position. They knew it was their mother who would attend those events with them. They did not expect their father's presence at such occasions. It was a sacrifice they all had to make.

Bill grew under the adoring eyes of the patients and was the center of attention for many as indicated in The Valmora Sun:

> Warning! Valmora pedestrians are cautioned to keep out of Billy Gellenthien's way these days. One of his Christmas gifts was a streamlined scooter and Billy is buzzing around corners like a small edition of the Super Chief. [1]

Editha's antics and preferences were well known, too. She had a teddy bear named "Blue Eyes" who went with her everywhere. In an article entitled, "The Young Skeptic," a reporter for The Valmora Sun wrote:

> When Editha recently announced, "Daddy, my Blue-Eyes isn't at all well — I'll have to take her into Las Vegas to be examined," it brought home that wistful old epigram that a prophet is unsung in his own land. [2]

Perhaps, however, Editha was displaying her understanding of the ethics of the doctor who knows it is unwise for him to treat members of his own household and sends them to a trusted colleague instead.

When some of the staff members decided to "fix up" her "Blue Eyes" to look as if the poor bear had been in a fight with a wild cat, Editha was furious. She didn't appreciate their sense of humor at taking her teddy bear and bandaging it up like a manikin in a first aid class.

But Editha sometimes put the pranksters in their place. A January, 1939 paper reported:

> Curt Brink didn't know what he was letting himself in for a few months ago when he staged a bit of ventriloquism for Editha Gellenthien with a Charlie McCarthy doll. Now since Editha got a Charlie for Christmas she expects Curt to make both dummies talk simultaneously. This double talk is too much for Brink who has decided he's getting more than he Bergened for. [3]

Editha kept busy, also, helping her mother entertain.

The children were given private instruction through the Calvert School until they were ready for high school. With headquarters in Baltimore, Maryland, the Calvert School provided all necessary materials through correspondence. Under private tutors, the children excelled. When they transferred to the public schools in Las Vegas, they were promoted beyond their age groups because of their advanced academic abilities. In fact, Editha graduated from New Mexico Highlands University when she was only 19 years of age — probably the youngest graduate Highlands ever had.

The Gellenthiens provided their children with varied educational experiences through travel, hobbies, ranch work, and books. Editha raised rabbits, and both children became familiar with the workings of a horse and cattle ranch. Both were expected to work in any capacity either at Valmora or at Gascon. They learned to cook, wash dishes, work in the office, the store, or the post office putting up the mail and putting the mailbag on the hook for the mail train. They learned to meet the new patients and to get along with people in general. Their mother encouraged them to learn to do anything well, never to be afraid of work, and never to be "too good" to do any job — a trait she had learned years before from her own parents.

Editha planned to become a veterinarian or a medical doctor. She was a brilliant student but complained that she wished no one knew her last name. As soon as her teachers learned she was Dr. Gellenthien's daughter, they expected nothing less than perfection from her. She was able to measure up to their expectations with persistence and hard work, however, for she had inherited ability and talent from both parents, learning scientific thinking from her father and social and domestic skills from her mother. Alice taught her to be as versatile as she was — able to wear jeans and help a cow have a calf at four p.m., then be dressed for dinner at the best restaurant by seven. Just as Alice operated Gascon ranch largely by herself, caring for the stock on the range and acting as hostess to the visiting doctors, Editha began full time ranching in 1962 when she and her husband moved to Gascon. They cared for horses and cattle and provided a resort area for visitors.

Editha was awarded the Highlands University Distinguished Alumna Award in February of 1975, having graduated in 1954 with a biology major. She served on the University's Presidential ad hoc student recruitment committee and served on the Governor's Commission for Higher Education. Throughout the years she has been active in civic affairs. She was Director of the Las Vegas - San Miguel Chamber of Commerce and was instrumental in the founding of the Chamber's Movie Committee, serving as Chair. In 1974 she went to Hollywood with former Governor Bruce King to promote New Mexico in the movie industry. She was on the executive committee of the Northern Rio Grande - Adelante - Resource Conservation and Developmental Project, was a member of the advisory board of the

New Mexico Cattle Growers' Association, and served as Secretary of the Mora County Planning and Zoning Commission. She is active in P.E.O., Cowbelles, and many service organizations. She completed an E.M.T. course, becoming a Certified Medical Technician. Although she has given C.P.R. a couple of times and has been instrumental in providing first aid to neighbors, most of her "patients" are animals. She helps deliver calves, cares for the newborns, and nurses sick or injured pets and ranch stock. In reality she is the ranch "veterinarian." So far none of her patients have complained.

Editha married James Bartley on August 2, 1954. After Carl and Alice turned the Gascon Ranch over to Jim and Editha, the Bartleys successfully operated the Gascon cattle and guest ranch, 400 acres on the eastern slope of the Sangre de Cristo mountains. There they reared their three children, Sherry, John and Carl, and helped raise no less than 50 other children throughout the years.

Carl William inherited curiosity, independence, and the desire to learn from his parents. "Bill" graduated from junior college at New Mexico Military Institute, was commissioned as a 2nd Lieutenant, and earned his Bachelors degree from the University of Colorado in business and sociology. This led him to a large insurance company and he soon became the main adjuster for them for the state of Colorado. Bill married Melva Morse on September 12, 1958. They had two boys, Shane and Tom. At the age of 33 Bill returned to law school and was graduated *cum laude* from Washburn Law School in Topeka, Kansas in 1971. He specialized in criminal law and bankruptcies. After a divorce in 1977, Bill married Maralee Merrill Lane and he continues to practice law.

With two children, five grandchildren, and three great-grandchildren, Carl Gellenthien has reason to be proud of his family. But they are not his only family. The *hijos y hijas* of Valmora — sons and daughters — were numerous over the years. Whether they were called "graduates," "alumni" or "family," those "adopted" children carried the title proudly. They had achieved as much as a student laboring over college courses. They had maintained strict self-discipline, followed an exacting regime, taken prescribed "courses" and developed new skills and talent. They had not broken training and had won the coveted trophy of health, having overcome the enemy, TB.

Besides the patients who emerged from the protective wing at Valmora, however, there was another sort of alumni, little known to the rest of the world. These, too, were *hijos y hijas* "adopted" children of the Gellenthiens. They were a select group of young people who were assisted through school by Dr. and Mrs. Gellenthien.

The exact number of that group is not known. They, too, are part of the Valmora family. Some were given financial support. Some were given emotional support — encouragement and confidence. Some were given opportunities to advance through contacts made by the Gellenthiens. But all were the pride of Valmora because in one way or another they succeeded. The Gellenthiens must have sacrificed a great deal to put their own children as well as so many others through school. But to them education was the greatest gift one person could give another, and they wanted to help.

In Scrapbook #12, entitled "Valmora Alumni," one page sports the proud title, "Valmora daughters now registered nurses, graduated, August and September, 1964, Schools in Chicago, Denver, Albuqeurque." Newspaper clippings on that page show three young ladies from Las Vegas who were graduating from nursing school.

Letters of thanks are also included in the scrapbook, including one that is signed "Con amor [with love] your brat. Thanks for everything." Another says, "To Dr. G., My doctor, my teacher, my friend, and my Pop! With love and highest regard and respect, your Hija." A young man who became a doctor wrote that he would graduate with his M.D. soon, stating, "Your medical embryo is about to be released on the unsuspecting world."

Altogether, at least half a dozen medical doctors and scores of nurses received help and encouragement from the Gellenthiens in one form or another. Of all the young people Dr. G. worked with and helped, there were only one or two actual protégés. Dr. G. was a teacher to many but a mentor to only a select few. One of those was Robert Dewey Smith, son of George Dewey Smith and Christine Hursh Smith of Las Vegas. His master's thesis entitled, "The Action of Isonicotinic Acid Hydrazide on Ten Tuberculosis Patients at Valmora Sanatorium" was completed in 1952. He received his M.D. at the University of Colorado School of Medicine in 1957, served an internship at Charity Hospital in New Orleans and completed a three-year fellowship in Internal Medicine at the Mayo Clinic. Then he came to serve as Dr. Gellenthien's assistant at Valmora. He established a private practice in Las Vegas as well.

Dr. G. had lived with the spectre of death for years. He had seen patients and close friends fall under its pall. Chuck Mayo died in a bizarre accident when he was driving a tractor. His aorta was severed on impact and he bled to death. Dr. Grant Fairbanks, a brilliant speech and hearing specialist, died just after visiting Gascon Ranch when he choked on a piece of steak on his return trip home, traveling by air to California. An archeologist from Chicago came to examine the Pecos ruins and came down with what he thought was the "flu." He was sick on the plane home, was taken directly to the hospital, but died within hours before his illness was diagnosed. It was the discovered that he had handled a dead squirrel near Pecos and was bitten by a flea. He died of bubonic plague.

Thus, Dr. G. was prepared for death at any time. But he was not ready for the death of his protégé. Robert Smith died suddenly at the age of 36 of diabetes mellitus and cardiac ventricular fibrillation. As Dr. Brown had passed the torch on to Dr. Gellenthien, so Dr. G. had hoped to pass it on to Dr. Smith; but it was not to be.

Some years later Dr. G. ran across Dr. Smith's thesis which had been researched at Valmora. He opened a page to a photograph of a chest X-ray.

"Oh, I remember this patient," he said. "He was too far gone when we got him. He died."

Dr. G. remembered the patient just from seeing an X-ray, though the patient had been gone 30 years. He remembered, too, about Bob Smith as he closed the thesis slowly, almost reverently.

"He was a brilliant doctor. I wish he hadn't had to go."

Dr. G. put the thesis back in its place and returned to his office, alone.

NOTES

1. "Sun Spots," *The Valmora Sun,* January, 1939, p. 2., in Scrapbook 3, Valmora Library, Valmora, New Mexico, p. 23.
2. "The Young Skeptic," *The Valmora Sun,* January, 1939, p. 2., in Scrapbook 3, Valmora Library, Valmora, New Mexico, p. 23.
3. *Ibid.*

CHAPTER
XVIII

Arnica

Dr. Gellenthien hovered anxiously over a woman in labor at Valmora Hospital. He tried not to show that he was worried. He had put in a call for Dr. Gerritt Heusinkveld of Denver, the excellent obstetrician who had delivered his daughter Editha. But on this day, October 18, 1936, Dr. Heusinkveld was hunting somehwere in the Colorado mountains. Dr. G. knew he would have to deliver this baby without benefit of a specialist, and he didn't like it.

The patient was 35 years of age. She had given birth once before, two years ago. But now she was in trouble. After a long labor she had given birth to a healthy boy. The nurse, Georgie Claiborne, took the infant and cared for him as the doctor worried over the woman. Dr. G. called the nurse back to his side minutes later when postpartum hemorrhaging occurred. It was his worst fear, realized.

"We've got to stop this bleeding," the doctor said quietly. "Find a role of sterile gauze for a uterine pack."

The woman knew she was in danger. She was conscious and aware that she was hemorrhaging profusely. But she remained calm. The nurse returned with the gauze and stood by somberly while the doctor packed the patient's uterus. There were long moments of tense silence. Gellenthien monitered his patient's vital signs and watched for more bleeding. He prayed silently that the pack would work. It did. When the patient was out of danger, the doctor bent and lightly pushed the woman's hair back from her forehead. And then he gently kissed her.

The woman was his wife. He had just delivered their second child, Carl William.

Later Georgie complimented the doctor on his composure. He had worked calmly, showing no fear. His self-discipline, his control over his emotions in times of crisis, proved to be consistent with his professional training and experience. Not for a single second had he lost control.

"Doctor, you did a good job," she said. "You remained steady and calm when you knew your wife could be bleeding to death."

"Are you kidding?" he replied, surprised. "Didn't you notice my knees trembling? They turned to jelly. I thought I'd lose my pants!"

But his steady hands hadn't trembled, and he hadn't flinched for a second.

Later Carl mentioned the experience to Alice.

"Did you realize that if I didn't stop the bleeding you'd die?" he asked.

"Yes, I knew," she replied. "But I knew you were doing everything you could," she said matter-of-factly.

If Alice Gellenthien had been frightened, she hadn't shown it. She had come through the ordeal with British fortitude and courage. Carl said her English disposition never allowed her emotions to overwhelm her. Perhaps her trust in her husband's skill had something to do with her calm attitude, too. She believed that Carl Gellenthien was an extraordinary doctor.

Alice Brown had known there was something special about Carl Gellenthien when she first saw him arriving as a patient at Valmora. The attraction was mutual. Carl soon learned to recognize Alice's step in the hall and looked forward to her visits. He learned that the hospital's dietician was as much at home in the saddle as she was in the kitchen. In the kitchen she was a gourmet cook but in the corral she was a match for any cowhand. In fact, she did a large part of the ranch work herself, both at Gascon and at Valmora. She could wield an egg beater or a branding iron with equal skill. She could dress for a party in Chicago's most elite social circles or she could dress for ranch work like any "saddle slicker" and still retain that special dignity, that "class" that made her special. She loved horses and was an excellent trainer and rider. Like her father, she was a good appraiser of horseflesh. When it came to trading or selling, she'd always say, "A horse is worth what you can get for it."

Perhaps some of Alice's independence of spirit had grown out of necessity. When her mother was killed on the bridge, Alice's world was shattered. She and her sister Margaret had barely escaped death themselves. And it was upon Alice's young shoulders that the responsibility of running Dr. Brown's household and rearing her younger sister fell. She was fourteen years of age. She became her father's most reliable helper, her sister's best friend. But she had to drop out of school and continue her studies on her own when she could. She was a self-educated woman who loved to read everything from news magazines to poetry, novels, and biographies. It was her steady, self-reliant, constancy that made her father adore her and that, perhaps, attracted Carl Gellenthien to her. She was, as it has been said, the catalyst that drew him out of his illness, gave him the will and the spirit to overcome his illness and to forge out a secure future for himself, one that included her.

When Carl's father, Charles Gellenthien, met Alice for the first time, he took Carl aside to talk to his son about his role as a young husband. He told Carl what a fine young woman Alice was, how impressed he was with her character and personality. He told Carl he approved of his choice of a life partner and would gladly loan Carl the money for a wedding ring.

"One more thing, Carl," he added. "If you ever have marital problems — it will be *your* fault."

Charles was a very perceptive man. He knew that Alice was a sweet-tempered woman, not easily provoked. Carl was reminded of the old Jewish proverb: "Do not make a woman weep, for God counts her tears."

Alice and Carl were married on April 12, 1928 at Valmora. Carl had been appointed medical director, leaving Dr. Brown free to do the administrative and public relations work for which he was so suited.

Carl soon found the perfect pet name for Alice. He called her "Arnica." *Arnica* is any asteraceous plant of the genus arnica, *A. Montana* of Europe. It is a tincture of the flowers of *A. Montana* and other species of arnica used as external application in sprains or bruises — a linament. Because arnica is a soothing linament used to ease the aches and pains caused by external blows and bruises, it seemed appropriate for Carl to call his wife by that name. Alice was his soothing and comforting salve, "arnica." At the end of a tiring day, after he had gone through the many discomforts and irritations of every day life, she would soothe him and ease his mind. She had the comforts of home ready to greet him when he had been battered about by the cares of the outside world. When life was difficult and he met with adversaries, when he felt "beat up" and bruised, Alice was always there to comfort and to soothe. His anger or his hurt soon dissipated under the balm of her calm and cheerful spirit.

"Used as a salve arnica helps to promote the healing of wounds, bruises, and irritation."[1] That is just what Carl's Arnica did for him. From the moment they had met, when Carl was flat on his back in the hospital with tuberculosis, Alice had been his arnica.

"I couldn't have climbed the ladder of success without her," Dr. G. said. "She was my support, my help, my solace, my — well, my arnica."

Alice was gentle and kind to animals as well as people, and they were attracted to her. Dr. G. shared his wife's fondness for horses and for all animals. He never hunted because the Gellenthiens did not want to destroy life needlessly. The following item appeared in local papers:

Notice to the public

No hunting

Notice is hereby given that all persons are prohibited from hunting game birds or animals on the Gascon Ranch, Rociada, New Mexico, and the Valmora Sanatorium, Valmora, New Mexico, located in Mora County, New Mexico.

Any person entering upon said premises for purposes of hunting or to kill any game birds or animals will be prosecuted according to law.

Signed:

C.H. Gellenthien

Pub. Oct. 2, Nov. 4, 11, 1963. [2]

Alice took in stray cats and dogs. At one time she had as many as 40 cats. Nothing could make her temper flare like seeing an animal mistreated. But Alice did not have the quick Latin temperament, the kind that flares up instantly and dies down just as quickly. Hers was the slow, seething English temperament of her English and Irish ancestors. Anyone unlucky enough to be on the receiving end of her anger had probably been justly chastized before he even realized she was upset. Such was the case when Alice discovered that Dr. Benjamin Goldberg, assistant to Dr. Brown one summer, was doing away with some of her cats. The man's disdain for cats was obvious, though he knew they were Alice's pets.

Nearly everyone went swimming in the Coyote Creek swimming hole every afternoon in the summer time. One day Alice observed Dr. Goldberg swimming. She went upstream a little and poured bluing in the water hole from the edge of the creek, hidden by a bush. When the professor came out, he was dyed blue. At first he thought he was cyanotic! He couldn't figure out why anyone would tamper with the swimming hole until someone dropped the hint that he would do well to leave Alice's cats alone.

One of the orphaned kittens saved by Alice was a feisty little guy. He was dying when Alice found him and nurtured him back to life and health. He was so grateful to the family that had given him a home and saved his life that he became an especially affectionate pet. Alice named him "Tommy Atkins" after a character in one of Rudyard Kipling's poems. Of all the kittens and cats that shared the Gellenthein home, it was Tommy Atkins that Editha and Bill

276

remembered best years later. The children grew up surrounded by animals — dogs, horses, cows, rabbits, deer, and a goat named Heidi — but it was Tommy Atkins that they remembered because of his special affection and courage.

"It seemed he knew we had saved his life and wanted to show his gratitude," Editha said.

Perhaps because of his difficult early days his health was frail. At any rate, he developed pneumonia. He lay, the center of the concerned family's attention, fighting a losing battle with his illness. Alice fussed over him when necessary and left him alone when she could, knowing that sick cats like to be left alone in a quiet place. The children were admonished to keep away from him, but they stood at a measured distance and looked at him in sympathy.

"Poor Tommy Atkins, hurry and get well," they said.

And the doctor, between visiting patients at the hospital and going out on his calls, examined the kitten, gave the diagnosis, and said, "You can never tell about cats. They have a lot of resilience. Maybe he'll pull through." If he had been able to provide any treatment to save the ktten, seeing his wife's concern, his children's fear, and the kitten's suffering, he would not have hesitated a moment to administer the remedy. But only nature could determine the little creature's fate.

The entire family watched the last pitiful breaths of the sick kitten. He was purring. Tommy Atkins was always purring. Editha thought it was his way of showing his gratitude. Even as he must have known he was dying, he purred. And he didn't stop until his last breath.

The doctor was amazed. "He knew he was dying and he was purring. He died purring," he repeated. "If we human beings could go out that way —"

The doctor continued to show his love for wildlife was well as for domestic animals. In June of 1984 he stopped on his way home from a seminar to free a roadrunner. The bird had become stuck in some fresh tar which the highway department had put down near Valmora. As soon as Dr. G. released the bird, it ran off. It had escaped unharmed except for a few missing feathers.

Sherry Bartley came to stay with her grandparents when she was in elementary school. Gascon Ranch was so remote that it was a hardship for the Bartley children to travel so far to Las Vegas for school. Living at Valmora, Sherry could catch the bus at Watrous. Her grandfather drove her the four miles every day, though sometimes they missed the bus and he had to chase it to get her on. Along the way to the bus every morning, Sherry was drilled in her multiplication tables. At the house her grandmother taught her to cook and help with household tasks. When Sherry fell off a sled, flying down a hill through the snow, she broke both her wrists. Then it was her turn to be waited on.

Alice was a good teacher for Sherry. She herself had learned responsibility at an early age. As a self-educated woman, Alice valued education. She had a keen intellectual curiosity about every subject. Her life had always revolved around the home and the family. As her father's housekeeper and cook, her sister's chief nanny, and the hospital dietitian, she was busy with domestic affairs. But she also helped her father with public relations work, traveling to Chicago to promote Valmora, helping prepare and distribute the Christmas gifts, being hostess to dozens of business and social events. Alice passed her abilities along to her children and grandchildren, along with the special kind of inner strength so many successful women possess. It was that strength that supported and encouraged her husband and family and which was put to the ultimate test when the fmaily home was struck by lightning in 1952.

Alice was in town, the children were in school, and Carl was working at the hospital across the way. When he saw the flames and smoke, he ran across the field to the house, but it was too late. For anyone who has not lost everything in a single moment, it is difficult to understand the shock and grief the Gellenthiens went through. Imagine the shock of coming home from a short shopping trip to find nothing but ashes left of your home. Even the family pets, two dogs and two cats, were sacrificed to the unmerciful fire. Alice's new wedding ring, the one Carl had purchased after their marriage when he could ᵤfford a more expensive diamond, had been in her dresser drawer in the bedroom. It, along with her other jewelry, was gone. Later Carl shifted through the cold ashes trying to find the diamond. But as he searched though the melted glass, twisted metal, and dusty residue, the ashes irritated his lungs and he began to cough violently. He hemorrhaged as he stood there in the ashes and decided that everything of material value was gone; he had to accept it. But they had each other and their health. There are some things fire cannot destroy.

Carl had his work to return to; the children had their studies. Alice probably suffered the most, for her home was her work. Only the items that were in the clinic or hospital, in the Valmora library or at Gascon ranch were saved. Everything else familiar to her was gone. Yet Alice found the strength to overcome the devastating loss, even to grow from it. At the age of 51 she was able to start all over again. The Gellenthiens moved into Dr. Brown's old adobe house next to the hospital.

When Carl and Alice moved into the old house next to the clinic, Alice began to make the place a cheerful, comfortable home. Alice was always the bastion of strength for Carl. She made the transition after the fire easier for him. Now he could walk a few steps across the way and be in his office. She always had dinner or lunch waiting, though she never knew when he would be home. If he was out half the night on a call, she knew that he would be home when his work was finished. Sometimes, of course, he was delayed due to bad weather conditions or bad roads. A reporter for *The Spirit of Valmora* composed a short description of Dr. G.'s work in "The Lost Ford or No Wife to Guide Them."

> ...O.B. Stork calling for aid, Doctor Gellenthien responding, one Sunday morning when the weather was fine. Some of you fellows want to go along? We may not get back until evening. Room for three.[3]

So Franz, Schwendinger and Glanneschi all decided to go to the small settlement, Cherryvale, 20 miles away, through Shoemaker, past the church, the schoolhouse, the "lake" and over the mesa.

> The Doctor's work kept him all day in a little one room hut, with facilities almost as primitive as those which must have existed at that Bethlehem Birth of two thousand years ago. The three who went for the ride spent the day at the combination home and schoolroom of the settlement's teacher, a Spanish-American, who fed and entertained them...[4]

At seven o'clock that evening the doctor was finished and they started back for Valmora.

> The Ford car has been endowed with many virtues but a sure homing instinct is not one of them, as you shall see. Driving to Cherryvale in the morning sunlight and with another car to follow was one thing. Driving back at night, even with careful directions from their guide of the morning, quite another.[5]

The story goes on to tell of the drive from one house to another. They ended up back at the house where the stork party had been held, then at the schoolteacher's house after driving around again.

> The poor man (the schoolteacher) had had a full day, what with guiding and entertaining, and had retired. But he realized that if he was to have any lasting peace he must personally conduct these city-bred Americanos, who were helpless after dark without red and green lights to aid them — or a Western-bred wife in the driver's seat. He therefore dressed, got out his own car and accompanied the blue Ford until it was safely in a lane with a fence on both sides and headed for Valmora. So the four men got home that midnight and crept into their cold beds.[6]

Such incidents, which seemed an adventure to the three men who accompanied the doctor, were commonplace. Alice never watched the clock. She knew her husband could take care of himself on his calls. Her job was to make life pleasant when he came home, regardless of the hour. How many Christmas Eves, New Years' celebrations and birthdays did she spend alone? How many colorful birthday cakes did she make and serve the children unaided? How many candles were blown out year after year under her supervision alone? How many childish prayers did she alone hear when she put the children to bed? Yet she took it all in stride. Alice understood that being alone with the children comes with the territory when one becomes a doctor's wife.

Early in the 1960s Alice was driving the station wagon, loaded down with groceries, a crate of eggs, and sacks of chicken feed, through Watrous when a small whirlwind or "dust devil" caught the hood of the vehicle. It apparently had not been securely latched. The windshield was totally obstructed. Alice had seen a car headed her way, so she veered to the right to avoid a collision and turned the station wagon over in a bar ditch. Some of the Highway Department workers found her and took her to Valmora. Carl had to put Alice in the bathtub before he could examine her. The eggs and sacks of feed had broken and she was soldily covered with debris. Later Carl said she looked like she'd been "tarred and feathered."

Alice called for her son-in-law, Jim Bartley, to come over and help lift her onto the X-ray table so Carl could get pictures. She trusted Jim's strong arms and didn't want anyone else to lift her. There were no fractures, but she was a mass of solid bruises. She was put to bed and asked Sherry to come over and do the household chores for the next few days. Sherry felt it was an awesome responsibility, but she was glad she was able to help her grandmother.

The State Police came to the house to make out a report shortly after the accident. They needed to question Alice. Carl had given her a special medication. They found her in bed drinking a glass of whiskey. They understood.

Alice had always expected to be a widow. Before she married Carl, she was told he might live only two years. She was willing to accept that. Even after he was apparently cured, she never knew when a train wreck, an airplane crash, or an auto accident might take him. He traveled a great deal and his work was sometimes dangerous. Carl always kept his papers in order and up to date so she might be provided for when he died. He put the vehicles in her name so that she'd have no problem when he was gone.

Indeed, besides his tuberculosis, Carl had several serious illnesses along the way. He had his appendix out in the early days when even that operation was not always successful. Then he had hemorrhoid surgery, later the removal of his gall bladder, and finally in 1972, he had to have surgery for an enlarged prostate that he feared was malignant. Fortunately, it was not cancerous, but the surgery was traumatic. Afterwards he hemorrhaged and nearly died in spite of blood transfusions. He then developed hepatitis as a result of those transfusions. He had never been so close to death.

Carl and Alice wanted to be prepared, for he knew he could die at any time after that fateful day in 1924 when his TB was diagnosed. Alice showed the Carl the spot where she wanted her final resting place, a steep hill overlooking the valley at the top of the canyon wall. She wanted her ashes scattered there. Yet neither of them expected that she would die first.

On the morning of December 27, 1973, Alice awoke in the early hours with pains in her back and shoulder. Carl checked her vital signs and told her she must stay in bed. Alice said she would be just fine after a day of rest. She called Editha at Gascon Ranch to ask her to send Sherry over later to help with the household chores.

"Are you sure you're all right?" Carl asked, not wanting to leave her to go to work. Alice assured him that she was fine. She urged him to go on over to the hospital and have breakfast there. Mary Valdez, Benny's wife, cooked for the staff and served breakfast every morning in the hospital kitchen. Carl reluctantly went over to the hospital. hospital.

When Carl returned, Alice was still in pain. He again checked her blood pressure and pulse and was about to suggest that they get her to a hospital when suddenly Alice went into cardiac distress.

Carl knew what was happening now, but there was nothing he could do. Even if Alice had been in a hospital at the time, there would have been little anyone could do. The coronary occlusion was sudden and deadly. All the doctor could do now was hold his wife in his arms. He held her tightly, closely, for a long time, long moments after the heart had ceased to beat. She, like Elizabeth Barrett Browning, was privileged to die in her husband's arms, cherished and adored. It was no wonder that Elizabeth whispered, as she died, "It is beautiful." Few women are so fortunate, so blessed, as to be so loved. That love was the bridge that carried her over.

As Carl listened for Alice's heartbeat and found none — his own heart racing incredibly under the terror that gripped it — there was a sickening silence. The heartbeat of his life was still.

Suddenly there was a thundering, cracking noise like timber falling on ice or steel splitting stone: a crack, a thud, a snap. At the same time sudden darkness struck like a shade snapped down over the window. Quick as the snap of a whip — darkness and the silence of the tomb. The blackness was the oblivion of shock. The noise was the shattering of his broken heart with its reverberating shock waves wheeling through his nervous system in earthquake-like spasms.

After that everything became mechanical. Carl picked up the phone and called Editha.

"You'd better come on over," he said evenly. "Your mother's gone."

Carl's voice sounded so normal Editha had no idea what he meant. She had just talked to her mother on the phone. She thought her father meant that Alice had gone out to the kitchen to fix breakfast or gone outside against the doctor's judgment and that he wanted Editha to come over and help manage things. The idea that Alice might have died did not register.

"Gone where?" Editha questioned.

"Her heart stopped beating," the doctor replied.

Editha heard the cracking noise then too. She realized that her father's heart was broken.

When Editha and Sherry arrived Carl was calm and composed. All the arrangements had been made. Editha wondered how her father could be so calm until she realized that in his state of shock he was acting mechanically. He fell back on his years of training, years of dealing with death. He knew what was supposed to be done automatically. He had guided so many others through the valley of the shadow. He knew the path well.

"In spite of the fact that he was doing all the right things, not appearing upset or out of control, I knew that his heart was broken, literally shredded," Editha said.

There is a degree of pain that is beyond feeling. Just as there are sounds beyond the range of the human ear, so there is a pain beyond perception. When physical pain has reached the zenith of its intensity, the body lapses into unconsicousness or death and so feels no more. Or if death is impossible, the brain releases its endomorphs and so in the throes of agony, the pain, though the source is still present, is no longer perceived. So, too, when the emotional pain — the pain of the heart or the spirit — has reached comparable intensity, the soul, too, lapses into a kind of unconscious numbness and can feel no more for a time. The circuit breaker never fails when the circuit is overloaded.

So it was when Dr. Gellenthien experienced the sudden, unexpected loss of his wife. He remained in shock for a long time, though he was able to function by all outward appearances quite normally.

He went on with his usual work load, but inwardly he remained stunned. One day he was walking down the street when an old friend greeted him. Carl did not recgonize him. He hardly acknowledged the greeting. The numbness finally wore off and the anesthetized spirit began to feel again, but only after Carl lost himself again in his work and the great healer of time had a chance to function. He gradually began to be aware of the world. But he never got over the dread of going home after finishing up at the office. The house no longer seemed like a home. It was "an empty barn," cold, desolate, barren. His Arnica was no longer there.

Carl lost weight. He hardly noticed what he ate if he ate at all. The survival rate of widowers is low. Carl survived for the sake of his work. But his eyes reflected the grief of his soul. The pain he had endured was evident though he did not become morbidly maudlin or wretched as some men do. Yet when he thought of Alice his face was touched with a shadow of his loss. The pain a soul can endure is immeasurable. The loss of a beloved wife must be comparable to the greatest physical tortures the body has been subjected to in the devices which man in his inhumanity to man has ingeniously perfected.

Recent research lists "loss of a spouse" as the number one stress factor a person can experience. For a doctor, it must be especially traumatic, for the loss most likely is accompanied with an element of guilt or a feeling of failure when he is present at the death. He must wonder if he, who spent a lifetime turning death away, could not have done something to save the one he loved the most. Such feelings were expressed in *Polly* when Dr. Maybright's wife died in childbirth and he had been unable to save her.

> I think, father, what really upset Polly so was when she heard that you — you were there. Polly thinks, she always did think that you could keep death away...I think...that was what quite broke Polly down — losing mother, and losing faith in your power at the same time. [7]

The words of his oldest daughter enlightened Dr. Maybright and the doctor went to see his grief-stricken daughter, Polly.

> "Father...I have been in a dreadful, dreadful dream since Mother died," Polly explained. "The most dreadful part of my dream, the blackest part, was about you...You were there, Father, and you let her die."
>
> Dr. Maybright put his arm around the trembling child, and drew her close to him.
>
> "Not willingly," he said, in a voice which Polly had never heard him use before. "Not willingly, my child. It was with anguish I let your

mother go away. But, Polly, there was another Physician there, greather than I."

"Another?" said Polly.

"Yes, Another — and He prescribed rest, forever more."

All her life afterward Polly remembered those words of her father. They calmed her great sorrow, and in many ways left her a different child. [80]

Like Dr. Maybright in the novel, Dr. G. knew that the Great Physician Himself was there and that He knew what He was doing. Still, the loss was sudden and shocking and undoubtedly accompanied by some doubts — the constant "what ifs" that plague the grief-stricken.

Carl closed off the bedroom. He left things just as they were when Alice died — her sewing basket, closets, photographs. "I embalmed the house," he said later, realizing what he had done. He forced himself to live severely and simply, not unlike a monk. The self-imposed severity was part of his early grief. With the help of his family and friends, the doctor gradually began to see that it was all right to buy a jacket or a pair of socks. Life could go on.

In the waiting room of Dr. G.'s office there are various artistic works — oil paintings, a Navajo diorama set behind glass — all gifts from grateful patients. But the art that captures the eye and holds it the longest is the large painting of a woman looking down from her place on the north wall. No other painting adorns the wall; it belongs solely to her. Her face is bright even when the small lamp above the painting is not turned on. She wears blue jodhpurs, a yellow blouse, brown gloves, and holds her riding crop in her right hand. Obviously this dignified young lady is a skilled horsewoman.

The beautiful oil painting hanging in the medical office was given to Valmora by Curt Brink, who left for his Chicago home on March 9th (1939). The subject is an attractive Western girl standing beside her saddle and bridle and was painted by Curt's younger brother, Jack. This makes a very appropriate and enhancing addition. Curt's kindness and thoughtfulness in giving this gift are deeply appreciated. [9]

Alice Gellenthien served as the model for this portrait in 1938. Through the years it has been thought of as a portrait of Alice, though it is not an exact likeness of her, especially in its facial features. Yet the artist has captured the quiet dignity of Alice in a pensive moment. On her face is the hint of a smile. At the next moment it may break through and fill the room with laughter. But that moment has not yet come. It is there, waiting for the next second. Her face has been captured by the aritst at the precise moment before a smile comes.

284

The artist has captured a moment as a photographer does, a glimpse of a character frozen in time. He has captured the face of the sweetheart, wife, mother, companion, friend, horsewoman — all the things she was, seen by the suggestive stroke of his brush. One is reminded of Keats' appreciation of artistic beauty in his "Ode on a Grecian Urn," expressing the wonder of the captured moment made eternal by the artist:

She cannot fade...
  For ever wilt thou love, and she be fair!

More happy love!...
  For ever warm...
    ...and for ever young. [10]

The painting of the young woman has hung in the reception room for years. Some say it is not Alice. Yet the portrait brightens up the hearts of those who knew Alice and remember her, so similar is the woman in the portrait to Alice herself. It creates a spark of curious wonder in the hearts of those who did not know her.

"Look there," a patient will say. "That's the doctor's wife...that's a picture of his Alice."

Carl used to climb the mountain where Alice's ashes were scattered to pay tribute to the monument there. He stopped making the steep climb up the canyon wall after his 80th birthday. There was little need. He had the site memorized. The true memorials had been left in the hearts of those who loved her.

Carl himself wrote the inscription that was placed on the bronze plaque which is set in cement and stone at the base of the rock monument. Benny Valdez and the doctor built the monument themselves, carrying cement and water and rock to the site. The stone overlooks the entire Valmora valley. The plaque reads:

Alice Brown Gellenthien
January 7, 1901   December 27, 1973.
"Unto almighty God
I commend the soul
Of my beloved wife
Alice
And according to her wish
I have spread her ashes
Upon
The lands of Valmora
Which have been her cherished
and
Only home on earth."

February 17, 1974 — Carl H. Gellenthien, M.D.

Alice's death certificate listed the cause of her death as "Myocardio Infarction," "Coronary Thrombosis" and "Arteriosclerosis." Though the cause of her death was not an uncommon one, the way Alice lived her life and faced her death was as rare as Keats' marble maiden who "cannot fade, forever warm, forever young."

The brisk canyon winds, the driving rain, the gentle snow, and the pounding hail: those natural elements of the wilderness have not disturbed the monument. A hundred years from now, barring catastrophic conditions, it will still be there — a thousand years — and more. Should some archeologist find it then he might wonder at the fact that through the centuries human nature does not change. Men, under all conditions and in all times, some of them physicians, mourn and endure the loss of their beloved wives. He might wonder who this Carl H. Gellenthien, M.D. was. Why did he go to the trouble of placing a momument there, at the precipice overlooking the valley? What kind of woman was this Alice to have deserved such a special memorial? He might wonder how she had lived and how she had died. He might wonder that men of that past era — the Atomic era — a dark and treacherous time in the history of mankind, could have loved so deeply while their history books were filled with accounts of war and violence. He might wonder if this man, this medical doctor, had been loved as deeply as he had loved. He might even wonder if somehow that love had endured.

NOTES

1. John B. Lust, *The Herb Book*, N.Y.: Bantam Books, Inc., 1974, p. 101.
2. Newspaper clipping in Scrapbook 4, Valmora Library, p. 13.
3. "The Lost Ford or No Wife to Guide Them," *The Spirit of Valmora*, December, 1930, p. 3., in Scrapbook 3, Valmora Library, p. 41.
4. *Ibid.*
5. *Ibid.*
6. *Ibid.*
7. L.T. Meade, *Polly: A New-Fashioned Girl*, *op.cit.*, pp. 13-14.
8. *Ibid.*, pp-. 18-19.
9. "Cuff Notes," *The Valmora Sun*, April, 1939, p. 4., in Scrapbook 3, Valmora Library, Valmora, New Mexico, p. 29.
10. Foreman, *op. cit.*, pp. 295-297.

EPILOGUE

Once again, the condemned man waited in a small hospital room for the hour of his death.

Room 3B32 was not a prison cell, for the man had committed no crime. His executioner was not the hangman or the firing squad. His death sentence was not mandated by the laws of men.

Whether delirious and feverish or convulsed in paroxysms of coughing, the wasting frame of the man languished hour after hour in the private room. The exiled man had seen the pale countenance staring back at him from the mirror — the face of pneumonia etched across his own.

The man was Carl Herman Gellenthien. The year was 1984. The small room was one of many sanctuaries of hope at St. Vincent Hospital in Santa Fe, New Mexico. In Room 3B32 Carl Gellenthien saw the pallid image of his enemy, saw the mask of death across his face.

Yet, he did not die. Somehow, one day soon after his confinement, a subtle change began to take place. How or why he did not know, but the elderly man knew he was to be granted another reprieve. He knew he would have to earn it. But there was no doubt. He would fight the enemy and he would win.

Carl Gellenthein knew the fight he was up against. He understood his enemy. He had been a medical doctor for 57 years. He had seen many elderly patients succumb to pneumonia.

On January 3, 1984, Dr. G. had slipped on the ice ouside a house near his home and fallen. He drove himself home in spite of the pain, certain he had fractured some ribs. He sent a message to his friend Dr. Zigmund W. Kosicki, an orthopedic surgeon, to let him know he would be coming into St. Vincent Hospital as soon as possible. Dr. Kosicki was waiting at the emergency room when Dr. G. arrived. Dr. G.'s X-rays revealed several broken ribs, a separated shoulder and a hip injury.

If he had been a younger man, Dr. G. might have been sent home. But the risk of pneumonia in an elderly person suffering a fracture was too great. Dr. Kosicki called in Dr. Charles A. Riley, a specialist in internal medicine and pulmonary diseases. Yet even with the best of care, Dr. G.'s condition worsened. Three days later pneumonia gripped him. His lungs, already scarred with TB, filled with fluid. But although death clutched at him, the enemy did not pull him away. His foe waited for him to face it squarely in Room 3B32. He did.

Dr. G. had fought many battles before and won. But now his age was against him. He slipped into a delirium, a world of fantastic nightmares where reality and dreams blend into a never-never land of horrors, a long hall of mirrors distorting the rational into the terror of the unreal.

Once before, Dr. G. had developed pneumonia following surgery when he had his gall bladder removed. At that time, too, delirium gripped him. But he never forgot he was a doctor. He heard a commotion in the emergency room down the hall from his private room and thought it was time for him to go to work. He asked Lupe, the friend who was sitting in his room with him, to help him get down to the emergency room to take care of the patients — not realizing that he was a patient!

The delirium did not occur at first. It waited until the toxins of pneumonia and the combined forces of various medications had time to merge in a grotesque clash. The first two days Dr. G. enjoyed the visitors who dropped by to wish him well. One welcome visitor was Father Edward Byrne, Chaplain at St. Vincent who had come from Ireland to "take the cure" years before. After supper one evening he came in and sat by the bed and talked with Dr. G. about the days when TB was the greatest enemy of mankind.

"You saved my life," the priest said. "I was dying of TB when I came to you. Now I've been here all these years as chaplain. I'll be retiring soon."

"Yes, we beat TB," Dr. G. said. "We fought and fought. And we finally won."

Yet even as he spoke, the bacilli in the doctor's lungs thrived. He would be treated with penicillin, the great lifesaver of the 20th century, but he was to face the greatest battle of his lifetime. And his physicians, though they were his best friends, could not give him the youth that would have made the battle easy. They could give him medication and care, but they could not roll back the years that made him so vulnerable to the deadly enemy. Dr. Kosicki's concern deepened as his friend's condition worsened.

"I wish there was something I could do," he said. The undertone of his statement was the tortured frustration felt by doctors when they cannot help those they care about the most. It is a kind of haunted, quiet agony which cannot be shared. He had just examined the patient and had left the nurses' desk. "There just isn't anything I can do. My hands are tied."

There was one thing he could do, however, and he did it. He was there. He was a friend. He cared.

It was that same kind of caring which exerted a mysterious force in Carl's life at the age of 24. As family, friends, colleagues, and staff members showed their concern and love, that same Force began to surround the patient. The darkness of his disease had almost totally enveloped him when a small light appeared. The light grew as he reached out and nourished it with hope. As it grew larger and brighter, it dispelled the darkness of despair.

The light came in many forms: a daily phone call from his granddaughter Sherry Becker at home in Arizona, a visit from his daughter Editha from Gascon Ranch, and a cheerful "hello" from Patty Reilly, secretary in the hospital's Education Division, as she popped into the room for the 9th time. It came in Dr. Kosicki's morning visits as he dropped in with the newspaper for his patient to read. It came in the cheerful advice of Dr. Bergere A. Kenny, Director of the Medical Seminars for Physicians, which Dr. G. always attended. It appeared when Librarian Jane Knowles made sure he had plenty of reading materials. And it was there when well-wishers like Dr. Weldon Dunlap, an ophthalmologist to whom Dr. G. had referred patients, dropped in to see how he was doing. The nurses, X-ray technicians, respiratory therapists and other staff members who showed their concern became a part of that growing light. Indeed, the mystery of love is greater than the mystery of death. And while that Force had played a significant role in Carl's recovery from TB in 1924, the battle he now fought was much fiercer, for it was the critical grip of deadly pneumonia that clutched his aging body, bringing with it a variety of acute complications.

That night of Friday, January 6, 1984 was the turning point, for it was then that the enemy was defeated. As Carl lay in his feverish sleep, sometimes awake, other times dreaming, he remembered the last two years. His thoughts drifted to the last trek he had taken with his Los Rancheros Visitadores friends. And then he thought about the last AMA meeting he had attended in Chicago. He had visited his old neighborhood while there, seeing the familiar places and reminiscing about the old days.

Dr. G. thought of the many hard-working local families he had known for so many years. He thought of Mollie Lucero who had grown up as Mollie Archuleta in Watrous. Her grandmother had been a midwife and had delivered many babies in the Watrous, Shoemaker and Valmora area. She had been a great friend of Dr. G. Mollie began her career with the railroad as a young woman in 1943. Her husband, Frank Lucero, had worked for the railroad until his retirement in 1969. Mollie became the Regional Freight Manager for Las Vegas and Santa Fe, responsible for the efficiency of the Santa Fe Railroad Company in her area. When Dr. G. came in to take the Amtrak to Chicago in 1983, Mollie insisted on driving him down to the car he would be getting on so that he wouldn't have to walk nearly the entire length of the train.

"I don't do this for everyone. But Dr. G. is part of the family!" she said.

Dr. G.'s "family" extends from the villages of New Mexico to the heart of downtown Chicago. However, the numbers of his long-time friends has dwindled in the last few years. At the AMA Convention in 1983, Gellenthien sat almost alone in the long row which had been roped off and designated, "Past Vice-Presidents and Past House of Delegates." Only two others sat in the long row with him, and only three or four sat in the row in front of him. The empty seats around Dr. G. were evidence of how many had gone on, leaving their places vacant. He alone remained of his old group, and the loneliness was poignant.

"Isn't it sad to see him sitting there surrounded by all the empty chairs?" a friend remarked. "Nearly all his old colleagues are gone now."

"Yes, but Dr. G. says he's learned to make friends among the younger sets," another replied.

"Oh, but it can't be the same," the first declared. "You know, when he dies, a species will be extinct. He's the last of his kind."

Yet even as a young man Carl prepared to meet death, confronted as he was by TB. Over 57 years ago, in his address to his graduating class at St. Luke's in Denver, he said, "We are unable and unequal to the task of bidding farewell."[1] After so many years have gone by, Dr. G. can still quote the poem he cited in the conclusion of his speech that day:

"Life we've been long together,
Through pleasant and through cloudy weather;
'Tis hard to part where friends are dear;
Perhaps 'twill cost a sigh, a tear;
Then steal away, give little warning.
Choose thine own time
Say not 'goodnight'
But in some brighter clime

Bid me 'Good Morning.'"[2]

Carl thought of that verse as he lay struggling against pneumonia. The doctor wondered if now he faced that moment of death he had held off for so many years. Once he had scribbled down a note and tucked it away in a scrapbook:

Do we secretly rage at the years of sublimating our own needs when we take care of the needs of others?

Down at the core, do we desperately want relief from the body and the nerve-racking pressures we bear with — seeking injury or death as a way out?

Do we attend the dark mystery of death so often that we're finally tempted to confront it directly, personally?[3]

He had never, like some physicians, become so overburdened with the task of caring for others that he had sought a way out. Death had always been the enemy. He had fought it personally and he had fought for those too weak to fight. Now he wondered if he must face his foe and finally lose the battle.

That fateful Friday night death determined to take him at last. Dr. G.'s room was silent except for the bubbling of the oxygen that gently blew its life support into the fragile, scarred lungs. The doctor's breathing was heavy with pain. He slept, coughed, then slept a few more brief moments until another paroxysm overtook him.

While Dr. G. struggled for each breath, many prayers were being formed in different ways and in different places. A black lady from Albuquerque had called to make her usual appointment and had heard that the doctor was in the hospital. She asked her entire church to pray for Dr. G. While Protestant believers formed prayer chains, many Catholic and Jewish friends prayed as well. Each prayed in his own way, but all asked the same God to be merciful and allow the doctor to recover and return to his practice. The prayers of the doctor's family and friends took many different forms. But perhaps it was the plea of the poor people of Mora County that struck closest to the Heart of One who visited the homes of the poor, healed the sick, fed the hungry, and held babies in His arms nearly 2000 years ago. ago.

"Who will take care of us if Dr. G. is gone?" they asked. "There is no one to replace Dr. G. Please God, let him return to us."

Dr. G. resumed his practice in February and took up his usual busy schedule immediately. He attended the Los Rancheros Visitadores' annual trek in the spring of 1984 as he had been doing since 1932. He attended the New Mexico Medical Society's annual meeting in Santa Fe in the spring. And he again attended the AMA Convention in Chicago in June of 1984, in addition to numerous continuing education seminars in various places.

Soon after his return home from the hospital, someone in Las Vegas started a rumor that the doctor had died. A patient from Glorieta called to find out if it were true and was relieved to learn that the doctor was home from the hosptial, back in his office seeing patients as usual. The woman made an appointment and came in later that week.

"I'm glad to see that you're not dead," she told the doctor.

Dr. G. quoted Mark Twain in his reply: "Rumors of my death have been largely exaggerated."

And though he can laugh about it, Dr. G. becomes very serious when he speaks of his recent illness. "The BOSS has been good to me. I wouldn't be here today if it hadn't been for Him. Today is a gift from God, a day I shouldn't have. But if I can help someone along the way, it is my way of telling God *thanks.*" Each day is another opportunity to give the gift of compassion back to God. Dr. G. was able to continue his work because the prayers of so many were answered when the Great Physician heard them in His compassion. No one saw Him, for He could not be seen by human eyes. And yet His Presence entered the room and stood at the bedside of Dr. Carl Gellenthien.

The first week after his return to Valmora, Dr. G. saved a man's life when he suffered a heart attack in the middle of the night and Dr. G. was the only doctor he could reach. Dr. G.'s gratitude was returned in full payment as he continued his practice.

NOTES

1. Carl H. Gellenthien, "Au Revior." Manuscript of speech delivered at Commencement, 1927, graduating class of St. Luke's Hospital, Denver, Colorado, in *RX, 1927 Yearbook,* 1927, n.p.
2. *Ibid.*
3. Handwritten note in Scrapbook 3, Valmora Library, Valmora, New Mexico, p. 10.

BIBLIOGRAPHY

BOOKS

Bunyan, John. *Life and Death of Mr. Badman and The Holy War*. Ed. John Brown. Cambridge: The University Press, 1905.

Cousins, Norman. *Anatomy of an Illness as Perceived by the Patient*. New York: W.W. Norton & Company, 1979.

de Kruif, Paul. *The Fight for Life*. New York: Harcourt, Brace and Company, 1938.

Dickens, Charles. *The Life and Adventures of Nicholas Nickleby*. New York: Hurst and Company Publishers, n.d.

Dubos, Rene and Jean Dubos. *The White Plague: Tuberculosis, Man and Society*. Boston: Little, Brown and Company, 1952.

Dunlop, Richard. *Doctors of the American Frontier*. New York: Ballantine Books, a Division of Random House, 1965.

Foreman, H. Buxton, ed. *The Poetical Works of John Keats*. New York: Thomas Y. Crowell & Company, 1865.

Guinn, William. *Death Lies Deep*. New York: Gold Medal Books, 1955.

Lust, John B. *The Herb Book*. New York: Bantam Books, Inc., 1974.

Mann, Thomas. *The Magic Mountain*. Translated by H.T. Lowe-Porter. New York: Alfred A. Knopf, 1939.

Meade, L.T. *Polly: A New-Fashioned Girl*. Chicago: M.A. Donohue & Company, n.d.

Mooney, Elizabeth. *In the Shadow of the White Plague*. New York: Thomas Y. Crowell Publisher, 1979.

O'Brien, Bonnie Ball. *Promises Kept*. Nashville, Tennessee: Broadman Press, 1978.

Orlandi, Enzo, ed. *The Life & Times of Chopin*. Translated by C.J. Richards. Philadelphia: The Curtis Publishing Company and Arnoldo Mondadori Editore, 1967.

Schweitzer, Albert. *Out of My Life and Thought*. New York: Henry Holt and Company, 1949.

Sontag, Susan. *Illness as Metaphor*. New York: Farrar, Straus and Giroux, 1978.

The Holy Bible. Nashville, Tennessee: Crusade Bible Publishers, Inc., 1975.

Trilling, Lionel, ed. *The Selected Letters of John Keats*. New York: Farrar, Straus and Young, Inc., 1951.

Watson, Lillian Eichler, ed. *Light From Many Lamps*. New York: Simon and Schuster, 1951.

ARTICLES AND PERIODICALS

Gellenthien, Carl H. "Altitude and Artificial Pneumothorax." *The Journal of the American Medical Association* (March 2, 1940), pp. 727-728.

_____. "New Methods in the Treatment of Tuberculosis." Reprinted in *Industrial Medicine* 16 (March, 1945), 1-6, in Scrapbook 3, Valmora Library, Valmora, New Mexico, p. 69.

Hayakawa, S.I. "The Good Old Days — You Can Have Them." *The Saturday Evening Post* 246 (January/February, 1974). p. 42.

"Milestones," *Time* (February 10, 1947), clipping in Scrapbook 1, Valmora Library, Valmora, New Mexico, p. 133.

Ober, William. "Did Chopin Really Die of TB? Diagnosis Reconsidered." *Diagnosis* 3 (November, 1981), pp. 15-16.

"Parallel Cases, Tuberculosis: George Bodington," *MD* (March, 1964), p. 195, clipping in Scrapbook 10, Valmora Library, Valmora, New Mexico, p. 7.

"Parallel Cases, Tuberculosis: Hippocrates," *MD* (March, 1964), p. 195, clipping in Scrapbook 10, Valmora Library, Valmora, New Mexico, p. 7.

"The Power of Art Over Disease," *Robins Reader* (Spring-Summer, 1982), p. 6.

"Tuberculosis: A Menace and a Mystery and $4,500,000 in Christmas Seals." *Life Magazine* (November 29, 1937), pp. 30-31.

Witter, Evelyn. "The Story of Raggedy Ann." *The Book-Mart* 9 (April, 1983), p. 3.

Wright, Paul. "Valmora: The Wilderness Retreat." *New Mexico Highway Journal* IX (May, 1931), pp. 18-20.

NEWSPAPER ITEMS

Addington, Neil. "Crews Hunt More Bodies in Wreckage." *Santa Fe New Mexican* (Santa Fe, New Mexico), September 5, 1956, n.p., clipping in Scrapbook 6, Valmora Library, Valmora, New Mexico, p. 53.

"Alumni News." *The Valmora Sun* (Valmora, New Mexico), December, 1938, p. 3., in Scrapbook 3, Valmora Library, Valmora, New Mexico, p. 21.

"Alumni Potpourri." *The Valmora Sun* (Valmora, New Mexico), April, 1939, p. 3., in Scrapbook 3, Valmora Library, Valmora, New Mexico, p. 29.

"AMA's Washington Office — Its Legend and Its Legacy." *American Medical News* (Chicago, Illinois), June 18, 1982, p. 9.

"A Real Santa Claus," *The Las Vegan* (Las Vegas, New Mexico), 1932, n.p., clipping in Scrapbook 1, Valmora Library, Valmora, New Mexico, p. 42.

"A Volcanic Experience of Mr. Bohannon." *The Valmora Sun* (Valmora, New Mexico), November, 1938, p. 7., in Scrapbook 3, Valmora Library, Valmora, New Mexico, p. 19.

Baumann, Edward and John O'Brien. "Capone's Old Hotel Now Just a Tomb?" *Chicago Tribune* (Chicago, Illinois), June 18, 1981, Sec. 1. pp. 20-21.

"Bullet's Artless Comment: George Washington — C.M. Garland," n.p., (February 24, 1924), n.p., in Scrapbook 1, Valmora Library, Valmora, New Mexico, p. 57.

Cheney, V.S. "Early History of Valmora Reveals Pioneer Effort." *The Valmora Sun* (Valmora, New Mexico), June, 1939, p. 1, in Scrapbook 3, Valmora

Library, Valmora, New Mexico, p. 33.

"Chicagoans at Dinner to Boost Sanitarium for the Tubercular," n.p., October 1, 1931, n.p., in Scrapbook 1, Valmora Library, Valmora, New Mexico, p. 17.

"Christmas Week and New Year's Day Joyous Events," *The Valmora Sun* (Valmora, New Mexico), January, 1939, p. 1, in Scrapbook 3, Valmora Library, Valmora, New Mexico, p. 23.

"Cuff Notes." *The Valmora Sun* (Valmora, New Mexico), December, 1938, p. 4, in Scrapbook 3, Valmora Library, Valmora, New Mexico, p. 21.

Curtis, John B. "'Giant Hand' Crushes Train Like Accordion," in Scrapbook 6, Valamora Library, Valmora, New Mexico, p. 50.

Dickinson, William B. "Santa Fe's Chief Rams Mail Train," in Scrapbook 6, Valmora Library, Valmora, New Mexico, p. 52.

"Earlier Journalistic Efforts Recounted: Former Papers More Intimate But Less Comprehensive in Scope," *The Valmora Sun* (Valmora, New Mexico), January, 1939, p. 1, in Scrapbook 3, Valmora Library, Valmora, New Mexico, p. 23.

Edwards, Willard. "Johnson Puts Off Shutdowns by VA," in Scrapbook 3, Valmora Library, Valmora, New Mexico, p. 54.

"Famous T.B.'s." *The Buzzer,* in Scrapbook 3, Valmora Library, Valmora, New Mexico, p. 71.

"Frank Borman, Barry Morris Goldwater, Frederick Brant Rentschler and Wernher von Braun to be Enshrined." *National Aviation Hall of Fame.* Issue 2 (Dayton, Ohio), 1982, p. 1.

Gellenthien, C.H. "Adios Amigos, Dios Valla Con Ustedes." *The Valmora Sun* (Valmora, New Mexico), June, 1939, p. 1, in Scrapbook 3, Valmora Library, Valmora, New Mexico, p. 33.

_____. "Dr. Gellenthien Inaugurates Series of Health Articles: Stresses Intelligent Cooperation Between Doctor and Patient." *The Valmora Sun* (Valmora, New Mexico), November, 1938, p. 5, in Scrapbook 3, Valmora Library, Valmora, New Mexico, p. 19.

_____. "Factors Bearing on Prognosis Are Many and Sundry: Resistance and Patient's Intelligence Take Precedence." *The Valmora Sun* (Valmora, New Mexico), March, 1939, p. 1, in Scrapbook 3, Valmora Library, Valmora, New Mexico, p. 27.

_____. "Gellenthien Says Climate Is Great Aid." *The Health City Sun* (Albuquerque, New Mexico), November 20, 1931, p. 1.

_____. "'Rest,' The Most Important Aid in 'Curing' T.B." *The Valmora Sun* (Valmora, New Mexico), January, 1939, p. 1, in Scrapbook 3, Valmora Library, Valmora, New Mexico, p. 23.

"Gellenthiens in West Indies Trip." in Scrapbook 3, Valmora Library, Valmora, New Mexico, p. 1.

"Help Provided for Needy in Snowbound Area: Crew Works on Clogged Roads." *Las Vegas Optic* (Las Vegas, New Mexico), January 12, 1939, p. 1.

"Helping Santa Claus." *The Spirit of Valmora* (Valmora, New Mexico), December, 1930, p. 3., in Scrapbook 3, Valmora Library, Valmora, New Mexico, p. 41.

Hudson, Herbert. "Rough For While." in Scrapbook 6, Valmora Library, Valmora, New Mexico, p. 41.

"Human Error Cited in Train Accident Claiming 20 Lives." in Scrapbook 6, Valmora Library, Valmora, New Mexico, p. 47.

Johnson, Vivian. "It's All in a Day's Work." *The Valmora Sun* (Valmora, New Mexico), February, 1939, p. 7, in Scrapbook 3, Valmora Library, Valmora, New Mexico, p. 25.

Kleist, H.E. "Bird Home Builders Bravely Overcome Many Difficulties: Life Does Not Always Run Smoothly for Our Feathered Friends." in Scrapbook 1, Valmora Library, Valmora, New Mexico, p. 72.

"LBJ Heeds Capitol Hill Criticism, Orders New Study of VA Hospitals." in Scrapbook 3, Valmora Library, Valmora, New Mexico, p. 54.

McFarland, R.M. "All's Quiet on Boy Gang Line; 'Y' is Reason." in Scrapbook 1, Valmora Library, Valmora, New Mexico, p. 83.

"Modern Methods of Tuberculosis Discussed: Valmora Medical Superintendent Tells of Development by Science in Fighting Disease." in Scrapbook 1, Valmora Library, Valmora, New Mexico, p. 57.

"More About the Christmas Party." *The Valmora Sun* (Valmora, New Mexico), January, 1939, p. 8, in Scrapbook 3, Valmora Library, Valmora, New Mexico, p. 23.

"Need Blood to Save Sick Man at Sanatorium," (Las Vegas, New Mexico), in Scrapbook 1, Valmora Library, Valmora, New Mexico, p. 43.

n.t., n.p., n.d., caption for photograph of the wreck at Springer Siding, in Scrapbook 6, Valmora Library, Valmora, New Mexico, p. 32.

n.t., n.p., n.d., clipping in Scrapbook 1, Valmora Library, Valmora, New Mexico, p. 42.

"New Resident Physician Arrives." *The Valmora Sun* (Valmora, New Mexico), November, 1938, p. 3., in Scrapbook 3, Valmora Library, Valmora, New Mexico, p. 19.

Nicholas, Dorothea. "Division Street 'Y' Marks First 50 Years of Work." *Chicago Daily Tribune* (Chicago, Illinois), September 29, 1960, Part 5, p. 4, in Scrapbook 1, Valmora Library, Valmora, New Mexico, p. 87.

"Optic Sends Food to Isolated Area." *Las Vegas Optic* (Las Vegas, New Mexico), January 11, 1939, p. 1.

"Plays Santa Claus for All Mora County's Children in School Tomorrow Afternoon: Dr. W.T. Brown of Valmora is Presenting gifts to Over 1,000 Little Folks." (Las Vegas, New Mexico), December, 193/, in Scrapbook 1, Valmora Library, Valmora, New Mexico, p. 25.

"Pneumothorax Patients Should Consult Doctor Before Taking Trip in Airplane." in Scrapbook 1, Valmora Library, Valmora, New Mexico, p. 139.

"Ransdell Announces Retirement." *Baptist New Mexican* (Albuquerque, New Mexico), June 12, 1976, p. 1.

"Research Work of Gellenthien Gets National Notice: Article in Medical Journal Tells of Findings in Aviation Medicine Field." (Las Vegas, New Mexico), April 22, 1942, in Scrapbook 2, Valmora Library, Valmora, New Mexico, p. 6.

Roberts, Oral. *May Newsletter* (Tulsa, Oklahoma), May, 1982, pp. 1-2.

"Santa Fe Fireman Shocked." *Albuquerque Journal* (Albuquerque, New Mexico), in Scrapbook 6, Valmora Library, Valmora, New Mexico, p. 53.

"Statistical Report Tells Graphic Story." *The Valmora Sun* (Valmora, New Mexico), February, 1939, p. 1., in Scrapbook 3, Valmora Library, Valmora, New Mexico, p. 25.

"Sunshine Often Difference Between Life and Death in T.B. Treatment Says Gellenthien." in Scrapbook 1, Valmora Library, Valmora, New Mexico, p. 110

"Sun Spots." *The Valmora Sun* (Valmora, New Mexico), January, 1939, p. 2, in Scrapbook 3, Valmora Library, Valmora, New Mexico, p. 23.

"'Swing Your Partner' — and Break a Leg." in Scrapbook 2, Valmora Library, Valmora, New Mexico, p. 48.

"The Lost Ford or No Wife to Guide Them." *The Spirit of Valmora* (Valmora, New Mexico), December, 1930, pp. 3-4, in Scrapbook 3, Valmora Library, Valmora, New Mexico, p. 41.

"The Young Skeptic." *The Valmora Sun* (Valmora, New Mexico), January, 1939, p. 2, in Scrapbook 3, Valmora Library, Valmora, New Mexico, p. 23.

Thompson, Fritz. "The Flood." *Impact, Albuquerque Journal Magazine* (Albuquerque, New Mexico), March 15, 1983, p. 4.

"Today in Albuquerque." (Albuquerque, New Mexico), December 31, 1931, in Scrapbook 1, Valmora Library, Valmora, New Mexico, p. 21.

"Valmora in Chicago." *Las Vegas Optic* (Las Vegas, New Mexico), October 10, 1932, p. 4.

"Valmora Resort Widely Known." *The Valmora Sun* (Valmora, New Mexico), November, 1938, p. 1, in Scrapbook 3, Valmora Library, Valmora, New Mexico, p. 19.

"Valmorans Report Frolic at Recardo's." *The Valmora Sun* (Valmora, New Mexico), November, 1938, p. 1., in Scrapbook 3, Valmora Library, Valmora, New Mexico, p. 19.

Vivian, Walter T. "Along the Banks of the Gillinas." *Las Vegas Optic* (Las Vegas, New Mexico), September 5, 1956, in Scrapbook 6, Valmora Library, Valmora, New Mexico, p. 53.

_____. "Worst for Veteran Newsman." *Las Vegas Optic* (Las Vegas, New Mexico), Spetember 5, 1956, p. 1, in Scrapbook 6, Valmora Library, Valmora, New Mexico, p. 43.

W.E.D "The Old-Timers' Column." *The Boscobel Dial,* June 31, 1933, in Scrapbook 1, Valmora Library, Valmora, New Mexico, p. 84.

"Weelum." "Weelum Enjoyed the Valmora Banquet." in Scrapbook 1, Valmora Library, Valmora, New Mexico, p. 17.

"Who's Who at Valmora Past and Present." *The Valmora Sun* (Valmora, New Mexico), December, 1938, p. 4, in Scrapbook 3, Valmora Library, Valmora, New Mexico, p. 21.

_____. *The Valmora Sun* (Valmora, New Mexico), January, 1939, p. 4, in Scrapbook 3, Valmora Library, Valmora, New Mexico, p. 23.

_____. *The Valmora Sun* (Valmora, New Mexico), February, 1939, p. 4, in Scrapbook 3, Valmora Library, Valmora, New Mexico, p. 25.

_____. *The Valmora Sun* (Valmora, New Mexico), March, 1939, p. 4, in Scrapbook 3, Valmora Library, Valmora, New Mexico, p. 27.

_____. *The Valmora Sun* (Valmora, New Mexico), June, 1939, p. 4, in Scrapbook 3, Valmora Library, Valmora, New Mexico, p. 33.

REPORTS

Annual Report of the National Tuberculosis Association for the Year Ending March 31, 1961. *The People Behind the Big Push.* New York, New York: National Tuberculosis Association, 1961.

Gellenthein, Carl H. "Discharge from Treatment" Form 1784 Standard, Santa Fe Hospital Association. Report record in Scrapbook 6, Valmora Library, Valmora, New Mexico, p. 64.

_____. Handwritten notes reporting injury, in Scrapbook 6, Valmora Library, Valmora, New Mexico, p. 64.

_____. *Official Superior's Report of Injury.* September 10, 1936, in Scrapbook 6, Valmora Library, Valmora, New Mexico, p. 65.

_____. Report sent to Dr. O.L. Hanson, AT & SF Hospital Association, Topeka, Kansas; Dr. John R. Winston, Medical Director, At & SFRR, Chicago, Illinois; Mr. C.B. Kurtz, Superintendent, Colorado Division, AT & SFRR, La Junta, Colorado, April 29, 1967, in Scrapbook 6, Valmora Library, Valmora, New Mexico, p. 66.

Stoudt, J.L. Handwritten note in Scrapbook 6, Valmora Library, Valmora, New Mexico, p. 64.

"Total Patients Treated and Discharged from September 15, 1927 to September 15, 1963." Report in Scrapbook 11, Valmora Library, Valmora, New Mexico, p. 27.

BOOKLETS AND LEAFLETS

B.D.J. *I've Been to Valmora.* Leaflet in Scrapbook 2, Valmora Library, Valmora, New Mexico.

Brown, W.T. *Valmora Industrial Sanatorium, Valmora, New Mexico: Patients Upon Entering the Institution, Subscribe to the Following Rules and Regulations.* Booklet 2, in Scrapbook 5, Valmora Library, Valmora, New Mexico, p. 53.

_____. *Valmora .Sanatorium.* Booklet 7, in Scrapbook 1, Valmora Library, Valmora, New Mexico, p. 2.

Brown, W.T. and C.H. Gellenthien. *Valmora Sanatorium.* Booklet 4, in Scrapbook 1, Valmora Library, Valmora, New Mexico, p. 3.

Gellenthien, Carl H. *The Valmora Guide.* Booklet 5, in Scrapbook 1, Valmora Library, Valmora, New Mexico, p. 32.

_____. *Valmora Sanatorium.* Booklet 6, in Scrapbook 3, Valmora Library, Valmora, New Mexico, p. 47.

La Junta, The Meeting Place, Now Watrous, New Mexico, According to W.J. Lucas — Why Ft. Union and Other Papers. Leaflet from City Museum, Las Vegas, New Mexico.

Stopping at the Stevens. Stevens Hotel Company, Chicago, Illinois, November

20, 1930, Booklet in Scrapbook 1, Valmora Library, Valmora, New Mexico.

"The Oath of Hippocrates." *Hippocrates: Ancient Medicine and Other Treatises*, n.p., n.d., n.p.

Valmora Sanatorium: An Invitation. Booklet 1, 1916, in Scrapbook 5, Valmora Library, Valmora, New Mexico, p. 60.

UNPUBLISHED MATERIAL

"Arthritis." Unpublished mimeographed sheet. Recipe used at the Mayo Clinic, Rochester, Minnesota, in Scrapbook 3, Valmora Library, Valmora, New Mexico, p. 49.

"Average Temperature & Pulse of 129 Cases." Valmora, New Mexico, in Scrapbook 11, Valmora Library, Valmora, New Mexico, p. 50.

Diehl, Eric. "Valmora: Tonic for Tuberculosis." Unpublished manuscript winning first place in New Mexico's statewide Calvin Horn Scholarship Contest and selected by the Committee of the New Mexico Historical Society, April, 1981, Las Vegas Robertson High School, Las Vegas, New Mexico, p. 7.

Emerick, Lois Reiser. "Valmora: The Story of an Institution." Unpublished Masters Thesis, Department of History and Social Sciences, New Mexico Highlands University, Las Vegas, New Mexico, p. 1962.

Gellenthein, Carl H. Handwritten note in Scrapbook 3, Valmora Library, Valmora, New Mexico, p. 10.

_____. Handwritten note to Marge Shea, September 17, 1956, in Scrapbook 6, Valmora Library, Valmora, New Mexico, p. 19.

_____. Handwritten notes composed following the accident at Springer Siding, September 5, 1956, in Scrapbook 6, Valmora Library, Valmora, New Mexico, p. 17.

_____. Typed notes written up after the accident at Springer Siding, in Scrapbook 6, Valmora Library, Valmora, New Mexico, p. 62.

INTERVIEWS

Bartley, Editha. Gascon Ranch, various dates, and Las Vegas, New Mexico, various dates, June 10, 1981 through July 30, 1984.

Davis, Waldo. Las Vegas, New Mexico, October 21, 1983.

Ewert, Earl. Gascon Ranch, June 15, 1981.

Frank, Paul. Santa Fe, New Mexico, September 20, 1981.

Gellenthien, Carl H. Valmora, New Mexico, various dates, and Las Vegas, New Mexico, various dates, December 29, 1980 through December 30, 1984.

Iacomini, Tony, Valmora, New Mexico and Las Vegas, New Mexico, various dates, October 24, 1981 through February 17, 1984.

Kosicki, Sigmund, Santa Fe, New Mexico, various dates, May 5, 1984 through July 30, 1984.

Lucero, Mollie, Las Vegas, New Mexico, July 12, 1984.

Meyer, Irma, Valmora, New Mexico, various dates, June 10, 1981 through December 20, 1983.

Mortimer, H.M., Albuquerque, New Mexico, April 12, 1981.

Shields, Lora, telephone interview, November 28, 1983.

Valdez, Benny, Valmora, New Mexico, April 15, 1983.

Walters, Harold, Santa Fe, New Mexico, June 17, 1983.

OTHER SOURCES — Poetry, Quotations, Songs, Stories, Speeches, Letters

Barkers, S. Omar. "Mountain Cemetery." *Sunlight Through the Trees*. Las Vegas, New Mexico: Highlands University Press, 1954, p. 47.

Browning, Elizabeth Barrett. *Sonnets From the Portuguese*. New York: Harper & Row, Publishers, n.d.

Churchill, Winston, quoted in *Medical Aspects of Human Sexuality* 16 (November, 1982), n.p.

Dowson, Ernest. *The Poems of Ernest Dowson*. London: John Lane, The Bodley Head, MDCCCV, p. 2.

Edsall, Fay B. "Johnny." *Impressions of Valmora*, July, 1937, poems in Scrapbook 1, Valmora Library, Valmora, New Mexico, p. 81.

_____. "The Doctor." *Impressions of Valmora*, July, 1937, in Scrapbook 1, Valmora Library, Valmora, New Mexico, p.80.

Gellenthien, Carl H. "Climatological Data Chart." Framed chart in Dr. Gellenthein's office, Valmora, New Mexico, n.d.

Hunt, James Henry Leigh. "Abou Ben Adhem." quoted in Ralph L. Woods, ed., *A Treasury of the Familiar*. New York: the Macmillan Company, 1943, p. 41.

O'Shaughnessy, Arthur. "Ode." quoted in Ralph L. woods, ed., *A Treasury of the Familiar*. New York: the Macmillan Company, 1943, p. 269.

Runyan, Damon. "Doc Brackett." quoted in Audry Stone Morris, ed., *One Thousand Inspirational Things*. Chicago: Peoples Book Club, 1958, pp. 38-9.

Whitman, Walt, quoted in Lillian Eichler Watson, ed., *Light From Many Lamps*. New York: Simon and Schuster, 1951, p. 87.

LETTERS

Calhoun, James S. to Orlando Brown, May 20, May 23, 1850, in Scrapbook 3, Valmora Library, Valmora, New Mexico, p. 51.

Dixon, Arthur to Mrs. A.M. Claiborne, March 2, 1953, in Scrapbook 5, Valmora Library, Valmora, New Mexico, p. 50.

Gellenthien, C.H. Letter in Scrapbook 20, Valmora Library, Valmora, New Mexico, p. 21.

_____ to D.J. Davis, June 6, 1927, in Scrapbook 11, Valmora Library, Valmora, New Mexico, p. 3.

_____ to G.J. Fellroth, April 15, 1958, in Scrapbook 3, Valmora Library, Valmora, New Mexico p 3.

_____ to Cecil Hope, September 11, 1957 in Scrapbook 6, Valmora Library, Valmora, New Mexico, pp. 16-17.

_____ to Thomas G. Morris, February 10, 1965, in Scrapbook 3, Valmora Library, Valmora, New Mexico, p.55.

_____ to Mr. and Mrs. Fred W. Wolter, October 23, 1956, in Scrapbook 6, Valmora Library, Valmora, New Mexico, p. 20.

Gellenthein Carl and Alice. "1957 — For Alice and Me." Letter written at Valmora, New Mexico, December, 1957, in Scrapbook 4, Valmora Library, Valmora, New Mexico, p. 25.

Gorsline, Kay, to Dorothy Beimer, November 27, 1982.

Johnson, Vivian B. to the editors of *Life Magazine*, December 6, 1937, in Scrapbook 2, Valmora Library, Valmora, New Mexico, p. 71.

Lagrave, Lou to Dorothy Beimer, January 2, 1982 in Scrapbook 18, Valmora Library, Valmora, New Mexico, p. 47.

SPEECHES

Gellenthien, Carl H. "Au Revoir." Manuscript of speech delivered at Commencement, 1927, graduating class of St. Luke's Hospital, Denver, Colorado, in *RX, 1927 Yearbook*, 1927, n.p.

_____. "Socialized Medicine is the Keystone in the Arch of Communism." Manuscript of speech in Scrapbook 4, Valmora Library, Valmora, New Mexico, p. 81.

_____ "Statement of Carl H. Gellenthien, M.D., President of the New Mexico Medical Society, Presented to the United States Senate Committee on Education and Labor." Reprint from *Rocky Mountain Medical Journal*, September, 1946, pp. 1-2, in Scrapbook 3, Valmora Library, Valmora, New Mexico, p. 35.

Rial, William, Y. "Who's Your Doctor?" Manuscript of speech delivered at the American Medical Association's Annual Convention, Chicago, Illinois, June 19, 1983.

Sheen, Fulton J. "The Physician, the Clergy, the Patient." Manuscript of speech delivered at the American Medical Association's Annual Convention, Atlantic City, New Jersey, June 17, 1963.

INDEX

306

ACKNOWLEDGMENTS

Harper & Row: for *In the Shadow of the White Plague* by Elizabeth Mooney; copyright © 1979 by Elizabeth Mooney. W.W. Norton: for *Anatomy of an Illness As Perceived by the Patient* by Norman Cousins; copyright © 1979. Little, Brown and Co.: for *The White Plague: Tuberculosis, Man and Society* by Rene and Jean Dubos; copyright © 1952. Random House: for *The Magic Mountain* by Thomas Mann, translated by H.T. Lowe-Porter; copyright © 1939 Alfred A. Knopf, Inc. Broadman Press: for *Promises Kept* by Bonnie Ball O'Brien; copyright © 1978. Random House: for *Doctors of the American Frontier* by Richard Dunlop; copyright © 1965 Ballentine Books. A.L. Fierst: for *Death Lies Deep* by William Guinn; copyright © 1955, Gold Medal Books, Fawcett Publications. Farrar, Straus & Giroux: for *Illness as Metaphor* by Susan Sontag; copyright © 1978. Brandt & Brandt Literary Agents: for "Doc Melhorn and the Pearly Gates" by Stephen Vincent Benet, from *The Selected Works of Stephen Vincent Benet*; copyright © 1938, copyright © renewed 1965. New York University Press; Dover Publications; *Impact, Albuquerque Journal*; Evelyn Witter; *American Medical News*; S. Omar Barker; *Diagnosis*; Simon and Schuster. Harcourt Brace Jovanovich: for *The Fight for Life* by Paul de Kruif; copyright © 1937, 1965. Diana Trilling: for *The Letters of John Keats*, edited by Lionel Trilling; copyright © 1951.